A DEVOTIONAL

Words of Life

Hearing God's Voice Today in the Psalms

Advantage™
INSPIRATIONAL

Linda Winter-Hodgson

Words of Life by Linda Winter-Hodgson
Copyright © 2010 by Linda Winter-Hodgson
All Rights Reserved
ISBN: 1-59755-030-2
ISBN 13: 978-1-59755-030-7

Published by: ADVANTAGE BOOKS™
                www.advbookstore.com

Unless otherwise indicated, Bible quotations are taken from *The Holy Bible*, New International Version. Copyright © 1973, 1978, 1984 by International Bible Society, Zondervan Corporation. All Rights Reserved.

Library of Congress Control Number: 2010920454

Cover design by Pat Theriault

Cover Artist: Judy (Langemo) Roth
Watercolor cover art inspired by a Scott Gibson photograph
Photo of author on back cover by Danter Photography, Morris MN

First Printing: February 2010
10 11 12 13 14 15 16   10 9 8 7 6 5 4 3 2 1
Printed in the United States of America

Words Of Life

It is my hope that while reading these pages, you will be filled with words of life. Truly, God's word is living; it is active; it came to dwell among us in Jesus Christ.

Listen to the words as you read them. Eat them. Chew on them. Roll them around on your tongue. Take them inside your body and inside your spirit as one would eat the Bread of Life. Let the words nourish and strengthen your inner person just as food nourishes and strengthens your outer person.

We need food each day. Fresh food. Good food. We need God's words each day. Fresh words. Good words. Words of life.

Let us savor His Word; take it into our hearts, bite by bite, until we're filled to overflowing. Then may our own words be less and less our own, and more and more of Christ's, as they spill over from our satisfied hearts-filled to the brim with "words of life."

> Sing them over again to me,
> Wonderful words of life;
> Let me more of their beauty see,
> Wonderful words of life;
> Words of life and beauty,
> Teach me faith and duty.
>
> Beautiful words, wonderful words,
> Wonderful words of life;
> Beautiful words, wonderful words,
> Wonderful words of life.

(From the hymn, "Wonderful Words Of Life," by Philip P. Bliss, 1874)

Words in Books

the
written word
is
such a good thing,
isn't
it?
the way it is on the page
and
the way it is in your head
when
you
read it.
the way it comes into your eyes
and
the way it sounds in your mouth
when
you
roll it around
in there.
and
the way it makes you feel
when
someone
reads it to you
out
loud.

Linda Winter-Hodgson

Words of Life

Hearing God's Voice Today In The Psalms

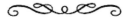

Psalm 1 "But his delight is in the law of the Lord, and on his law he meditates day and night" (v.2).

A very slow, quiet, meditative reading of the Psalms over 13 months has been such a blessing to me. It is this reading that has caused me to write a devotional book. On my own, I have no "new thoughts" to offer anyone, but if this prompting to write a book is from God, perhaps He has some thoughts to share through me, that might bless others. That is my hope.

As you read, go slowly. Throw out time tables. *Delight* in the law of the Lord! Meditate on His words day and night.

Sit in your favorite chair and ask God to make His voice more familiar to you. He will do it. He is faithful.

God desires to change us "from one degree of glory to another," (II Corinthians 3:18 RSV) to be more like Him. As we sit quietly each day and spend time in His word, He will change us to be more like Jesus.

Dear Jesus, As I read slowly through your Psalms, your Word, cause me to hear your voice. Speak to me as a familiar friend. I delight in You! Amen.

Psalm 2 "The kings of the earth take their stand and the rulers gather together against the Lord, and against his Anointed One. 'Let us break their chains,' they say, 'and throw off their fetters'" (v. 2-3).

The Lord laughs at these words. Verse 4 of Psalm 2 says that He "scoffs" at the idea of man freeing man. The kings and rulers of the earth may say that they can "break the chains" and "throw off the fetters" that bind mankind, but Jesus says in John 8:36 that only "if the Son sets you free" will you be "free indeed."

As I read the above scripture verses of Psalm 2, I think of the Berlin Wall, and of the freedoms that resulted when it was announced in 1989 that the Wall would no longer serve as a barrier between East and West Germany. Certainly we applaud these freedoms and rejoice in them.

But Psalm 2:10 says, "Be wise." Remember that no king or ruler or political leader of this earth has the power to free our hearts from guilt or from the sins that so easily shackle them. No earthly man or woman can make our hearts clean, and give us perfect peace inside. No person on earth can break our chains and throw off our fetters. God laughs at such presumption.

If you are bound today with chains of anger or unforgiveness, with fetters of fear or despair, let Jesus come into your heart. He is the King. He alone has the power to free you. He can do it. He has already done it when He died and rose from the dead to pay our debt completely. In Him we are free indeed!

Dear Jesus, You are my King. Come into my heart, please. Break any chains and throw off any fetters that bind me. Forgive me for my sins. Thank you for making me "free indeed!" Amen.

❦

Psalm 3 "But you are a shield around me, O Lord; you bestow glory on me and lift up my head. To the Lord I cry aloud, and he answers me from his holy hill. Selah" (v. 3-4).

Usually I am a fairly calm person. My home is calm, and fairly clean, and in order. I like it that way. It gives me peace and a feeling of being in control of my surroundings.

Today nothing around me is calm. I am struggling to maintain my composure and my inner peace. Nothing tragic or earthshaking is going on in my life. No, just common, everyday kinds of upsets seem to be happening all at once, and they threaten my peace of mind. Maybe you can relate.

Let's see, first there was the car. Notice I said, "was." It died last week, "never to be revived," according to our auto mechanic. Well, that was OK. We had a second vehicle, a pick-up truck. Notice I said, "had." Yesterday it wouldn't start, so today it is in the auto mechanic's garage. That leaves my husband and me stranded at our home two miles out in the country, with no vehicle. Our friends and family are coming to our rescue, giving us rides to town and to work, but two broken down vehicles make for more stress and less calm!

Then there's the bathroom. Remember how I said common, everyday upsets can threaten peace of mind? The bathroom in our house is being remodeled. No big deal. Except that there's noise, and mess, and no shower, and lots of fine, powdery Sheet-rock dust floating all over the house.

You've got the picture. Not much calm in my house today. Not much control over my surroundings. And in the midst of all this comes Psalm 3, verse 3, "But you are a shield around me, O Lord; you bestow glory on me and lift up my head. To the Lord I cry aloud, and he answers me from his holy hill. Selah."

That "Selah" is important. It means "Stop." "Wait." "Let this sink in."

So I will. I will cry aloud to God and He will answer me. He will answer you, too.

List all of your circumstances to God today. List the upsets, great and small. And after the list, add these words: "But you are a shield around me, O Lord."

Let Him surround you and shield you from all that steals your calm. Let Him be a buffer around your heart. A bubble. A shield. The turmoil is outside the bubble. It can bump up against your shield, but it can't get inside. God is your shield. He is my shield. Behind the shield is calm.

Selah.

Lord, thank you for being my shield. Thank you for promising to answer from your holy hill. Whether my upsets are small, or insurmountable, you are a shield around me. In Jesus' name, Amen.

Psalm 4 "In your anger do not sin; when you are on your beds, search your hearts and be silent. Selah. Offer right sacrifices and trust in the Lord" (v. 4-5).

Lord, this week I was angry. I got angry, and I thought of this verse, and I should've been silent, but I wasn't.

I was anything but silent. I was loud and complaining and irritable.

Lots of things went wrong with our remodeling project, and our house is still a mess, and I got sick, and my husband was gone, and the list went on and on.

You knew the list, Lord. You knew my complaints before I voiced them. You even knew that sometimes so many things will go wrong in our lives that we *will* get angry, but you cautioned, "In your anger do not sin."

In your anger do not go around complaining and crabbing to others. In your anger do not curse God. In your anger do not give in to despair.

Well, I blew it. I did those things that I wasn't supposed to do.

You gave us a formula in Psalm 4 to handle anger rightly. "Search your hearts and be silent."

That is so hard to do, Lord. It is a sacrifice. A *right* sacrifice. The sacrifice of silence may be a right sacrifice when I am angry.

You commanded it in your word in Psalm 4. Maybe next time I'll do better. With your help, Lord, I know I will.

You forgave me this time like you do every time I fail. I confessed my sin to you, and your forgiveness washed over me, and you've forgotten my sin completely. I have a clean slate. A fresh start.

Next time I am angry, God, help me to offer to you the "sacrifice of silence." Help me not to curse or complain. Help me instead to follow the advice of Psalm 4, verse 5: "Offer right sacrifices and trust in the Lord."

Dear God, help us to trust you when we are angry, and when we have lots to be angry about. In our anger, let us not sin. Let us offer instead, the sacrifice of silence. May we learn not to stuff our anger inside, but not to complain, either. We bring our anger to you, God. We trust you to handle and make right all that causes it. In Jesus' name, Amen.

Psalm 5 *"Spread your protection over them, that those who love your name may rejoice in you" (v. 11b).*

When I first underlined this verse in my Bible, I had dear friends who were living as missionaries in Peru. The conditions in Peru were dangerous, and this verse stuck out as a word of comfort regarding my friends' safety. I felt compelled to pray these words of Psalm 5 aloud for my friends, and I did.

The friends have since returned to the U.S., and are now serving God in this country. I don't know all of the dangers or near-dangers they faced in Peru, but I do know that God urged me to pray this prayer for them while they were there. I know He answered. I know He kept them safe.

Do you know anyone today who needs protection? Has the Holy Spirit placed anyone on your heart for whom this prayer might be relevant today? If so, don't hesitate to pray. The Lord responds to our cries for others, and for our own needs, too. He hears our prayers.

Psalm 5 gives us a beautiful picture of God spreading His protective arms over those who love His name.

Even when we are separated by distance from those we love, we can take comfort in God's ability to answer this prayer.

Dear God, please "spread your protection over (names of those the Holy Spirit lays on your heart), that those who love your name may rejoice in you." In Jesus' name, Amen.

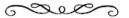

Psalm 6 "The Lord accepts my prayer" (v. 9b).

I'm behind today.

Behind in my writing. Behind in my correspondence. Behind in visiting some people I need to visit.

I'm behind because I'm sick. Flus and head colds have struck our house four times in the past few months.

You know what it's like. To be behind. To feel sick. Maybe you and your family are even facing serious illness. Serious falling behind. Serious fear.

The psalmist understands. He tells us about it in Psalm 6. He needs healing because his "bones are in agony" (v. 2). He is "worn out from groaning" (v. 6). His eyes are "weak with sorrow" (v. 7).

But in the midst of all that comes verse 9. "The Lord has heard my cry for mercy; the Lord accepts my prayer."

Whether you're feeling behind in your work, or sick and "weak with sorrow," the Lord accepts your prayer. He doesn't condemn you. You might condemn yourself. You might feel guilty for falling behind. You might feel despair over getting sick so often. You might feel like giving up.

But God says no. Don't give up because you've fallen behind. Don't despair over illness. Don't give in to condemnation.

Cry out to God.

He accepts our prayers.

He hears our cries for mercy.

If God accepts us, we can accept ourselves.

If you've given up on a project because you've fallen behind, pick it up again today. Ask God if it's worthwhile. If it is, pursue it. He accepts you. So what if it's late? God gives second chances. Lots of chances. Start again. Finish the work. God will accept it. He accepts your prayer. He accepts you.

If you're in despair over illness today, read Psalm 6. Pray to God. He will hear your cry just as He heard the psalmist. He will accept your prayer.

Dear Lord, if I've fallen behind, help me to finish what you've given me to do. If I am sick, help me to trust you. Please heal me. Please help me when I fall behind. I know you hear my cries for mercy. I know you accept my prayer. I will rest in that knowledge today. In Jesus' name, Amen.

Psalm 7 "I will give thanks to the Lord <u>because of his righteousness</u>" (v. 17a). (underlining mine)

Why should having a righteous God make us thankful?

Well, let's see, maybe Isaiah 64:6 can help us out. "All of us have become like one who is unclean," it says, "and all our righteous acts are like filthy rags."

Hmm. OK. So, we're unclean. So our righteous acts are like filthy rags compared to God. Still doesn't make me feel very thankful. How about you?

Let's look further. Let's see where else God speaks about righteousness in His word. After all, we all need reasons to be thankful. Let's track this one down.

Isaiah 61 has more to say on the subject. "I delight greatly in the Lord; my soul rejoices in my God. For he has clothed me with garments of salvation and arrayed me in a robe of righteousness" (v. 10).

What do you think? Are we getting closer? I think so. These garments, this robe, let's think about them for a moment.

In order to give something to someone, we have to have it first. Garments of salvation. A robe of righteousness. Let's look in our closets. Ever had one of those? Me neither. But God does.

He owns salvation. He bought it. He paid for it with Jesus' blood. He has it. He can give it away.

And righteousness? He's got that, too. He possesses it. It's one of His attributes. Righteousness is God's to share.

And He does. Lavishly. Lovingly. He clothes. He arrays.

Those are not words of a pauper, my friend. Those are the words of One who can afford good threads.

And He offers them to you and me. Every day. Every morning and every evening. After every sin, every mistake, God says, "Here, try this on. Put it on over your failures. It'll cover. It'll fit. My robe of righteousness. I bought it for you. Sure it was expensive. It cost my Son's blood. But I wanted to do it. I love you. It's a gift from Me to you."

"I will give thanks to the Lord because of *His* righteousness."

Thank you Lord, that righteousness is yours to give. You possess it. And you share it. I need it, Lord. Today and every day. Put on me the garments of your salvation. Cover me. Clothe me. My heart rejoices today as I put on such a beautiful robe. In Jesus' name, Amen.

Psalm 8 "From the lips of children and infants you have ordained praise because of your enemies, to silence the foe and the avenger" (v. 2).

Excuse me. I'm not sure I read this verse right. Did you?

I've heard the first part many times. "From the lips of children and infants you have ordained praise . . ."

But wait a minute. There was no period, no mark of punctuation there in my Bible. The sentence goes on! Let's read that again.

"From the lips of children and infants you have ordained praise because of your enemies, to silence the foe and the avenger."

I had to read that twice this morning. Three times. And I still didn't get it. Why would God need the praises of infants and children to silence His foes? Why doesn't He do it himself? Why would God ordain praise from children "because of His enemies?" Who are God's enemies, anyway?

I didn't know the answers to these questions, but they bothered me this morning. I read this verse and it struck me as important. God's words tend to do that to a person! So I asked. I asked these questions to God. I sat in my rocker quietly and listened, and this is what He said.

"My enemies are your enemies. My enemies are anything and anyone that sets itself or themselves up against Godly ways. My enemies get in the way of my people praising me. My enemies bring despair, discouragement, and dishonor to Me and to my people. "

I thought about that and Melinda came to mind. Amy did, too. Melinda is 9 years old. Amy is 10. They are two of my piano students.

Sometimes being a piano teacher (or being a school teacher, a mom, a dad, a homemaker, or any kind of career person) can be depressing. Sometimes there are few rewards and slow progress. Sometimes insecurity and discouragement can set in. Sometimes this gets in the way of praising God. Hmm. Sounds like an enemy to me.

That's where Amy and Melinda come in. You see, they're children. You couldn't pick them out in a crowd. They're not different or famous. Yet from their lips, and from the lips of all children, God has ordained praise because of his enemies.

He showed me that one day, and I still have the letters in my scrapbook to prove it. One is from Melinda. One is from Amy.

One says:
Dear Linda,
I like you very much!
You are very much fun!
You are very nice!
piano student,
Melinda

The other one is pasted on the next page in my scrapbook:

Dear Linda,

You are the best piano teacher I ever had. I'm glad my mom picked you as my piano teacher. Your piano student,

Amy

P.S. I like your dogs and cats!

Do you know what those two letters did? They silenced my enemies! They were from the lips of children, and they were filled with praise! They took my discouragement and turned it into joy! They silenced my foe of insecurity that day. That's what the praises of children can do.

God knew that. That must be why He ordained it. Because of His enemies. Because of our enemies.

If you have children in your life today, your own, or other people's, listen to them. God has ordained special words and sounds from their lips! Even infants can silence God's foes! He has ordained it. He has promised it. Listen to some "foe-stoppers" today!

Dear Lord, today let me listen for the praises you have ordained from the lips of children and infants. What a privilege you have given them! They silence your enemies! They silence my enemies! May their praises be unhindered today.
In Jesus' name, Amen.

Psalm 9 " ...You have sat on your throne, judging righteously." (v. 4b) [and] "...he has established his throne for judgment" (v. 7).

What do you think of when you read these words? What feelings come over you? Fear? Trepidation? Uncertainty? Vengeance? Smugness? Peace? Relief?

It all depends on how you view God's justice. God's judgment. God's throne.

Psalm 9 has much to say on the subject. It divides us, all of us, into camps.

On one side, there are "the oppressed," "the afflicted," and "the needy." There are those who "know [God's] name." There are those "who seek [God.]"

On the other side, there are "the wicked," and "the enemy." There are "the persecutors." There are "the nations that forget God."

We've all read about these two camps throughout history. We read about them today in our newspapers.

Holocausts.

Genocide.

Slavery.

Warfare.

Aggression.

Abuse.

All of these have two camps:

The oppressed	The wicked
The needy and afflicted	The persecutors
Those who seek God	Those who forget God

Sometimes we despair of God's justice in our world. Sometimes we don't see it. But it's there. Not always in our timing. But the promises of God's righteous judgment are there. They're in Psalm 9.

Let's look together at these promises and be encouraged by them.

For the oppressed and the needy, God promises in v. 18: You will "not always be forgotten."

For the afflicted, God promises in verses 12 and 18: "He who avenges blood remembers: he does not ignore the cry of the afflicted." [and] "The hope of the afflicted will not always perish."

For those who seek God, the Lord promises in v.10: They will "never be forsaken by the Lord."

Isn't that good news? Sometimes people's hope perishes, but it won't always be that way! God is just. He avenges blood. He remembers the needy. He renews the hope of the afflicted. He doesn't forsake those who seek Him.

We need to know that today. We need to know it in light of history. We need to know it for the future. We need to know it for the Last Days.

It is not up to us to avenge. To play God. To punish the wicked. That is God's job. "He has established His throne for judgment" (v. 7).

Let's look further at God's promises in Psalm 9.

For the wicked, God promises in v. 16: They are "ensnared by the work of their hands."

For the persecutors, God promises in v. 15: They will "fall into the pit they have dug."

For those who forget God, God promises in v. 17: They will "return to the grave."

That's good news, too. We need to know that evil will be punished. That good will triumph. That God wins. That justice prevails.

It does. But lest we get haughty, or boastful, or smug as we consider God's justice, let us think, too, of the words in Isaiah 1:18 where God says, "Come now, let us reason together . . . though your sins are like scarlet, they shall be white as snow; though they are red as crimson, they shall be like wool."

Doesn't sound like justice, does it? At least, not *our* kind of justice. God's is different. Thank goodness!

He will punish the wicked.

He will judge the nations.

He will send some to hell.

That is God's justice.

But consider; so is this:

He allowed Jesus, innocent and sinless, to be condemned to death in our place.

He said to the thief on the cross, "Today you will be with me in paradise."

He says to you and to me, "If you confess your sin, I am faithful and just to forgive" (I John 1:9). And, "At just the right time, while we were still sinners, Christ died for the ungodly" (Romans 5:6).

That, my friend, is also God's justice. Different from ours. Ready to forgive. Even the undeserving. Because, you see, all of us are undeserving. From the oppressed to the wicked. From the needy and afflicted to the persecutors. From the seekers to the forgetters. "All have sinned and fallen short of the glory of God" (Romans 3:23).

And so today, if viewing God's throne of judgment makes you feel fearful, or vengeful, or smug, draw closer. See the nail-pierced hands of the Judge. Embrace those hands. Be thankful for them. Hold on to them as hands that can save you. They can. They already have.

The blood that spilled from those hands spilled for you and me. It redeemed us. It bought us back from the hellish side of judgment.

Look at that throne again.

Approach it.

Boldly.

Confidently.

Look at it through the shed blood of Jesus.

We will be judged. Mark that well. But if our sins are under the blood, confessed, covered, and forgiven, then we need not fear.

"Come now, let us reason together," says the Lord. Not our reasoning. Not our justice. But His.

Thank you, Lord, that your justice says, "Though your sins are like scarlet, they will be white as snow." Whichever camp I'm in today, Lord, help me to confess my sins. Help me to repent. Help me to stand before Your throne of judgment, washed with Jesus' blood, and to view it then as Your throne of grace. In Jesus' name, Amen.

Psalm 10 "But you, O God, do see trouble and grief; you consider it to take it in hand" (v. 14a).

Has your grief ever gotten out of hand? Too deep? All consuming? Beyond your control?

How about trouble? Has it ever come raining down on your head? Too fast for you to rise above it?

Trouble and grief.

They are partners. Overwhelming, destructive partners.

I know because they overwhelmed me and almost destroyed me in 1987. That was a bad year for me. A bad year for my family. My father died, my dear aunt died, and my sister and her husband got divorced.

A friend told me that year that trouble often comes in "three's." I'm not a superstitious person, and I know her prophecy isn't always true, but I will say that in 1987, it felt like she was right.

Three troubles.

Three reasons to grieve.

Together they overwhelmed me. They almost destroyed me.

I went into a depression that turned into an anxiety disorder. I went to doctors and psychiatrists, and took pills and went to therapy sessions. Some of them helped and some of them didn't. I went up for prayer in our church. I cried. I was scared. I was hard to live with. I thought I'd lose my mind.

Sounds like my grief was out of hand, doesn't it? It was, and I knew it, and that made me more scared and angry at myself. That didn't help. But God did.

He saw my trouble and grief.

He sees yours, too.

He sees it; He considers it; He takes it in hand.

Isn't it comforting to know that God, the Ruler of the universe, *considers* our grief? That means He ponders it. He "thinks about it in order to understand or decide," according to Webster's. He "keeps in mind" our troubles and grief. And that's not all.

God also "takes it in hand." That's the best part. That's the part of Psalm 10:14 that I like most. When our trouble and grief is beyond our control, God takes it in His. He takes it "in hand." "In hand" means "possession or care." God takes our troubles and our grief into His possession. He takes over. He takes control.

It may not happen right away, but my friend, take heart; it will happen. Even now God is considering your grief. He is deciding how best to help you. He sees trouble and grief. That is a promise from His living Word.

Hang on to that today. Please don't give up. I almost did. Many times. In 1987, and in 1988, and many times since when troubles have overwhelmed me. No one could've told me in the midst of grief and depression and anxiety that anything would ever look good again. But it did. It does. Part of your grief and sadness may remain, but it won't always overwhelm you. It will be in control. It will be "in hand." God's hand. It will be manageable somehow. Please wait and see what God will do.

Our aunt Eleanor did, and her story is an encouragement.

Eleanor was married to my husband's Uncle Gordon. They were very much in love with each other, and they loved the Lord. Eleanor dreaded the day when one of them might die first and leave the other to grieve.

That day came one morning when Gordon was in his 70's. Eleanor called him for breakfast, but he didn't come. She went to the bedroom and found him dead in their bed. Eleanor told us, "I told the Lord right then, 'Lord, you're going to have to help me handle this, because I can't.'"

"A feeling like warm oil came over me right there in the bedroom," she told us later. "From my head to my feet, I felt God's presence pour over me, and it hasn't left since." That was one year later, when we visited her on the West Coast, that Eleanor told us her story.

I'm not minimizing her grief or her troubles since Gordon's death. Most of us will never know the pain and anguish suffered by others who are going through trouble and grief. But I do know that Eleanor wasn't completely overwhelmed. God took her grief in hand. He didn't take it away, but He did promise to see it, to consider it, to take it in hand.

As God considers your situation today, know that He will so the same for you. He may do it in ways that are unique to your troubles and your grief. He may do it in ways you can't see or imagine or even believe. That's OK. God's actions don't depend on our capabilities. He is capable. Even when we're not.

Know that He is seeing.

Know that He is considering.

Know that He will take in hand your trouble and grief.

Take control of my grief, O Lord. Take over, that it might not get the best of me. Let it not overwhelm me. Thank you, Lord. Thank you. In Jesus' name, Amen.

Psalm 11 "When the foundations are being destroyed, what can the righteous do?" (v. 3).

Pray.

Stand firm.

Be a light.

Trust God.

Those are things we can do when foundations are being destroyed. I believe they are things we are supposed to do.

They sound simple, don't they? Maybe too simple. Ineffective, perhaps, against the forces of evil. Against crumbling principles and mores of society, what can these four little things do?

Praying.

Standing firm.

Being a light.

Trusting God.

I believe they can change everything and anything.

Oh, society will continue to have wickedness. That won't change until Jesus returns. But we don't have to run. To flee. To be afraid. To cover our heads in despair. We don't have to worry about the righteous becoming ineffectual, or extinct.

Read all of Psalm 11 today to see what I mean.

God says that if we take refuge in Him, no one can say to us, "Flee like a bird to your mountain," or, "When the foundations are being destroyed, what can the righteous do?"

We can do a lot!

We can take refuge in God!

He wins!

The wicked will lose!

"Upright men will see His face!" (v. 7b).

Those are promises of hope when we see evil around us. And in light of those promises, I believe God is asking us today to do those four things I mentioned earlier.

When we see evil or wickedness at work, on television, in government, in our communities, we can pray. Really pray. Ask God to change it. We can stand firm. Don't compromise. Be holy. Let righteousness and love shine. Be a light. We don't have to beat people over the head with our opinions. We can reflect Jesus' love. We can touch those around us with examples of compassion, gentleness, and truth. Then we can trust God. He can do it. He is righteous. He loves justice (v. 7). He is in His holy temple. He is on His heavenly throne (v. 4). God is in control.

If we are Christians who take refuge in the Lord, no one, no matter how powerful, can say to us, "Flee like a bird to your mountain."

No one can ask, "When the foundations are being destroyed, what can the righteous do?" Because, dear saints, we can do a lot!

Dear God, there is wickedness all around me. Yet I need not flee. I take refuge in You. I bring before You today the unrighteous situation that bothers me most. It is on my heart. Help me to pray about it now. Help me then to stand firm. Teach me how to be a light in this situation. Help me to trust You. In Jesus' name, Amen.

Psalm 12 " ...we own our lips - who is our master?" (v. 4b).

Do you know who is speaking these words? The psalmist says in verse 3 that it is those with "flattering lips" and "boastful tongues."

Contrast that with the Lord's words. They are "flawless," "refined," and "purified" according to verse 6.

It is arrogant to think that we own our lips, that our words have no master. Words are living things. God's words. Our words. All words have one Master: Jesus Christ. He is the Word (John 1:1).

When flattering lips and boastful tongues have hurt me, or deceived me, or lied to me, I am well aware of the power of words. Words can kill.

When God's words bring healing and life and peace to my soul or to a situation, I am well aware of the life-giving power of words. Words can heal.

"The words of the Lord are pure words." So begins a well-known, oft-sung scripture song. It goes on, "Like silver tried in the furnace of the earth, the words of the Lord are pure."

Pure.

Flawless.

Refined.

Oh, that our words were like His!

They can be. It takes practice, and spending time in God's word. Soaking it in. Eating it. Letting it nurture us. Fill us. Then and only then can our words be like God's. Life-giving. Flawless. Refined. Webster's calls that "made free from impurities; purified; cultivated; elegant."

"A word aptly spoken is like apples of gold in pictures of silver," says a proverb of the Lord (Proverbs 25:11).

To be "aptly spoken" our words must be rightly timed. Not only must they be pure, they must be appropriate. A compliment or word of encouragement may not be heard if spoken when the hearer is too busy.

How about praying about *when* we should speak? Not only about *what* we should speak.

A favorite song in an old piano lesson book has these lyrics: "Don't talk; Don't talk; Don't talk if you've nothing to say!" Those words speak especially to a person like me, whose favorite past time is to *talk*!

Talking is not bad. It can be joyful, fun, and revealing of our inner selves.

But let's be careful. Let's not pretend that we own our lips. Let's acknowledge that our Master, and the Master of our lips, is Jesus. Let's ask Jesus not only *what* words to speak, but also *when* to speak and when not to. Let's read His words and become familiar with them. Let's allow Him to refine our words, to remove the impurities in our speech. Let's let our words, spoken, written, or sung, be adorning to our hearers, "like apples of gold in pictures of silver."

May God grant it. In Jesus' name, Amen.

Psalm 13 "I will sing to the Lord, for He has been good to me" (v. 6).

Maybe you don't feel that the Lord has been good to you. Sometimes we don't. Sometimes we look at our possessions, our talents, our health and our situations, and we still feel we've come up short.

Maybe that's how the psalmist felt when he wrote the first part of this psalm. "How long, O Lord? Will you forget me forever? How long will you hide your face from me? How long must I wrestle with my thoughts and every day have sorrow in my heart? How long will my enemy triumph over me?" (v. 1-2).

Doesn't sound like cause for singing, does it? It doesn't even sound like these verses belong in the same psalm as verse 6. But they do.

The psalmist has found an answer for some of his toughest questions: *Look at what God has done for you.*

In the midst of life's toughest questions, we can still sing to God because *He has been good to us.*

He has given us Jesus.

He has given us His Word, the Bible.

He has said that His mercies are new every morning (Lamentations 3:22-23).

He has promised eternal life in heaven to all who trust Him.

He has given us a future and a hope (Jeremiah 29:11).

You can add to this list of good things God has done for you. Each of our lists will be different. But the list above is the same for all who believe. No matter what your big questions are today, nobody can take these good gifts of God away from you. They are yours. They are mine. They are reasons for singing.

I don't know what kind of a singer you are. Maybe you're an "in the shower only" singer. Maybe you're a professional singer. Whatever kind of singer you are, you can sing to the Lord because He has been good to you. Your circumstances might not always show it. Your questions might not all get answered. But God has been good to you and to me.

Sometimes dwelling on that goodness of God brings answers to hard questions in itself. Sometimes singing to the Lord in the midst of tough questions brings us out of the doldrums. Out of the depths.

Sing to God today.

Please do it.

Sing a song you know.

Make one up.

Think about all the ways God has been good to you, past and present. Incorporate them into your song. See what it does for you. I know it will bless God! And you might be surprised at how it blesses you!

I'm going to try it right now!

Dear Lord, please help us to find answers to our questions. If part of the answers lie in praising you and remembering your goodness to us, let us do that more often. Let us do it today. I will sing to you, Lord, for you have been good to me. In Jesus' name, Amen.

Psalm 14 "...for God is present in the company of the righteous" (v. 5b).

I like that terminology: "the company of the righteous." Don't you? It comforts me. Company always does that.

Company of any kind can be comforting. The company of a friend. Of a spouse. Of a child. Of a visitor to the hospital. Of a pet.

My company each day for the past year has been a dear calico cat named "Rumplestiltskin." I've called her "Rumple" or "Stiltskin" for short. She has slept beside me on her spot, an upholstery-covered bench, every morning as I have read and written and had my quiet time with God.

Today she is gone. I let her out of the house the evening before last as I always do, and for some reason she has not come back. I've searched and called and prayed, but still my company is gone.

It is a lonely feeling when company is gone. We need others. That's why God commanded that we not neglect fellowship. Fellowship of the saints. Fellowship of the righteous. And sometimes fellowship of our furred and feathered friends.

Fellowship combats loneliness. It gets us thinking of something or someone other than ourselves. Psalm 14 even says that fellowship or "the company of the righteous" "overwhelms" evildoers (v. 4-5). There is strength in company. "Where two or more are gathered together," God says, "there am I in the midst of them" (KJV). That is why evildoers are overwhelmed, you see, because "God is present in the company of the righteous."

It may sound foolish, but in the quiet of my own home, when my husband was at work, and Rumplestiltskin was my only company, God honored that and He drew near. He was present in our company, and both my cat and I knew God's peace.

This Sunday I am looking forward more than usual to going to church. I want to be in the company of the righteous. Maybe because one of my own dear companions is gone, I need other company more than ever. Maybe I just need to be with others for a while to combat loneliness.

God will be there. Whether 2 are gathered or 2,000, He has promised to be in the company of the righteous. May His presence in our company be our comfort today.

Lord, please bring company to the lonely today. You choose the company, God. You know best. In Jesus' name, Amen.

Psalm 15 "He who does these things will never be shaken" (v. 5b).

What things? What things can we do in order to gain God's promise that we will "never be shaken?" Let's read the list and find out.

> Do what is righteous.
> Speak the truth from your heart. (v. 2)

Have no slander on your tongue.

Do your neighbor no wrong.

Cast no slur on your fellow man. (v. 3)

Despise a vile man.

Honor those who fear the Lord.

Keep your oath even when it hurts. (v. 4)

Lend your money without usury (an excessive rate of interest).

Don't accept a bribe against the innocent. (v. 5)

There's the list. How did you do? I'll be honest. I bombed out in verse 3 today. Tomorrow may be different. Our sins change each day. But today as I read the list, I got stuck on verse 3. "Have no slander on your tongue." "Cast no slur on your fellow man." I did that yesterday. No need to go into detail. No need to mention names. My heart knows I did wrong. God knows it, too.

He asks me to confess my sin, and He is faithful and just to forgive. So I confessed today. As I read this psalm, I confessed.

I want to live on God's holy hill. I want to dwell in his sanctuary. That's the other promise of Psalm 15. If we follow God's list, with His help, we can live on His holy hill. We can dwell with Him. And we will never be shaken.

Which verse in the list tripped you up today? If one did, don't give up. Confess it to God. He is so faithful to forgive! He wants us to live on His holy hill. We know we're there when He washes the guilt away.

That's a holy feeling. A holy hill. Let's live there today, on God's hill. Let's keep our walk blameless. Let's confess our sins and let Jesus' blood cover the past. Let's try harder to follow the list in Psalm 15, so that we will never be shaken.

Dear God, it feels good to live on your holy hill. I'm there today because you forgave me. You welcomed me to your holy hill when I confessed my sin. I can dwell in your presence today because you give second chances. You forgive. Thank you. Help me to reread this list often. By your grace and continued sanctification in my life, help me to do better at following Your orders. Thank you for your promise that if I do, I will never be shaken. In Jesus' name, Amen.

Psalm 16 "As for the saints who are in the land, they are the glorious ones in whom is all my delight" (v. 3).

Who are the saints in your life? Psalm 101:6 says, "My eyes will be on the faithful in the land, that they may dwell with me; he whose walk is blameless will minister to me."

People don't have to have died to be called saints. Saints are those who are living among us who follow Jesus and His ways. Saints are those who love God. Saints are those who love their neighbors. Saints are faithful, and their walk is blameless.

Saints. They may be old or young. Women or men. Pastors or lay people. Mothers or fathers. Sisters or brothers. Grandmas or grandpas. Uncles or aunts. Neighbors or those living far-off.

Saints. Men and women who love God, and it shows in their lives.

Don't those people minister to you? They do to me! Just thinking about them ministers to me!

I think of Uncle Al who, at age 93, still ministered to his sick wife. When she was in the hospital, Al was by her side, leaving only occasionally to eat meals and catch a few hours sleep. For 63 years of marriage, Uncle Al and Aunt Alice were by each other's sides, in sickness and in health, loving one another. They were saints in the land, dear friends, and thinking about them today ministers God's love to me.

Thinking about my mother does that, too. She is a saint. Oh, she wouldn't call herself that, but God would. And I would. She isn't perfect. But then, saints aren't perfect. Saints are Christians. Christians showing the love of God in their lives.

That's my mom. Always showing God's love. Through phone calls to see how her kids are doing. Through homemade soup brought to neighbors and shut-ins. Through visits to family and friends.

Those are saintly duties, friends. Those are acts of love. Those are things we do as Christians, not to gain heaven, but to bring a little of heaven to earth.

Saints are all around us. They are encouraging. They are loving. Psalm 16 even says that they are "glorious!" They are our "delight!"

Put your eyes on some saints today, won't you? Put your mind on them, too. Look for them. Think about them. Let them minister to you and be your delight!

Lord God, today I choose to put my eyes on the faithful in the land. I choose to think about your saints. Let their walk encourage my own. Let my walk be saintly, too. In Jesus' name, Amen.

Psalm 17

You'll notice that there is no verse in italics on top of the page for today. That's because I couldn't choose one verse out of Psalm 17 to examine. They all seemed to fit together too closely.

Just like the human body. It fits together closely. Each part has a job to do. Each body part can be used for evil or for good.

That's what Psalm 17 talks about. The parts of our bodies. Our eyes, our ears, our lips, our mouths, our hearts, and our feet. It talks about God's body, too. Psalm 17 speaks of God's eye, His ear, His hand, His wings, and His face. They all fit closely together. And each has a job to do.

Let's look at those jobs today. Let's look at the psalmist, the wicked, and God, according to Psalm 17. Let's see how each one uses the body and its' parts.

The Psalmist

lips	v. 1 pray a righteous plea
	are not deceitful
heart	v. 3 is probed and examined by God
	is found blameless by God
mouth	v. 3 has resolved it will not sin
feet	v. 5 have held to God's paths
	have not slipped
eyes	v. 15 will see God's face
	will awake to see God's likeness

The Wicked

hearts	v. 10 are closed up and callous
mouths	v. 10 speak with arrogance
eyes	v. 11 are alert, to "throw the righteous to the ground"

God

ear	v. 1,6 hears our prayers
eyes	v. 2 see what is right
lips	v. 4 speak words that keep us from the way of the violent
hand	v.7 saves all who take refuge in Him
	v. 14 saves us from wicked men whose reward is in this life
eye	v. 8 keeps us as "the apple of his eye"
wings	v. 8 hide us in their shadow
face	v. 15 will be seen by the righteous when we "awake" from death

All the parts of our bodies can be used for good. They can communicate with God. They can be kept clean from sin. They can also be used for evil. They can become calloused. They can hurt others. They can hurt God.

God's body protects ours. It acts as a refuge for the righteous. It hides us, saves us, and keeps us.

May we use our bodies to serve God and communicate with Him. He is ready to hear us, to see us, and to speak with us.

Dear God, thank you for keeping me as "the apple of your eye." Thank you for "giving ear" to my prayers. Thank you for saving me "by your right hand." Thank you for hiding me "in the shadow of your wings." Help me to use my body in the way you intend. Keep my heart clean. Keep my feet from slipping and my mouth from sinning. May I one day see your face. In Jesus' name, Amen.

Psalm 18 "I love you, O Lord, my strength" (v. 1).

Have you ever asked the Lord to help you love him?

Deuteronomy 6:5 says, "Love the Lord your God with all your heart and with all your soul and with all your strength." (NIV)

We cannot love God that way on our own. In order to "love God with all of your strength," God has to be our strength. He has to give us that strength and that ability to love Him. That's why David, in Psalm 18, after telling God that he loves Him, then calls God his "strength."

The dictionary describes "strength" as "the state or quality of being strong; intensity."

Have you ever loved anyone strongly, with intensity? Your mom or dad? Your boyfriend or girlfriend? Your husband or wife? Your friend or relative? That love can be very strong. Very intense. That is the way we are supposed to love God.

He desires that we talk with Him and spend time with Him the way we do with those we love. He desires to be invited as a special guest to our every meal, walk, conversation, date, gathering, and celebration. He desires to be intimate with us. He desires to be loved.

Isn't it neat that our God desires to be loved? We all know what that's like. We can relate to that. We all desire to be loved.

That makes it easier to understand how God wants to be loved. It's not hard to love God. It's simple.

Think of what makes you feel loved:

> someone paying attention to you
> someone talking with you
> someone listening to you
> someone spending time with you
> someone writing to you
> someone saying "I love you" to you

God wants that, too.

I think He smiled when David wrote Psalm 18, verse 1: "I love you, O Lord, my strength." I think that made God glad.

If you've never really loved God, please don't despair. You see, God is the *source* of love, so He can help. He knows that people have trouble with love. They fall into it. They fall out of it. God sees that, and He understands it. Better than human beings ever will, I think! But His love is not like that. It is unchanging. Immovable. Forever. "I have loved you with an *everlasting love*," says God (Jeremiah 31:3).

The God who loves us that way can also help us to love Him more. He *wants* to help us. He wants to be our source of love when ours runs out.

Are you "out of love" today? Empty? None left to give?

Are you short of love for your spouse? Your sister? Your brother? Your relative? Your friend? Your enemy? Your God?

Please tell God about it. He is the source of love. "God *is* love" (1 John 4:16). He can give you more when your storehouse of love is low or empty.

Be honest with Him. Confess that you don't love Him enough. He can handle it. He already knows. God wants to help us love Him more.

We might be surprised at how readily God answers that prayer. We may be surprised at the new levels of intimacy we can gain with our God. We may find deeper feelings of love than we knew were possible towards God and towards one another. We may find new joy in delighting in God as He delights in us. We may find a new best friend.

Thou, my best and kindest Friend,
Thou wilt love me to the end.
Let me love Thee more and more,
Always better than before.
In Jesus' name, Amen.

(from *Now The Light Has Gone Away,* hymn text by Frances R. Havergal, 1869.)

Psalm 19 "The law of the Lord is perfect, reviving the soul" (v. 7a).

You wouldn't think that laws could revive your soul. We humans tend to think that laws are hard, oppressive, and punishing.

God doesn't see it that way. He gave us laws to help us, to lift us up, and to "revive our souls."

His laws are perfect.

Let's look at God's most basic and important laws today. We've heard about them ever since Sunday school days. Ever since we were children, God's laws, the Ten Commandments, have been impressed upon most of us. But sometimes we need a review. A refresher. A reviver.

That's what the Ten Commandments can do. They can revive our souls. By reading them and following them, we can be refreshed.

Let's look at one through ten in Deuteronomy 5:7-21 (NIV).

1. You shall have no other gods before me.
2. You shall not make for yourself an idol.

3. You shall not misuse the name of the Lord your God.
4. Observe the Sabbath day by keeping it holy.
5. Honor your father and mother... so that you may live long and that it may go well with you.
6. You shall not murder.
7. You shall not commit adultery.
8. You shall not steal.
9. You shall not give false testimony against your neighbor.
10. You shall not covet your neighbor's wife. You shall not set your desire on your neighbor's house or land... or anything that belongs to your neighbor.

There they are. God's laws. All laid out to help us "prosper and be kept alive" (Deuteronomy 6:24). They're pretty basic, really. Lots of common sense. But if we forget them or don't obey them, all hell breaks loose. Literally. Our lives deteriorate. Become chaotic.

If we *keep* God's laws, "all goes well with us" (Deuteronomy 6:18). Our souls are revived. That's why Psalm 19 says, "By them [God's laws] is your servant warned; in keeping them there is great reward" (v. 11).

If you don't know the rewards of keeping God's laws today, please take a look at them. Read them over again. Begin putting them into practice.

It's never too late to start. If you've started but failed (We all do!), ask God's forgiveness. Confess your failings in keeping God's laws. He will forgive you for Jesus' sake.

Then start again to keep the Ten Commandments. They are for today. They are not out of date. They never will be. They are perfect, reviving our souls.

Dear Lord, help me to keep your commands. Help me to do what is right and good in your sight, so that it may go well with me.* Thank you that in the keeping of your laws there is great reward . . . a reviving of my soul. In Jesus' name, Amen.

- *First part of prayer is a paraphrase of Deuteronomy 6:17-18.*

Psalm 20 " ... may the name of the God of Jacob protect you" (v. 1b).

What is "the name of the God of Jacob?" Moses asked that same question in Exodus 3:13.

He said to God, "Suppose I go to the Israelites and say to them, 'the God of your fathers has sent me to you,' and they ask me, 'What is his name?' Then what shall I tell them?"

God said to Moses (Exodus 3:14), "I AM WHO I AM. This is what you are to say to the Israelites: 'I AM has sent me to you.'"

Isn't that comforting? God didn't call Himself "I WAS," or "I USED TO BE," or "I WILL BE AFTER AWHILE." He said, "Tell the Israelites that the God of their fathers, the God of Abraham, Isaac, and Jacob, the great I AM has sent me to you."

I AM means present tense. It means now. It means God is with us.

God was with Jacob; He was with Moses; and He is with us today. He is ever-present. He is I AM.

Isn't that a good name for God? That's a name you can run to. Anytime. As Proverbs 18:10 says, "The name of the Lord is a strong tower; the righteous run to it and are safe" (NIV). The name of the Lord protects us. It covers us. It gives us identity. Recognition. Respectability. Legitimacy. God's name does all that!

Have you ever known anyone in your community with a really good name? Respectability comes with certain names because those folks have earned it. Perhaps you come from a family who has a good name in your community.

I don't mean clout or false pride or pompousness. Some folks pretend to have good names, but in reality, their names are associated with dishonesty, pompous wealth, and undeserved clout in the community.

No, good names don't mean that. Good names are those who, through generations have come to be known as honest folks. Hard working. Neighborly.

I inherited a name like that. It was through nothing I did. I didn't deserve it. I was born with a good name. Both of my parents and their parents before them had worked hard to make for themselves a good name.

My grandparents on both sides came from Germany. They came here to America with little. They were humble and hardworking. They did not cheat or steal. They did not beg. They raised their children to know and love the Lord. They helped their neighbors. They helped found churches that are still standing and active today, long after my grandparents' deaths.

How do I know all of this? Because good news travels. Good names are remembered. Fondly. With admiration. With respect.

That's how I grew up hearing about both the names of my mother and my father.

My mother's name was Petersen, and my father's name was Winter. Mom tells the story of her father, H. Martin Petersen. He had learned the trade of a baker in Germany, and came here in 1906 at the age of 19. He came alone. He had one dollar in his pocket. H. Martin immigrated to Traverse County in west central Minnesota, where his friend, Sigfried Hinricksen, already had a farm. Sigfried and H. Martin had known each other in Germany before Sigfried had come to America. H. Martin rented land in Traverse County, and with no prior experience in the occupation, became a farmer. In 1917, he married my grandmother, Sophie Koch. They never made much money, but he and Sophie raised three children during the Depression years of the 1930's. During one of those years, H. Martin's entire grain crop fit into one wagon box.

My mom remembers going to town with her father that year. She and her brother, Roy, were just little kids. They hopped into the horse-drawn buggy with their dad, and drove the eight miles to town. Their only mission on that trip was to buy butter for Sophie to use at home. When they got to the creamery, my mom and Roy stayed outside on the sidewalk to play. Their dad went inside but soon came back out with tears in his eyes. The price of butter had gone up. He asked if my mom or Roy had enough money in their pockets between them to make up the difference. They didn't. So H. Martin and his children turned around and drove the eight miles back home without butter. They couldn't afford it.

Those years were tough; too tough for an American in the twenty-first century like me to comprehend.

But still today I hear the stories. I hear about H. Martin Petersen, my grandpa, and the good name he had despite tough times. I hear about how he paid his bills and didn't live beyond his means. I hear about how he went without and still did not complain.

I hear about how years later, after the Depression was over, my mother's sister, Bernita, went looking for a job. She was single yet, and needed to support herself. She had no resume, no previous job experience. She went to the lumber company in her hometown, and asked for employment. "What Petersen are you?" the company's owner asked. "There are so many Petersens."

"I'm H. Martin's daughter," Bernita answered.

"H. Martin's daughter?" came the response. "You've got the job!"

A good name. A good reputation. An honest way of life.

Those are things we can inherit. Those are things we can pass on. From one generation to the next.

God did. He gave us His name. When we give our lives to Christ, we become heirs. Heirs of Christ. We inherit eternal life, and all the riches of God's kingdom. We put on Christ's name.

It is a respectable name, the name of Christ. It opens doors for us. The door of peace. The door of joy. The door of heaven.

It also comes with a great responsibility. The responsibility to live honestly. To follow Christ. To be godly. It is a hard name to live up to. Harder than Petersen or Winter or any other earthly name. But we don't have to keep God's good name by ourselves. The great I AM is present to help us.

He forgives us when we fail. He protects us. He adopts us. He puts on us the name of His Son.

"You're mine," God says of His children. "You are my people who are called by my name" (2 Chronicles 7:14).

Dear Lord, I know that "a good name is more desirable than great riches," and that "to be esteemed is better than silver or gold" (Proverbs 22:1). Whatever my earthly name is, I thank you that I have inherited the good name of Christ. Help me to live my life according to all that your name implies. Thank you for being "I AM," God. Always present. Always with me. May the name of the God of Jacob protect me and all of those I love, all of my life. May your good name be passed on to all those who come after me. In Jesus' name, Amen.

Psalm 21 "O Lord, the king rejoices in your strength" (v. 1b).

Have you ever rejoiced in another's strength? People often admire strength that is greater than their own. We take comfort in knowing that what we can't do, something or someone else can.

The horse is a beautiful example of strength that goes beyond our own. A horse's muscles when running or pulling are miraculous to watch. Many people find pleasure simply in looking at and marveling at a horse's strength.

A tractor, which has even more power than a single horse, can be fascinating to watch as well. Just this past summer I had the opportunity to marvel at a huge Steiger tractor's horse power as it pulled a combine out of our neighbor's field. The combine was stuck in mud in a flooded field, and as the Steiger pulled, smoke and exhaust poured into the air. I wondered if even a huge tractor with four sets of dual tires could budge that combine, but it did! Slowly and steadily, moving at a crawl, the combine started to move out of the mud, and soon was rolling again on its own power.

Human muscle, too, can move mountains, it seems, and can be used to bring help and comfort to others. I remember a particularly stormy Minnesota winter during which my mom and I got our car stuck in a snowdrift. Our tires slid off of the road, and we were quickly embedded in a deep drift in the ditch. We were literally helpless on our own. We could not rock the car out; it was entrenched too firmly. We could not push the car; our strength was insufficient. We could not go for help; the nearest farm was too far away for us to walk there in sub-zero temperatures.

So, we waited. Someone with greater strength than our own was bound to come along. And they did. After 20 or 30 minutes, our neighbors, two brothers, came driving along the same road. Both were in high school, around 16 and 18 years old. They were strong and muscular, able to move mountains, or, in this case, *cars!* (ours!) Within moments, Mom and I and our vehicle were free of our snowdrift, *and* our predicament! Two strong sets of backs, arms, and legs of our neighbors had given us all the strength we needed. They were strong and they were willing to help.

God is the same. He is strong and He is willing to help. He can move mountains, or more practically sometimes, combines or cars!

He can move problems, too. Insurmountable problems. Problems that go far beyond what we can move in our own strength.

God can move mental mountains. ("I can't." "I'm no good." "I'm not smart enough.") He can move physical mountains. (Sickness. Fatigue. Pain.) He can move emotional mountains. (Anxiety. Doubt. Fear.) He can move spiritual mountains. (Fear of judgment. Doubt of salvation. Lack of trust in God.)

That's how strong God is. He can move all those mountains, and more!

It takes a letting go on our part. An acknowledgment of strength greater than our own. A *rejoicing* in God's strength! Part b of our Psalm verse today says, "How great is his (the psalmist's) joy in the victories You give!" God gives the victories in our lives. It is *His* strength that is "made perfect in our weaknesses" (II Corinthians 12:9). That's why the apostle Paul rejoiced in his own weaknesses. The weaker he was, the more God's strength had a chance to be of use.

When we are strong (and we *are* strong in a lot of areas), God's strength does not show itself. Oh, He *provides* the strength. He gives it to us. After all, without Him we can do nothing. "In Him we live and move and have our being" (Acts 17:28). But we do have our own strengths. We can at times rely on those strengths and talents that God gives.

But when those strengths run out, when they fail us (and they will), then only *God's* strength can see us through. Then a surrendering of our will takes place. Then *dependence* comes into play. Then we cry out to God and say, "Help!" "I'm stuck in the mud." "My car is down too deep!" No amount of rocking or pushing on our own strength will move the mountain before us.

If you've never been there, then this meditation won't make sense. Then your own strength, so far, is sufficient.

But mark this page in the book, will you? Because one day, you'll want to come back here. You'll want to remember that "the king rejoiced in *God's* strength." That His strength comes in when ours goes out. That His grace is sufficient.

Sometimes in life that's all there is. God's grace. God's strength.

Ours is gone. Ours is insufficient. That place feels terrible.

But it feels good to let God's Steiger-like strength pull us out of the mud. It feels good to let Him do the work until our wheels are rolling again.

Your wheels will roll again, dear fellow Christian. They may be stuck tight now, but they will move. God will get you going again. His power will do it. He will pull until you're ready to crawl forward on your own strength.

And when you are ready, you will know what it means to rejoice in God's strength. You will crawl forward, and then roll forward more easily, and then, God willing, you may even steam ahead at full speed!

If you have ever divorced, or failed in school, or lost a loved one, or been in financial crisis, or had a mental or nervous breakdown, or gone through treatment for chemical dependency, I think you'll know what I mean.

If you haven't, praise God! Life is hard enough *without* losing or lacking our own strength. But if you have lost yours, or if yours is lacking, take comfort today in a strength greater than your own. Rely on it. Trust it. Let it pull you along until your own strength is renewed.

Maybe you will need only a horse's strength to pull you out of your situation today. Maybe you will need a tractor's strength. Maybe you will need a person's strength. Maybe you will need God's strength.

Whichever source of strength you need today, wait for it. It will come. Then rejoice in it!

O Lord, I rejoice in your strength! In Jesus' name, Amen.

Psalm 22 "Yet you are enthroned as the Holy One; you are the praise of Israel. In you our fathers put their trust; they trusted and you delivered them. They cried to you and were saved; in you they trusted and were not disappointed" (v. 3-5).

"Yet you brought me out of the womb; you made me trust in you even at my mother's breast. From birth I was cast upon you; from my mother's womb you have been my God" (v. 9-10).

Psalm 22 is a psalm of contrasts. On the one hand, the psalmist feels forsaken by God. He cries out to God but does not get an answer. He is scorned by men, and God has not delivered him.

On the other hand, the psalmist hangs on to what he knows to be true of his God. He knows God is still enthroned as the Holy One. He knows that his fathers trusted God and were delivered. He knows that from birth he himself has trusted God.

Have you ever been in a place like that? It is an uncomfortable spot to be in. I remember being in that place when I returned to college after taking a break from it.

I went back to college as a non-traditional student. That means that I was older than three-fourths of the student population on campus. I was excited to go back and get a second degree; this time in vocal music. My first B.A. was in English Literature. But the excitement soon gave way to discouragement as I became sick for the first 3 weeks of school. First my neck muscles spasmed and pinched a nerve. Then I caught a cold and the flu and lost my voice. That's not good for a vocal major! Classes were hard for me anyway, and then I began falling behind because of illness.

And the real clincher was that I prayed long and hard about this before going back to school. I had peace in my heart about it and believed that God wanted me to do it. I even felt that God showed me a special scripture about the winds calming down when the disciples stepped into the boat. I took that to mean that the waves of illness and anxiety would calm down when I went back to college.

But they didn't. The waves didn't calm down for me at all. In fact, they seemed to be rising. I felt forsaken. I felt confused.

That's how the psalmist feels in Psalm 22. His sufferings and situation may have been much worse than mine, yet the feelings are similar. Where are you, God? Why don't you answer? Why have you forsaken me?

What a contrast then to begin verse 3 and verse 9 with "Yet." Did you notice that in our verses for today? Both sections of scripture start with the word "Yet." That word is a *key* when we feel forsaken by God. That word is a *foundation* to stand on when we are tried. It implies contrast. It implies "But." It implies, "There is another side to this coin."

Let's look at the other side in today's psalm. Let's see what follows "yet."

"Yet you are enthroned as the Holy One" (v. 3). That means that even when we feel forsaken and forgotten, God is still in control. No other force has taken over control of the universe or of our lives. This is still God's world. As Maltbie Babcock wrote in 1901 in the famous hymn *This Is My Father's World:*

> *This is my Father's world.*
> *O let me ne'r forget*
> *That though the wrong seems oft so strong,*
> *God is the ruler yet.*

There's that word again... "yet." This hymn writer knew something in 1901 that the psalmist knew in the centuries before Christ . . . God is in control!

Henry W. Longfellow knew it, too. In his famous poem *I Heard The Bells On Christmas Day,* Longfellow echoes our psalmist's contrast:

> *And in despair I bow'd my head;*
> *"There is no peace on earth," I said,*
> *"For hate is strong, and mocks the song*
> *Of peace on earth, good will to men."*

Then pealed the bells more loud and deep:
"God is not dead, nor doth He sleep;
The wrong shall fail, the right prevail,
With peace on earth, good will to men."

How's that for contrast? Longfellow knew it, too; God is still enthroned as the Holy One.

How about verse 9? "Yet you brought me out of the womb; you made me trust in you even at my mother's breast."

If you are a mature Christian, one who has walked with God for many years, you'll know what the psalmist means here. Things may feel bad today. You may feel forsaken. But if you look back over the course of your life, you will see God's hand.

Looking back helps sometimes when the present looks terrible. Look back in your life today. Did you meet Jesus as a child? Did He lead you? Protect you? How about your forefathers? Did they trust God? Did He deliver them? If your own ancestors didn't know or follow God, how about the Israelites, the "descendants of Jacob?" (v.23). We are all descendants of Jacob. All who follow Christ are children of Abraham. All Christians are children of promise. We have a rich history, friends. Whether we look back to our own childhoods to see God's deliverance and mercy or to the history of our ancestors, the Israelites, we see God's hand of deliverance. We see that we have a trustworthy God.

The word "trust" appears four times in our scripture verses for today. It appears after the word "yet." Perhaps that is significant. Perhaps we are being called to trust God even when we feel forsaken or sick or confused.

He may not have delivered us *yet*.

He may not have answered us *yet*.

But my challenge to you and to myself today is to *trust God*. To wait for Him.

He will make it better.

He will answer.

Stand on what you know today:

God is enthroned as the Holy One.

He brought you out of the womb.

He delivered our ancestors, the Israelites.

He will deliver us.

Dear Lord, I don't understand you sometimes. Sometimes I feel forsaken. Yet will I praise you. Yet will I trust you. Yet will I love you. In Jesus' name, Amen.

⌒⌒⌒⌒⌒

Psalm 23 "Your rod and your staff, they comfort me" (v. 4b).

Rod and staff: a stick or sticks used as a support, or as a symbol of authority (Webster's New World Dictionary of the American Language).

Tools of rescue. That's how I like to think of God's rod and staff. A shepherd needs tools like that. Sheep tend to get lost. To stray. To be in need of rescue.

A rod is usually straight. It supports; it steers; it guides; and it doesn't bend.

A staff is bent at the end. It has a crook. It can reach down; it can grasp; it can pull; it can save.

I like to think of the Holy Spirit as a rod, guiding us and keeping us in line. Defending against intruders. Keeping God's children in the way of truth. John 14:16 says, "And I will ask the Father, and he will give you another Counselor to be with you forever - the Spirit of Truth." And in John 14:26 Jesus continues, "the Counselor, the Holy Spirit, whom the Father will send in my name, will teach you all things and will remind you of everything I have said to you."

How's that for a "rod" of truth, of guidance, of support? A rod of truth doesn't bend, but it does gently lead and remind. It keeps us on a "path of righteousness" (Psalm 23:3).

God's staff does that, too. But it has another function as well. It is bent at the end. It can grasp and rescue. I like to think of Jesus as that staff, that tool of rescue. He reaches down with His strong right arm and rescues us from every peril; even death. His blood rescues us from the shadow of death.

Psalm 23 doesn't mince words about death and evil. "Even though I walk through the valley of the shadow of death, I will fear no evil," it says (v. 4a).

Valley.

Shadow.

Death.

Evil.

Those words are real. They suggest peril. A need for rescue.

Rod.

Staff.

Comfort.

Those words come next in the psalm. They are real, too. They suggest deliverance.

Rescue.

Comfort.

Confidence.

God's tools of rescue are unbeatable. His rod and staff can rescue us from *any* situation! Even death is no match for our triune God. Death's shadow may pass over us; it may even hold us in the grave temporarily. But praise God that "if that same Spirit that raised Christ from the dead dwells in us, then He shall quicken our mortal bodies" (Romans 8:11). That's rescue! That is our promise as Christians.

"For God so loved the world, that He gave His only begotten Son, that whosoever believes in Him will not perish, but have everlasting life" (John 3:16).

We need not fear evil, dear fellow Christians. We need not fear death nor its' valley nor its' shadow. God's rod and His staff, they comfort us.

Dear Lord, what other tools could rescue us from death but Jesus and your Holy Spirit? Thank you for your rod and your staff. May they guide me and grasp me whenever I am in peril. May they ultimately lead me through the valley of death without fear, into your loving arms. In Jesus' name, Amen.

Psalm 24 "The earth is the Lord's, and everything in it, the world, and all who live in it; for he founded it upon the seas, and established it upon the waters" (v. 1-2).

A meditation in scripture and verse: Genesis 1:1-10.

"In the beginning God created the heavens and the earth. Now the earth was formless and empty, darkness was over the surface of the deep, and the Spirit of God was hovering over the waters.

And God said, 'Let there be light,' and there was light. God saw that the light was good, and he separated the light from the darkness. God called the light "day," and the darkness he called "night." And there was evening, and there was morning --

the first day.

And God said, 'Let there be an expanse between the waters to separate water from water.' So God made the expanse and separated the water under the expanse from the water above it. And it was so. God called the expanse "sky." And there was evening, and there was morning -- the second day. And God said, 'Let the water under the sky be gathered to one place, and let dry ground appear.' And it was so. God called the dry ground "land," and the gathered waters he called "seas." And God saw that it was good."

> Are there
> oceans in the air?
> Gathered waters
> way up there?
> How did God
> found the earth upon the sea?
>
> Is this
> vast expanse of sky
> to be
> opened when we die?
> Does God who
> made the oceans care for me?
>
> When He
> hovered o'er the deep,
> Did God
> know His son would weep?
> Creation's Maker
> would be hung upon a tree?
>
> Dear God,
> as you made the earth,
> made the waters,
> gave them birth,
> Great Creator,

Will you hover over me?

by Linda Winter-Hodgson

Dear God, indeed you are the Great Creator. The earth is yours, the world, and all who live in it. Use your great creation power, please, in me. Create in me a clean heart. Make me to be all that your creation potential had in mind when you fashioned me. Help me to see You in earth and sky and sea. In Jesus' name, Amen.

Psalm 25 "Remember, O Lord, your great mercy and love, for they are from of old. Remember not the sins of my youth and my rebellious ways; <u>according to your love remember me</u>, for you are good, O Lord" (v. 6-7). (underlining mine)

Remember.
Remember.
What do you remember?

Your first birthday party with friends in elementary school? Fishing in a row boat with your dad? The taste of fresh-picked peas from the garden? The sound of your mother's voice as she sang?

Isn't it amazing how time can soften memories? Not all of them, of course. But often, we tend to remember the good times; the best times. That is how it should be.

God has a memory, too. He remembers "from of old." He remembers from the beginning. Back when things were perfect. The way He created them to be.

I like that phrase, "from of old," in verse 6 of today's psalm. I read a book called *The Education of Little Tree,* by Forrest Carter. The book is about the Cherokee Indians and their ways. The phrase "from of old" reminds me of the Cherokee ways. Indeed, their ways of living with nature are "from of old" in comparison with the white people's more "modern" ways.

Many things from of old are worth remembering. They are worth recalling. Worth pondering. God's love and mercy are two of those things. The psalmist asked God to remember His love and mercy "for they are from of old." And do you know what? I'll bet God did. When David asked God to remember, I believe God sat back and recollected. I'll bet He pondered and thought about how merciful and loving

He's always been, and then I'll bet God smiled.

It makes us glad to remember good things. It makes God glad, too.

Remembering fondly is a way of keeping good things close to our hearts.

That's why David goes on to say, "*according to your love remember me*, for you are good, O Lord" (v. 7).

David knew that not all of God's memories of him were good. David, like all of us, had been rebellious. He had parts of his youth that he'd rather not recall. They were embarrassing. Shameful. Sinful.

So he said to God, "Remember not the sins of my youth." Instead, David asked, "according to your love remember me."

That's how a father remembers a child. Not according to everything the child has done wrong, but according to how much he loves him or her. A parent remembers a child's first bath. A first loose tooth. A first haircut. When parents grow old, these are the things they fondly remember. Not the quarrels. Not the slammed doors. Not the harsh words.

That's how God is. He remembers us according to His love. Not according to our sins.

Have you ever noticed after someone dies, how the good memories and good times you spent together come flooding back at certain times? The good washes over the bad and fills up our minds with reminiscences to keep.

I like a certain passage from *The Education of Little Tree* in regard to memories. I want to share it with you today as you think of Psalm 25.

Little Tree, a 5-year-old Indian boy, has just helped his Grandpa bury their dog, Ol' Ringer. The dog has died while saving the little boy's life.

"And so we left him, under the water oak tree. I felt total bad about it, and empty.

Grandpa said he knew how I felt, for he was feeling the same way. But grandpa said everything you lost which you had loved give you that feeling. He said the only way around it was not to love anything, which was worse because you would feel empty all the time. Grandpa said, supposin' Ol' Ringer had not been faithful; then we would not be proud of him. That would be a worse feeling. Which is right. Grandpa said when I got old, I would remember Ol' Ringer, and I would like it - to remember. He said it was a funny thing, but when you got old and remembered them you loved, you only remembered the good, never the bad, which proved the bad didn't count nohow."

The bad "didn't count nohow."

That's how it is when our sins are buried under Christ's blood. God can't see them anymore. He can only remember the good, according to His love.

Dear God, when you remember me, may you like it. May it make you smile. Remember the good times we have together Lord. Hide the rest under Jesus' blood, never to be remembered. Remember me according to your love, O Lord, and help me to do the same for others. In Jesus' name, Amen.

⁓⦕⦖⁓

Psalm 26 "Test me, O Lord, and try me, examine my heart and my mind" (v. 2).

"Examine my heart and my mind."

Have you ever asked God to do this for you? Have you trusted Him enough to let Him do it?

I have. But not before tonight. Not really. I never really took the time. Let me explain, if you will.

As I read this verse in Psalm 26 tonight, I thought of my medical doctor. He's been examining me a lot lately.

You see, I've been having a great deal of trouble swallowing food for the past few months, and it's become a serious medical problem. I've lost lots of weight, and really didn't have much to lose to begin with. Lack of nutrition is affecting my mind, my thinking, my physical functioning, etc. So, I've been in the doctor's office a lot lately.

This week I had a 40-minute physical examination. If you've ever had a thorough physical, you'll know what I mean. There are blood tests, and neurological tests, and x-rays, and gynecological tests, and questions, and lots of jabbing and poking. Did I mention jabbing and poking? Some of the tests are painful and uncomfortable and some of them can be downright *embarrassing*. Anyway, you get the picture.

Well, my present doctor has been my physician for many years. And I have to tell you that even with all of the jabbing and poking and embarrassing tests, I never felt scared or uncomfortable in his presence. His nurse was in the room, too, and they both have seen my husband and I through lots of trying times. They are trustworthy people.

Sometimes they have to do things that hurt. Things I don't like. But I trust them.

When my doctor works on me, he is gentle. I ask him to be. He knows I am very sensitive to pain, and over the years he has learned what it takes to comfort me. I need lots of explanations. Lots of talking. A gentle touch whenever possible. My doctor knows me, and so he does the best he can to provide this kind of medical care.

As I read the words of Psalm 26, verse 2 tonight, I thought of my physician's gentle, caring examination, and it amazed me that through all of the physical exam in his office, I was not fearful of him.

So, tonight, as I felt God quicken this verse to my heart, I felt Him also ask, "Are you fearful of Me? Can I examine you, Linda? Can I test you and try you to see if there is anything wrong? Anything that needs fixing? After all, I am the Great Physician."

Then, I sat back in my rocker, and I said, "OK, God. Yes. You can examine me. You can probe me. Probe as deep as You like. I'm not embarrassed. After all, you've already seen it all anyway."

And do you know what? I found that I wasn't afraid of God, either. He knows me. Much better than any human doctor ever will. He is gentle. So gentle. So careful.

God has never made a wrong diagnosis. Be it a physical problem, a mental problem, an emotional problem, or a spiritual problem, God has never missed a step. And best of all, He not only diagnoses, He treats and heals, as well. God even does surgery if need be. He takes out the "tumors," if you will, that sometimes lie in our character.

Tonight I asked God for a complete physical. There was no charge, by the way! I believe He gave me one as I sat in my chair. I felt His presence. I gave Him the time He needed to do His job. I didn't get up. I didn't do anything else. I didn't rush God. I just sat there until I felt he was finished.

Sounds strange, I'm sure. But it's the truth.

I don't know if the tests are all back yet. Sometimes with physicians we have to wait for the results. But I know that whatever they are, God will let me know. All I have to do is listen.

Whether it's my swallowing problem, or a flaw in my character, or an emotional, physical, or psychological problem, God has the answer. He diagnoses, and He heals.

He may use doctors. He may not. He may heal instantaneously. He may treat us over a period of time.

But after tonight's examination by God, I know that I can trust Him. I know that He is the Great Physician. I know that He will examine and treat you, too, if you let Him. He will be gentle. He will be careful. He will be loving. So loving.

I think you'll be surprised.
When you're with a good doctor, there's no fear.
Just gratitude.
Just trust.

Great Physician, I allow You right now to examine me fully. Diagnose my problems, Lord. If I need surgery, please schedule me soon. Remove the bad and hurting parts from me. Renew my body, heart, soul, and mind. Please give me the courage to sit still long enough for You to thoroughly examine me. Thank you for being so gentle and so caring. I await your test results, Lord, knowing that you have a plan for my healing. In Jesus' wonderful name, Amen.

❧

Psalm 27 "One thing I ask of the Lord, this is what I seek: that I may dwell in the *house of the Lord all the days of my life, to gaze upon the beauty of the Lord and to seek Him in his temple" (v. 4).*

What do you like to gaze at? A sunset? A mountain? A sun catcher in your window? A knick-knack on your shelf? A photo of a friend? The face of one you love?

Today I am gazing at a Christmas tree. It is standing in our living room, decorated and lighted, awaiting the arrival of Christmas in just two more weeks. I enjoy so much looking at each ornament. Each one is from a special person in my life over the years. My husband's miniature village scene lies below the tree, lighted with baby-lights and rippling with white cotton snow. Honestly, I could gaze at it for hours. At night, with all other lights off, my husband and I sometimes do!

That's how it will be in heaven, too, except we won't be gazing at a Christmas tree. We'll be gazing at Jesus' face.

It will shine and sparkle more than any decoration. It will dazzle, but more than that, I think it will *invite*.

I believe that Jesus' face will invite our gaze. It will say, "Look at me. I love you."

It will be more beautiful and more pleasurable to look at Jesus' face than anything we can imagine.

David imagined it in Psalm 27. It is all he asks of the Lord. That he might "dwell in the house of the Lord *all the days of his life*, to gaze upon the beauty of the Lord."

All the days of our lives. What do you think? Will we get tired of gazing at Jesus?

I think not.

In fact, I know not.

Gazing at something beautiful is pleasurable. It is healing. It is soothing.

Beauty is important to me. Sometimes beautiful art work, beautiful music, beautiful natural wonders, or beautiful architecture do more for me than any words can. We are designed to enjoy beauty. It is here for our pleasure. It is also here for God's pleasure. He created it. We are to preserve it and enhance it whenever we can.

If you are blind, perhaps you might think this doesn't relate. And yet, I imagine blind people experience beauty and the need for beauty in their lives every bit as much as sighted people do. We all desire comfortable surroundings, if not to gaze at, then to feel, to hear, to smell, to taste. And, if one or more of those senses has been lacking on earth, in heaven all of our senses will be restored! We *all* can gaze upon the beauty of the Lord!

We can experience it. We can be surrounded by it. We can be healed in it. We will be *whole* in it.

That's heaven. Forever to look at Jesus' face. Forever to be in his company. Forever to be surrounded with beauty: The beauty of the Lord.

Dear Jesus, I know that Your word says that in heaven "there is a river whose streams make glad the city of God" (Psalm 46:10). I look forward to seeing that river, and I know it will make me glad; but more than that, I look forward to seeing Your face. I may glance away for a while at that river, or at my mansion, or at the other beauties in heaven, but always I know that my gaze will be drawn back to Your face. Amen.

Psalm 28 "Praise be to the Lord for he has heard my cry for mercy. The Lord is my strength and my shield; my heart trusts in him, and I am helped. My heart leaps for joy and I will give thanks to him in song" (v. 6-7).

Those of you who are reading these meditations in order will remember that in Psalm 26, I asked God, the Great Physician, to examine me. I said that the test results weren't back yet. Well, it's been a few weeks since then, and I think at least some of the test results are in.

There were no physical problems this time. My swallowing and eating problems seem to all be coming from stress. You know, "stress;" the big "s" word. We all have it to some degree in our lives. Some of us handle stress well, and some of us don't. I don't. At least not most of the time.

But do you know what? I'm getting better at it! That's the neat thing in the Kingdom of God. We can *always* get better! "My heart trusts in Him, and *I am helped*," says Psalm 28, verse 7.

I am helped.

That's what I feel like today. I'm not entirely cured yet. I still have some trouble swallowing food when I'm stressed. I still don't handle stress as well as I'd like. But it *is* better. I *am* helped.

Sometimes all we need are a few signs that things are going to get better. For me, those signs came during a three-week Christmas vacation since my writing about Psalm 26. During that vacation, I gained one quarter of a pound. That may not seem like much, but when you've been losing four pounds every week without wanting to, believe me, gaining one-quarter pound is a *big* deal! It's a little reminder that things can turn around. They can get better. It may take better management of my time, my job, my schooling, etc., but it can and will get better!

Another sign is the encouragement of friends and loved ones. For me, that has helped more than anything during this hard time of dealing with stress and its' symptoms. Friends and family have written notes, called on the phone, and prayed. They have been constant reminders of God's love for me through His body of believers.

Another sign to me that things will get better is God's Word, the Bible. All through the Bible, God's people went through seasons of "stress," if you will. Seasons of despair. Seasons of trouble. Seasons of hardship. Seasons of discouragement. The psalms are full of these seasons. That's real life. But the Bible is also full of descriptions of the seasons of abundance. Seasons of prosperity. Seasons of good health. Seasons of rejoicing. Seasons of praising. Seasons of victory.

That's why Psalm 28, verse 7 also says, "My heart leaps for joy and I will give thanks to him in song."

We won't always be "leaping" for joy. But isn't it great that sometimes, *we will!*

I'm not quite into a season of "leaping" yet with my swallowing problem, but I can say today with the psalmist, "My heart trusts in him, and I am helped."

That's a big first step out of a problem!

If you aren't there yet in your set of circumstances, don't despair. Life is a cycle of seasons. Some are hard and difficult. Some are easy and joyful. It was that way for people in the Bible, and it is that way for us today.

God *is* with us.

He *has* heard our cries for mercy.

We *can* trust in him and be helped.

Dear Lord, whether I am in the midst of a trial, or in the process of being helped, or in a season of ease and leaping for joy, help me to remember the cycles of life. Thank you for the written accounts of your people in the Bible who went though seasons in their lives similar to my own. Thank you for the psalms. In Jesus' name, Amen.

Addendum: I have to smile when looking back at the time when I wrote this meditation. Since then, my problem with swallowing food has not only gone away, I now have the opposite problem of eating *too much* food and having gained more weight than I'd like! God is faithful through all of the stages of our lives! I remember back now to the days when I prayed to gain even one quarter pound, and realize that sometimes a few extra pounds are not that big a deal to worry about!

Psalm 29 "Ascribe to the Lord the glory due his name" (v. 2a).

Have you ever done something and not gotten credit for it? How did it make you feel? Maybe you've hosted a party and no one realized or acknowledged all the work and effort you put into it. Maybe you've written a song and no one has sung or played it. Maybe you've written a poem or a story that has never been published.

Maybe someone stole one of your ideas and later took credit for it. Maybe you're a child who turned in a great project or assignment at school only to lose credit because of a mistake or a forgotten name on the paper.

There are all sorts of ways to lose the credit due our names. It happens to people all the time.

It happens to God, too.

Sometimes God miraculously saves people from a car accident and the news reports that those who escaped were lucky. Sometimes we look at the beauty all around us and attribute it all to Mother Nature. We forget that *God* deserves the glory.

If we feel bad when people don't acknowledge our work, think how God must feel when His work is not acknowledged. We sometimes deserve *some* credit for what we do, but God deserves *all glory; all credit* is due His name.

Every good and every perfect gift is from God the Father (James 1:17).

The psalmist recognized that truth when he said, "Ascribe to the Lord the glory due His name." Ascribing proper credit and thanks to God is part of worshipping Him. When we have learned to ascribe, or to assign, *all good gifts* as having come from God, then we are on our way to worship!

Dear God, all glory is due your name! You have made all things. All of your gifts are good and perfect. Please forgive me for forgetting to give you proper credit. Forgive me for forgetting to thank you. Help me to remember that all luck is really blessing, that all coincidence is really your hand at work in our lives, and that all of Mother Nature is really your creative handiwork. Today I choose to sit and meditate on what You have done, and to give You glory for it. I ascribe all glory to Your name, the name above all names. You deserve all glory and all credit, Lord. I worship You. In Jesus' name, Amen.

Psalm 30 "O Lord, when you favored me, you made my mountain stand firm; but when you hid your face, I was dismayed" (v. 7).

My sister has a neat custom which she does every year. On New Year's Day she reviews the past year in her mind, and chooses her favorite day. Sometimes she chooses two or three days. Days that stand out to her. Days that were special. Days that she'll remember as the best of that year.

I had one of those most memorable days on January 18th, 1994. It was a day when God "favored me." January 18th, 1994 was three days before a little ten-year-old girl named Jessica came to live with my husband and me. We would soon be adopting her as our daughter.

You might think that January 21st, 1994 would have been my choice for best day of that year, since that was the day Jessica actually came to join our family. And believe me, that day was one of my choices, too! But January 18th was special for me.

You see, it was 73 degrees below zero that day in Minnesota where we live. That's with windchill; without windchill, it was only 35 below! Because of those cruel, cold temperatures, *all* schools were cancelled by order of the governor of Minnesota. Even the university where my husband taught was closed that day! That meant Ken and I got to stay home all day together! We got to ponder and prepare for one of the biggest events of our lives . . . the arrival of a daughter!

Isn't God good to give us special days of knowing His favor? In all my life I had never felt God give me a day just to ponder and prepare. Maybe I had never needed one before. I don't know. But that day the thought kept coming to me that God was saying: "Just ponder. Just realize what I am doing. Think about all I have done to lead you throughout your life. Think about the fact that I have plans for you that you don't even know about! Think about the fact that I prepared this adoption for you and Ken and Jessica long before you even thought of it! Think of how I plan out lives; how I blend them together. Think about my sovereignty. Think about my love."

So I thought. I pondered. And it felt *so good!*

Have you ever done it? Just taken a day, a whole *gob* of time, just to ponder? It's a luxury, but it's worth it! It's worth it just to trace the path of God's love in your life.

Life hasn't always been rosy for me, believe me! And it won't always be rosy in the future. But God has never left me! He has never quit directing me! Sometimes He has let me wander around in the desert for a while, like the Israelites, but even then, He didn't leave me. Days like January 18th, 1994 remind me that even then, even during wilderness times, God had special days in mind. He had a plan. "A plan to give me a future and a hope" (Jeremiah 29:11).

I don't know when your special days of God's favor will come. I don't know what your best day of this year, or of any year, or of your life will be. Maybe there will be several. But I do know that whether we are in a wilderness time of wandering and feeling lost, or whether we are on top of the mountain, God has a special day of His favor planned for us in the future! He has *plans* for you, dear Christian friend!

My husband and I had to wait eight years for our special day of adopting a child. Maybe that is a short time in the plans of God. I don't know. It seemed long to us. But I am learning that God's best days are worth waiting for. I am learning to thank and trust God for special days of His favor. Days of pondering. Days of preparing. Days of resting in God's plans.

Dear Lord, thank you for favoring us with special days in our lives. Thank you for days when our "mountain" stands firm. Thank you for days when life feels solid and good! I know there will be many times ahead when my mountain won't stand firm. It will wobble. I will feel dismayed. Help me then to remember <u>the special days of your favor.</u> Help me to trust, and to wait for more of those good days. In Jesus' name, Amen.

⌁⌁⌁

Psalm 31 "How great is your goodness, which you have stored up for those who fear you, which you bestow in the sight of men on those who take refuge in you. In the shelter of your presence you hide them from the intrigues of men; in your dwelling you keep them safe from accusing tongues" (v. 19-20).

Intrigues excite interest or curiosity. They are plans or schemes of men which are secretive or underhanded. Intrigues include anything from idle gossip to secret love affairs.

People are interested in "the intrigues of men." That is why soap operas flourish. That is why sensationalistic magazines and newspapers survive.

God says that He will hide Christians from the intrigues of men. We don't have to get caught up in them.

It isn't easy to steer clear of gossip and intrigue and slanderous tongues nowadays. It may mean staying home from certain events. It may mean shutting off certain TV shows. It may mean "making it our ambition to lead a quiet life, to mind our own business and to work with our hands" (I Thessalonians 4:11 NIV).

That isn't easy in the United States these days. Life is often anything but quiet. But I believe that as Christians, we are still being called to do as the Bible says:

To live quiet lives (I Thess. 4:11)
To fear God (Psalm 31:19)
To take refuge in Him (Psalm 31:19)
To mind our own business (I Thess. 4:11)
To work with our hands (I Thess. 4:11)

If we make it our ambition to do even those five things, I believe we will see God's goodness in a special way. We will be kept safe from accusing tongues. We will be hidden from the intrigues of men. That is a promise from God.

Two of my best friends are teachers. They see and are exposed to many "intrigues" in their schools. Many of these intrigues are discussed in detail in the faculty lounge. There is slander and idle talk. Both of my friends have made decisions to pack a lunch and to eat elsewhere. They do not spend time in the faculty lounge. It has, in their schools, become a place of gossip. I admire them for their desire to lead a quiet, godly life. Steering clear of the intrigues of men is just one step on the road to that end.

I admire, too, the ways of my late father, Lorence Winter. Many times he made the difficult and unpopular decision for his family to stay home at night. There were endless school functions to attend, and many of our friends were gone to something most nights of the week. Dad's decisions for us to spend evenings together at home as a family were often met with opposition, especially from his kids! But when I look back on it, I see my Dad as a *guardian* of our family. He made it his ambition to lead a quiet life, to mind his own business, and to work with his hands. I learned that from him. We had plenty of friends and plenty of fun, but we also learned the joy of staying home together and spending a quiet evening. We played cards; we sang around the piano; we read; we visited. We were kept safe from many of the intrigues of men.

Our heavenly Father does the same for us as a family of believers. He guards us jealously from the intrigues of men. He keeps us safe from slander and gossip and schemes and busyness. He shepherds us. He desires that we take refuge in him, away from the world's busy pace. In the shelter of his presence we are safe from the intrigues of men.

Lord, may we experience the joy and peace of being "hidden away" from the intrigues of men. Help us, Lord, as we make it our ambition to lead quiet lives, to mind our own business, and to work with our hands. In Jesus' name, Amen.

Psalm 32 "I will instruct you and teach you in the way you should go; I will counsel you and watch over you. Do not be like the horse or the mule, which have no understanding but must be controlled by bit and bridle or they will not come to you" (v. 8-9).

Will you come to the Lord? Do you have to be *dragged* away from work and duties and recreation before you'll sit quietly with God?

I'm that way sometimes. Those are my dry spells. Times when I have not been at God's watering hole for a long time. Times without refreshment from His Word.

Those times are pretty bad. And usually the longer I stay away from God's word, the harder it is to get back. I feel guilty. I feel like God won't say anything to me in His Word, because He'll be punishing me.

"You haven't read the Bible for 3 weeks," (3 months, 3 years, etc., take your pick; whatever fits your situation!) I think I can hear God saying. "You haven't sat down and talked with me and listened to me, so now I'll never talk with you again."

Does that sound like God's voice to you? NO! That's the voice of guilt and of condemnation. God doesn't talk like that.

He may indeed feel bad when we haven't read the Bible or spent time with Him, but His words are different.

He says, "I will instruct you and teach you in the way you should go; I will counsel you and watch over you" (v. 8).

And earlier in Psalm 32, after the psalmist confesses His sin to God, God "forgives the guilt of his sin" (v. 5).

That's the kind of *friend* we have in God! One who forgives. One who *wants* fellowship with us. One who *wants* to talk to us in his Word.

God will not put a bit or bridle in our mouths. He will not drag us to His feet or to His Word. He will not force us.

But He does say, "*Come.*" He does *invite.*

He does this even when we've been away for a while. A few days. A few years. A lifetime.

God doesn't care how long. He's interested in *now.* He's interested in "forgiving the guilt of our sin" (v. 5), and getting on with His close friendship with us!

"Let's get on with it!" God says.

"I want to instruct you."

"I want to teach you."

"I want to counsel you."
"I want to watch over you."

No bits.
No bridles.
No force.
Just an open, anytime invitation from God to *come*.

What a friend we have in Jesus,
All our sins and griefs to bear!
What a privilege to carry
Everything to God in prayer!
O what peace we often forfeit;
O what needless pain we bear,
All because we do not carry
Everything to God in prayer.

(from the hymn *What A Friend We Have In Jesus* by Joseph Scriven.)

Psalm 33 "From heaven the Lord looks down and sees <u>all</u> mankind; from his dwelling place he watches <u>all</u> who live on earth - he who forms the hearts of <u>all</u>, who considers <u>everything</u> they do" (v. 13-15). (underlining mine)

"All" and "everything" are encompassing words. They are inclusive. They leave nothing and no one out.

"From heaven the Lord looks down and sees *all* mankind; from his dwelling place he watches *all* who live on earth - he who forms the hearts of *all*, who considers *everything* they do." Read that out loud, won't you? What does it mean to you? Do you believe it?

There are many Christians who don't. Many Christians don't believe that God cares about *everything* they do. Oh, the big things, maybe. But not the little things. Not the day to day, hour by hour, moment by moment things of life. God is too busy with the whole world to be bothered with those things, right?

Wrong. Psalm 33 says that God *considers everything* we do. He doesn't just see it; he considers it. He knows when a sparrow falls, my friend (Matthew 10:29). Our God cares about the *details* of our lives.

Recently I stayed on the 12th floor of a large hotel in a big city. There were 23 floors in all. As I looked down on the streets below me from my hotel room window, it seemed incredible to me that God knew at that precise moment the details of every person's life in every car and in every skyscraper's window.

The city can be overwhelming to me. I come from a farm in west central Minnesota. The land is flat, and the farms are miles apart. It's easier there, somehow, to believe that God considers the details of every life. There are fewer lives to consider! But in a huge city, with people and offices stacked on top of one another, how does God do it?

I have to admit that I don't know *how*, but I do know that *He does*. The Bible doesn't lie. His words are true. "From heaven the Lord looks down and considers *all* mankind. From the remotest jungle to the busiest city, God "watches *all* who live on earth." Isn't that comforting?

Sometimes we can feel insignificant. Lost in the crowd. Unnoticed.

But God says, "I notice." "I formed your heart." "I consider *everything* you do."

How should that knowledge affect our daily living? I believe that it is closely tied to prayer.

"Make my life a prayer to you," says a Christian song by Keith Green. "I want to do what You want me to." I believe that our lives, moment by moment, are to be lived as a prayer to God. Constantly. Always. Every minute. He cares about our every decision.

Yes, the choices are up to us. We can wear a red shirt or a blue one. We can take this road or that road. We can marry this person or that person.

But if our whole life is being lived as a prayer to God, His spirit will be affecting our choices. Our choices will affect others. God's love will be manifest through the details of our lives.

We can ask God to be part of our daily decisions, from the smallest to the largest. We can talk to Him in our minds *constantly*. He considers *everything* we do. There is no greater delight in daily living than to include God in every step.

Dear God, thank you for considering <u>all</u> that I do. Help me to take you with me to the grocery store, to the park, to my workplace. You are there already; make me aware of

Your presence so that I can know the joy of including you in every decision. Make my life a prayer to you, O God. In Jesus' name, Amen.

～≈℮℮℮～

Psalm 34 "Those who look to him are radiant; their faces are never covered with shame" *(v. 5). (underlining mine)*

What is your face covered with? What do people see when they look at you? When you walk down the street, and people catch your eye, what do they think of afterwards?

"Radiance" is a lovely quality. It means "shining brightly;" "beaming;" "issuing from a source as in rays;" "giving forth or sending out (happiness, love, etc.)."

Shining brightly. Beaming.

Is that what your face does? It probably can't on its own. Not even with makeup! But with God, it can! "Those who look to him are radiant!"

As a child, I had two nicknames which I remember fondly now as an adult. They were similar to one another: "Sunshine," and "Merry Sunshine." My Uncle Ray started the first nickname, and a lady in our church started the other. I remember so well crossing the aisle of our country church every Sunday after services to greet the people in the pews across from us. First I got a hug from Uncle Ray and Aunt Flo.

"Hello, Sunshine!" Ray would bellow, in his big, booming voice. Behind him a few rows back sat our neighbor lady.

"Good morning, Merry Sunshine," was her greeting every time, as she reached her hand across the pews to shake mine. I can still hear those voices, calling me those names.

"Merry Sunshine."

It makes me smile even now.

As a child, I didn't think much about those nicknames. But looking back, they must've had an impact, because I still remember them vividly many years later!

I am not boasting that I had such a beautiful or pretty face as to be called "Sunshine." Far from it! I inherited a big nose right along with the rest of my family! But Psalm 34 says, "My soul *will boast in the Lord*" (v. 2).

As a child, I knew Jesus, and it showed in my face! Jesus *radiates* from within us! We can't help but bring sunshine to the lives of others when Jesus is living within!

What a joy!
What a pleasure!
What a delight!
To have *God* inside!

"Lift up the light of your countenance upon us, O Lord," says Psalm 4, verse 6. With the light of God shining from within, our countenance, too, will radiate light. Our faces will show the love of God! They will never be covered with shame (Psalm 34:5).

Today when I take walks, I often see faces covered with shame. With guilt. With self-absorption. With self-centeredness. With anger. With get-outta-my-way looks. With hurt.

God sees these faces, too. He says, "Look to me. Only with Me living inside your heart can your facial expression change. It can shine. It can beam. It can radiate my love."

If you see a hurting face today, look at their eyes. Make contact. Show them Jesus in you. Even if it is only a brief glance, may they walk away feeling somehow brighter because Jesus' love shone on them.

Dear Lord, my prayer today is a children's song that I learned so long ago. May it be my lifelong promise.

> *I'll be a sunbeam for Jesus,*
> *To shine for Him each day.*
> *In every way try to please Him,*
> *At home, at work, at play.*
> *A sunbeam, a sunbeam,*
> *Jesus wants me for a sunbeam;*
> *A sunbeam, a sunbeam,*
> *I'll be a sunbeam for Him!*

(by Nellie Talbot)

In Jesus' name, Amen.

Psalm 35 "Contend, O Lord, with those who contend with me" (v. 1a).

A Christian friend of mine is in court today. She is fighting for her children. She is fighting for her reputation. She is fighting for her life. My friend is going through divorce.

She called and asked my husband and me to pray. Especially today. Especially when she is in court.

We have prayed for her and for her husband and for her children many times. She has prayed unceasingly. She has tried for years to make this marriage work. It is not our place, or any other person's place, Christian or non-Christian, to sit in the judgment seat when people are getting divorced or are going through other hard times. It is our place as Christians, to pray.

Today, on this court date for my friend, I prayed Psalm 35. I prayed it out loud; all of it; word for word. I put her name in every sentence. I placed this psalm prayer before God's altar, and asked that it would rise before Him as incense.

I know He heard. He is the great contender. God contends with those who contend with us. He fights for us.

If you have ever been slandered, or falsely accused, you will know what I mean. People can be merciless. They can "seek our life" (v. 4). They can be "ruthless witnesses" (v. 11). They can "repay evil for good" (v. 12). They can "slander without ceasing," and "maliciously mock" (v. 15-16). They can "hate without reason" and "devise false accusations against those who live quietly in the land" (v. 19-20).

Not a very pleasant list, is it? But it is true. Scripture says it can happen. People can be that cruel.

But the psalmist knows who to turn to in these circumstances. He knows God. God "turns back those who plot our ruin" (v. 4). God "rescues the poor from those too strong for them, and the poor and needy from those who rob them" (v. 10). God "delights in the well-being of his servant" (v. 27).

That is how we ought to be, dear friends. Not slanderous. Not ruthless. Not accusing. Not hateful. We ought to "delight in the *well-being* of God's servants." We ought to pray for it. We ought to seek it. We ought to rejoice in it.

Dear God, today I pray for all those who are contending. Please contend for them, O Lord. Please step in and fight for your servants. Please rescue them and bring about their vindication. May I, like You, O God, <u>delight</u> in the well-being of your servants. I *pray for the well-being of all your servants today. In Jesus' name, Amen.*

Psalm 36 "An oracle is within my heart concerning the sinfulness of the wicked" 1a).

An "oracle" is a prayer or revelation or statement. Have you ever had one of those within your heart?

The psalmist had an oracle within his heart concerning the wicked. To be honest with you, I have one, too. I didn't always have thoughts or prayers or revelations or statements about the wicked, but lately some things have happened within my own community that have caused me to formulate some statements about the wicked.

Oh, these people I'm referring to don't think that they're wicked. But that's the very revelation of the psalmist. The wicked "flatters himself too much to detect or hate his own sin" (v. 2). "There is no fear of God before his eyes" (v.1).

There's no need to go into detail about the wickedness I've encountered lately. Suffice it to say that I've seen greed, cursing, name-calling, inhumane treatment of animals, and inhumane treatment of people in my own community. And the sad thing is that in each instance of wickedness, those involved are not repentant. They do not detect or hate their own sin.

Now don't get me wrong. I know that *all* of us are wicked at heart. All of us are in need of Jesus' cleansing blood. All of us need to repent daily of our sins and wrongs. All of us need to walk in God's forgiveness.

But do you know the kind of wickedness I'm talking about? The kind the psalmist is talking about? The kind of wickedness where people have "ceased to be wise and to do good?"(v.3). The kind of wickedness where people "commit themselves to a sinful course and do not reject what is wrong?" (v. 4).

That's the kind of disregard for God that can be disheartening. It can cause Christians to feel overwhelmed. Outnumbered. Overpowered.

If you have ever been to a meeting and been one of the only ones to stand up for what you believe to be a righteous cause, you will know what I mean. Godly ways, loving ways, are not the ways of the world. They are not the ways of the wicked.

The psalmist knew that in his day, too. He chose to pray about it; he chose to write an oracle about it; he chose to compare it (wickedness) to God's love. After stating the facts about the wicked, the psalmist encourages himself (and us!) by stating the facts about God. What a contrast!

> God's love, he says, reaches to the heavens (v. 5).
> God's faithfulness reaches to the skies (v. 5).
> God's righteousness is like the mighty mountains (v. 6).
> God's justice is like the great deep (v. 6).
> God preserves both man and beast (v. 6).
> God's unfailing love is priceless! (v.7).

That's an oracle, too. That is a revelation or statement about God's love. That is an encouragement!

It is good to have within our hearts an oracle concerning the sinfulness of the wicked. It is good to understand wickedness and how it sets itself up against Godly ways.

It is also good to have an oracle within our hearts about the love of God. It is good to understand love and how it never fails (I Corinthians 13:8).

Next time we are at a meeting, friends, or in any situation where wickedness prevails, let us remember to keep an oracle in our hearts concerning that situation. Let us remember that God's love and righteousness and justice never fail. Let us remember to pray. Let us remember to keep the truth in our hearts about God's love. Let us write about it. Let us speak it out.

We need oracles concerning the sinfulness of the wicked.

And we need oracles concerning the all-powerful, unfailing love of God.

Dear Lord, today my prayer is the last three verses of our psalm, "Continue your love to those who know you, your righteousness to the upright in heart. May the foot of the proud not come against me, nor the hand of the wicked drive me away. See how the evildoers lie fallen - thrown down, not able to rise!" (Psalm 36:10-12).

Psalm 37 "Do not fret; it leads only to evil" (v. 8b).

That verse could've been written especially for me. I fret a lot. I worry.

Luke 12:25 says, "Who of you can add one moment to his life's course by worrying?" (Gideon Bible).

I know what the Bible says about worrying, and yet I do it. But verses like these help me. If you have a problem with worrying, they can help you, too. We can become people who worry less and trust more. God's living Word and life-changing power can do that.

What are some things we worry about? Luke 12 mentions food and clothes. Psalm 37 mentions evil-doers and their successes. Let's bring those things up to modern-day equivalents. We may not all worry about food in the sense of having enough, but how about these examples:

We weigh too much.

We weigh too little.

Either way, we can become obsessed with diets and diet plans. We can worry about our weight. Or, try this modern-day food dilemma:

We're having a party. What should we serve?

Will we have time to prepare the food?

Will there be enough variety?

Is the table set just right?

Is my house clean enough?

Sounds like worry to me!

Then there are clothes. Many of us in America have enough of those, but how about this scenario:

Clothing catalogs come in our mailbox. We want more than we can afford.

We see ads on TV. We want more. We worry.

Do I have the right clothes to fit in at school? At my job?

And how about evil-doers? Psalm 37:1 says, "Do not fret because of evil men or be envious of those who do wrong." Do you ever fret on this account?

How about:

When a law is passed by our government that you disagree with morally or politically? Do you fret, or trust God?

When someone cheats on their income tax and seems to be more well-off financially than those who are honest? Do we fret? Are we envious?

God says, "Don't be!" Don't be envious. Don't worry. Not only does it do no good, it leads to evil!

Have you ever thought of that? How fretting can lead to evil? I hadn't thought of it too much until today's scripture verse spoke to my heart. You see, the opposite of fretting is trusting. Verse 7 of Psalm 37 says, "Be still before the Lord and wait patiently for him; do not fret when men succeed in their ways, when they carry out their wicked schemes." Verse 3 says, "Trust in the Lord and do good; dwell in the land and enjoy safe pasture."

When we trust, we are still. We wait. We do good things. We enjoy safe pasture.

When we fret, we take matters into our own hands. We say, "If God isn't going to help me, I'll help myself." We jump ahead. We make poor choices. Rather than enjoying the safe pasture God has given us, we become discontented. We break out of the safe pasture into uncharted territory. We walk on dangerous ground.

Do you see the progression from fretting to doing evil? That's what Psalm 37 is all about: the difference between fretting and trusting. Between evil and good. Between the wicked and the blameless. "Do not fret," says God, "it leads only to evil."

That is a strong word to my heart today. I want to *trust* and not fret.

Dear God, so often I worry. I confess that as sin today. Please forgive me. Thank you. Please remind me not to fret, for it leads only to evil. Let me instead trust you, and let that trust lead to good. In Jesus' name, Amen.

<hr />

Psalm 38 "My bones have no soundness because of my sin" (v. 3b).

A lot of the psalms aren't very pleasant. They deal with pain and anguish and suffering and questioning and waiting. But then, so does life. Our lives encompass these things. Jesus' life did, too. Isn't it encouraging to know that the psalmist was just like us? And he and God cared enough about us to write about these experiences for future generations!

Today the psalmist is in agony. He has "no health in his body" (v. 7). To make matters worse, it's because of his own sin! Where is the good news in that?

Since I believe every part of the Bible contains *good news,* I believe we simply have to look for it when it isn't obvious.

So, where is the good news in David's admission that his "bones have no soundness because of [his] sin"? I believe that the very *awareness* of one's own sin is a good place to start in our daily walk with God. David knows God well enough to know that part of His love includes discipline. It includes consequence.

When we sin, there are consequences. It's kind of like getting sent to your room for doing wrong as a child. Yes, you can come back out soon. Yes, your parents forgive you and love you just the same. But the consequence of wrong actions still remains: you have to go to your room.

David understood that about God. He knew Him as a Father. A loving Father. One who loves us enough to be angry when we fall short of His best for us. One who disciplines us to put us back on a holy path.

That's what awareness of sin does. It puts us back on a holy path. It wakes us up! It says, "Hey! This isn't right!" "I need to change." "God isn't pleased!" "I want to please Him!"

What a good place to be! To want to please God!

David was there. He was in that place with God. He says in v. 18, "I confess my iniquity; I am troubled by my sin."

How happy God must be when He hears those words!

That's the whole point of consequences. Not to make us miserable after sinning, but to make us repent! To help us avoid the same sin, the same mistake, the same consequence in the future!

How sad when God's saints are no longer *troubled* by their sins. Then discipline cannot have its perfect work. Growth cannot take place.

But what *good news* for those who confess their sins and are troubled by them! What a vehicle to bring us closer to God!

Lord, thank you for awareness of sin. Please give me a soft, moldable heart that is troubled when I sin. Help me always to quickly repent. Please deal kindly with me, not according to my sin, but according to your mercy. May your consequences and discipline have their perfect work in my life. In Jesus' name, Amen.

Psalm 39 "Show me, O Lord, my life's end and the number of my days; let me know how fleeting is my life. You have made my days a mere handbreadth; the span of my years is as nothing before you. Each man's life is but a breath. Selah. Man is a mere phantom as he goes to and fro: He bustles about, but only in vain; he heaps up wealth,

not knowing who will get it" (v. 4-6).

Have you ever thought of yourself as a phantom? An apparition? One who appears only briefly, and then becomes invisible?

It is a comforting thought in a way. It puts life into perspective.

We "bustle about," as the psalmist says, during so much of life. What are we trying to do?

Make a name for ourselves?

Be noticed?

Heap up wealth?

Be remembered?

Get ahead?

All of our bustling about and going to and fro to accomplish these things, the psalmist says, is in vain. Kind of takes the pressure off, doesn't it? It does for me. When I let myself dwell on the fleeting nature of my life, there is an overwhelming sense of comfort, and of relief.

I struggle so often in life or "bustle," if you will, trying to:

> keep my house clean
> write more
> read more
> look nice
> have nice clothes
> get published
> be on time
> meet deadlines or standards or goals that I have set up for myself

Let's face it, if I died today, none of that would matter.

God has given me a prolapsed mitral valve in my heart to remind me of that. It's a valve that malfunctions at times, causing my heart to skip beats or beat too rapidly. This sometimes results in severe chest pains and sweating for me, and a feeling of exhaustion so great I must simply sit down and wait for strength to return.

The problem isn't life-threatening, but it feels like it is. And over the years, I've come in some ways to be thankful for this condition. I still pray that God will heal me of it, and maybe He will. I don't know. But in the meantime, every time I get severe chest pains, I am reminded that life is fleeting. I am reminded that sitting at Jesus' feet today is really the only thing needful. Having a soft and humble heart before God is all that counts. Asking His forgiveness for all of my sins is the only necessary question.

It took a lot of courage for David to make his request of God: "Show me, O Lord, my life's end and the number of my days; let me know how fleeting is my life."

Do we really want to know? To know that our time here is short? I believe that we do. Deep down. In our souls. That knowledge makes for eternal perspective. Eternal living. Not just for here and now.

Here and now is fleeting. Phantoms appear only to disappear.

Heaven goes on and on. God's love is from everlasting to everlasting. His forgiveness removes our sins as far as east is from west.

That is the kind of perspective we need. Eternal perspective.

In heaven there are no phantoms. There are only saints who once passed through earth on their way to their eternal home.

Dear God, please strengthen my eternal perspective. Let my days be calm, as I realize that eternity has already started. I have forever with You. In Jesus' name, Amen.

> *When we've been there ten thousand years,*
> *Bright, shining as the sun,*
> *We've no less days to sing God's praise*
> *Than when we'd first begun.*

(lyrics from the hymn "Amazing Grace" by John Newton.)

Psalm 40 "I waited patiently for the Lord; he turned to me and heard my cry" (v.1).

Are you a patient waiter?

I have a picture in my mind when I read this verse. There's a little girl tapping on the arm of her father. His face is turned the other way. His back is to her. She tugs at his sleeve. She talks to him. She knows that he hears, that he feels her tugging. Yet she has to wait. She does not know what he is doing. Why is it taking so long? Is he thinking? Is he talking to someone else? Is he involved in some "grown-up" business that she doesn't understand? Finally, he turns around and faces the little girl. He picks her up. He listens. He hears what is on her heart. He holds her close and hears her cry. Finally, she feels satisfied that she has been heard. She feels close to her father.

I had a father like that. He wasn't quick to give an answer. He had to think about it. He had to ponder. Sometimes he'd sit in the rocker and think. Sometimes he'd think on the tractor. Sometimes he'd tell me, "We'll see," or "maybe." Sometimes he'd sleep on it and let me know in the morning. It was frustrating for a little girl to have to wait. I remember.

"Can I go to the movie Friday night with Becky and Jackie and Lisa?" I'd ask.

"I don't know," Dad would reply. "I'll think about it."

"But all the other parents have said it's OK."

"I'm not all the other parents. I'll sleep on it and let you know."

That was like a death sentence to a little girl! There was all that waiting, and even then he might say no!

That was Dad, though. No quick answers. And usually, there was good reason for the waiting. It made for wise decisions. It gave Dad time to think. He and Mom could confer. Had we been gone too much lately? Did we need a night of staying at home? Was the movie a good one? Waiting gave time to find answers to these questions.

Waiting reminds me of Albin and Douglas, two bachelor brothers who farmed near us for years. They were in their seventies, and had lived together all their lives. They farmed together, cooked together, ate together, and shared a car together. But they were as different as day from night.

Albin was a talker. He jumped right in on any conversation. Douglas was a listener. He rarely said a word. But when he did, even Albin stopped to listen. Douglas' words were worth waiting for. They were gentle; well thought-out. The neighbors learned to wait for Douglas to speak. It took a while for him to be ready to say what was on his mind.

My husband is like that on matters of importance. Sometimes I'll ask him a question while we're driving in the car. He'll be silent for the longest time, just looking straight ahead. It almost drives me crazy! But then, just when I'm ready to erupt and say, "Why don't you answer me?" he'll turn to me with the gentlest answer, an answer that is often filled with wisdom, insight, and depth.

For the first years of our marriage, I think I missed out on a lot of those answers from my husband. I was impatient. I butted in. I got mad when I had to wait for an answer. I didn't realize what a gold mine his thoughts would bring me if I just gave him *time* to put them into words.

Impatience cheats us out of so many gold mines. We get mad and interrupt God, just when He may be getting ready to answer. In our eyes, God's answers may be slow in coming, but they are gold mines, well worth the wait!

Like the father with the little girl, God feels us tugging. We may look up and wonder why He is taking so long to answer. We may ask, "What is He thinking?" "Is God involved in some business that we don't understand?" Probably. His thoughts are higher than our thoughts. His ways are not our ways. We may have to wait longer and more patiently, but God will turn to us and hear our cry.

Dear God, so many times when I have waited patiently for You, You have answered me with a gold mine. Thank you. But even more times I have interrupted You. I've grown impatient and perhaps missed Your answer. Please forgive me. I know You're worth waiting for, God. Give me grace to wait patiently. I pray in Jesus' name. Amen.

Psalm 41 "Blessed is he who has regard for the weak" (v. 1a).

"Consideration; concern; respect and affection." All of these are definitions of "regard." But my favorite is the one in brackets in the dictionary. It says, "see RE - & GUARD."

So I did. Re is a prefix meaning "back; again; or anew." GUARD means "to watch over and protect; defend; a posture of readiness for defense; protection; to keep watch against."

The word regard says a lot! It is what we are to have for the weak. If we have it, we are blessed.

Regarding is something we are to do over and over again. Not just once or twice. You see, "RE" means "again; or anew." If you relocate, you move again. If you redecorate, you decorate again or anew. If you re-guard the weak, you guard them again, over and over, whenever the need arises.

The need arose in Minneapolis this winter when my husband and I were there for a music convention. My husband is a college choir director, and his group of 66 students was to perform along with many other college groups in a mass choir that evening. Before the performance, all of these young, exuberant students were free to wander around a little, to do some shopping, to get a bite to eat at one of the many downtown Minneapolis restaurants. My husband and I decided to take advantage of the free time, too, and headed off on foot in search of a restaurant.

Having walked only a few blocks, we realized that the neighborhood we were in was not the safest. To make matters worse, evening was already setting in, it was snowing, and there was a strong Minnesota winter wind.

Suddenly to our surprise, we saw standing a few feet ahead of us an elderly woman in bedroom slippers and a housecoat. She was shuffling along the sidewalk, her cold legs completely bare from the knees down. Every now and then, as a car went by on the street, she would attempt to step into the busy street. She seemed to be waving at a certain car that appeared, drove by, and then reappeared.

We watched for a moment, and determined that the woman must have come out of a nearby hospital emergency room, and was now trying to flag down her ride home.

There was no way she could've done it. The street had four lanes of steady traffic. There was no parking place near the curb where she stood. She was weak and unsteady on her feet. She tottered, and looked ready to fall. Her husband or driver kept circling the same block helplessly as the drivers around him sped past, slammed on their brakes, and honked their horns.

My husband and I were about to take the woman's arm when two college-aged boys stepped out of the crowd on the sidewalk. Without saying a word, one kindly took the elderly woman's arm, while the other stepped into the street. He bravely stepped right into the closest lane of oncoming traffic, and began motioning the drivers into the next lane. Some stopped, some honked, I'm sure some swore, but eventually the lane closest to the curb was clear, and the woman's husband could finally stop when he came around the block again. The young boy flagged him over to the curb, where the other college student helped the tottering woman into the car.

The whole thing took only a few minutes, but I remember it well. My husband and I felt relief. We felt proud of the college students, and we didn't even know them! They had stepped forward with regard for the weak when the need arose.

I think that's how God feels about us when we aid the weak. He even promises special blessings when we do! For those who have regard for the weak, Psalm 41 says:

The Lord delivers them in times of trouble (v. 1).

The Lord will protect them and preserve their lives (v. 2).

He will bless them in the land and not surrender them to the desires of their foes (v. 2).

The Lord will sustain them on their sickbed and restore them from their bed of illness (v. 3).

The weak are all around us in many forms:

They are in Nursing Homes waiting to be visited.

They are in hospitals and group homes and orphanages.

They are in the streets.

They are stuck or stranded on roadsides.

They are wandering, lost and homeless.

They are emotionally or physically or mentally or spiritually hurting people.

They are the unborn.

They are among all living creatures.

They are at animal shelters, abandoned.

They are in cages, neglected.

They are on highways, hit by cars and wounded.

All of the weak need our regard. Helping them once is not enough. "Re" means "again; anew." We must keep a posture of readiness to help the weak at all times. Like the woman on the Minneapolis street, they may appear before us suddenly. Like the two young boys who rescued her, we must always be ready to step in when help is needed. For when we regard the weak, we are blessed.

Dear Jesus, you had such regard for the weak that you came and died for all of us. Help me to keep my eyes open to see the weak and helpless around me. Help me to remember that many times, I am weak and helpless, too. Make me like those two college students, Lord; ready to show regard for the weak whenever the need arises. Amen.

———※———

Psalm 42 "As the deer pants for streams of water, so my soul pants for you, O God. My soul thirsts for God, for the living God. When can I go and meet with God?" (v. 1-2).

"When can I go and meet with God?" Is that our heart cry today? Are we jealous for our time with God? He is jealous for us. Exodus 20:5 says ". . . I, the Lord your God, am a jealous God." God wants nothing to stand in the way of our time with Him.

What keeps us from meeting with God? From sitting quietly and reading the Bible? From having daily devotions or private quiet times with God? What stops us from having these special, close times with our Lord?

Busyness
Sin
Guilt
Bad attitudes
Interruptions

All of these things contribute to lost time with God.

The psalmist knew what it was like to have dry times without meeting with God. He panted and thirsted for those times like a thirsty deer pants for water. I can see the psalmist stamping his feet like an irritated child and saying, "When can I go and meet with God?" The psalmist remembered a time when things were better. He even remembers "leading the procession to the house of God" (Psalm 42:4).

We can be leaders in the church and still go through dry times, dear friends. We can be Christians who have walked with God for years, and still experience great thirsting for God. We can feel parched and desperately in need of a drink from God's living water.

If we are not meeting with God daily in a time of solitude and prayer, let me suggest that the answer to this question, "When can I go and meet with God?" is NOW! Let's drop whatever else we're doing. Let's put aside the day's schedule. Let's confess sin and bad attitudes. Let's let the telephone ring when it interrupts us. *Let's meet with God!*

We can meet with Him at home, alone. We can meet with Him in our vehicles. We can meet with Him in bed before sleeping or before arising. We can meet with Him at church, too. The point is, let's do it!

Let's be as jealous for our meeting time with God as He is jealous for meeting with us.

He wants nothing to stand in our way. He has promised that when we seek Him, he will be found by us (Jeremiah 29:13-14). But we have to seek, friends. We have to take the time. We have to set aside meeting time with God.

Only you will know all of the rewards of your private times with God. He will show you things that pertain only to your heart, and to your situation. Others will benefit, too, as the fruit of quiet time with God grows in your life and is shared. But nothing can replace the time that is just "God and I."

My God and I go through the fields together;
We walk and talk, as good friends should and do.
We clasp our hands, our voices ring with laughter;
My God and I walk through the meadow's hue.

[From the hymn "*My God and I*" by I.B. Sergie, copyright 1935
Renewed 1963 by Austris A. Wihtol, Assigned to Singspiration, Inc.]

Psalm 43 "Send forth your light and your truth, let them guide me; let them bring me to your holy mountain, to the place where you dwell. Then will I go to the altar of God, to God, my joy and my delight. I will praise you with the harp, O God, my God" (v. 3-4).

What does it take to get to the place where God dwells? To live there every day? To be at His altar, the place of closeness and worship to God?

Psalm 43 says that it takes "light and truth." They will guide us. They will bring us to God's holy mountain; to the place where God dwells.

Light and truth are somewhat nebulous. They are not things we can put our fingers on. Perhaps their opposites can help us understand them more than anything else.

The opposite of light is darkness. Darkness hides. It covers. It is spooky and dangerous. It cuts back our vision.

The opposite of truth is lying. Lying hides or covers the truth. It is dangerous. It leads to more lies. It cuts back our vision. We can no longer see or think clearly when we do not know the truth.

Only God can send forth truth and light. He created them. In Genesis 1:3-4, it says, "And God said, 'Let there be light,' and there was light. God saw that the light was good, and he separated the light from the darkness."

In John 8:31-32, Jesus said, "If you hold to my teaching, you are really my disciples. Then you will know the truth, and the truth will set you free."

In fact, not only did God *create* light and truth, He *is* light and truth. Jesus says in

John 8:12, "I am the light of the world. Whoever follows me will have the light of life."

And in John 14:5-6, Thomas says to Jesus, "Lord, we don't know where you are going, so how can we know the way?" Jesus answers, "I am the way and the truth and the life. No one comes to the Father except through me."

Jesus was talking there of the way to heaven, but the same principles that applied to Thomas' question apply to our question. "What does it take to get to the place where God dwells? To get to a place of closeness to God on earth? To dwell at His altar? To live in his presence?

It takes a life of light and truth. It takes Jesus; the embodiment of light and truth.

If only Jesus were in our every situation. Then darkness would scatter. Then lying would flee.

Light and truth are the great exposers. They expose sin. They expose every form of human error and depravity. Greed, anger, malice, selfishness, lust, pornography, dishonesty, hatred. You name it. Light and truth expose it.

"If we walk in the light, as He is in the light, we have fellowship one with another" (I John 1:7). If not, we have no fellowship. Not with one another. Not with God.

The good news is that no matter how long we've walked in darkness, in one area of our lives, or in many, Jesus is the light bulb for that situation. All we need to do is ask: "Send forth your light and your truth, let them guide me; let them bring me to your holy mountain, to the place where you dwell."

God is delighted to do it! He is delighted when we ask! I believe that God likes nothing better than to send forth a beam of light and a dose of truth to our daily situations. He knows that it brings us closer to Him, and that's where he wants us to be!

"*Then* will I go to the altar of God, to God, my joy and my delight. I will praise you with the harp, O God, my God" (v. 4).

It's no fun to go to the altar of God if we're covered in darkness or lying. It's no fun if we've got things to hide. But when we ask God to send forth his light and truth; to clean out our minds and hearts and lives of every dark or unclean area, then we can approach His altar boldly. Happily. Joyfully.

Jesus is light and truth. He is not nebulous. He is real. He is tangible. He is concrete. He walked the earth in flesh and bones just like you and me. He bled real blood, and that blood cleanses and washes all of our sins away.

The result of God's sending light and truth into our daily lives is that we can now live close to Him. We can praise him! We can go to the altar of God. Not some far away altar in a church or tabernacle, but to the altar of God within our hearts. May that altar be flooded with truth and light. May we praise Him there, our joy, and our delight!

Dear God, please send forth your truth and light into every part of my life. Scatter darkness and falsehood. Bring me to the place where you dwell. There let me praise you, O God, my God! In Jesus' name, Amen.

⁓⸲⸲⁓

Psalm 44 "We have heard with our ears, O God; our fathers have told us what you did in their days, in days long ago" (v. 1).

Who are "our fathers?" I believe that they are all of the men, women, and children who have gone before us. They are especially those who have loved and followed the God of the Bible. All of us who follow Christ are children of Abraham. Whether Jew or Gentile, we are all children of promise if we know Jesus as Savior and Lord. Some of us were born into the house of Israel, others of us have been grafted into the kingdom of God.

Our fathers and mothers have much to tell about what God did in their days, in days long ago. Do we listen? If so, we can be encouraged and strengthened in our own walk with God. We can learn of God's provision, of His miracles, of His divine direction, if we "hear with our ears" His workings in the lives of our forefathers.

We have only to read Genesis and Exodus to learn of how God led and rescued the children of Israel. He brought them out of slavery in Egypt. He opened the Red Sea for them. He helped them cross over to another shore, to the promised land.

History since Bible times, too, is full of the stories of God's leading and rescue in the lives of our fathers. Think of some of the greats in history who have led lives of service to Christ. I think of the philosopher, Sir Isaac Newton, of the musician, Johann Sebastian Bach, of the hymn writers, Fanny Crosby, John and Charles Wesley, of the Sister and humanitarian, Mother Theresa. These are just a few names out of the thousands of Christians whose stories we can learn from. Reading their books and biographies, and hearing their music alone can lift our hearts to new heights in Christ!

Then there are our less famous fathers and mothers. Christians who have gone before us or who are still living but are of the older generation, who have lived through struggles in this life and have persevered in Christ. Who comes to your mind? Have you listened to their stories? Our farm homes and city apartments and senior citizen centers and nursing homes are filled with people whose stories we *need* to hear. Only through knowing their struggles and triumphs can we understand and persevere through our own. We are not living in a vacuum, friends. We are part of the great Christian faith and life since Adam and Eve. We have a purpose, and are part of a plan. We need to see that plan in context sometimes, or we may lose hope.

I think of the three cemeteries I visited recently on Memorial Day. Their gravestones alone had a story to tell of our forefathers. Many had dates of birth and death, and loving verses for children who had died before parents. Some children had died in infancy. Some parents had buried three children in two days, deaths the result of a plague or epidemic. Some spouses had outlived their partners by *sixty* years! I think of one stone in particular which showed the marriage date of a couple as 1928. In 1929, the husband had died. In 1985, the wife had died. Still, they were buried together, side by side. Think of it! I knew this family. I know of another woman whose husband died almost 40 years before her. She never remarried. I came to know her when she was in her seventies, and she lived to be ninety-four. She was not bitter. She radiated the love of God. She lived alone. She had one leg amputated at the knee. She spent each day in a wheelchair. Her circumstances may sound depressing, but her story is *uplifting*! She persevered. She told of her faith in God. She told of His provision. She said she was never alone. "Jesus is always with me," she said.

I can still hear those words of a ninety-four year old neighbor. I can hear them as I recall her saying them in her living room before she died. I can hear them echo through time as I stand over her grave.

Our forefathers and foremothers have stories to tell. Stories of how God brought them through. Our struggles are part of the big picture, dear Christian brothers and sisters. They are part of history.

One day others may hear our stories. They may hear of how God worked in our lives. They may be encouraged to persevere in their own walk because of what God has done and will do in our lives.

May we listen carefully and diligently to the stories of those who have gone before us. From Bible times to now, may we seek out their stories. May we hear what God did "in their days, in days long ago."

Dear God, I want to hear more of what You did long ago. Give me ears to hear and eyes to see what you've done in the lives of our ancestors. Help me to remember that You still work that way. From the Red Sea to now, You are faithful. May my story, too, be a legacy of your love and faithfulness. In Jesus' name, Amen.

Psalm 45 "My heart is stirred by a noble theme as I recite my verses for the king; my tongue is the pen of a skillful writer" (v. 1).

Is your heart ever stirred by a noble theme? The psalmist was stirred by the excellence of the king. The king was getting married, so the writer wrote a psalm in praise of the king for his wedding day. What better inspiration for writing than the excellent character of someone we know?

That's how it is with our God. His character is excellent. He, too, is getting married. God's bride is *us:* the Church. Verses 6-7 of our psalm are even applied to Christ, our bridegroom, in Hebrews 1:8-9. "Your throne, O God, will last for ever and ever; a scepter of justice will be the scepter of your kingdom. You love righteousness and hate wickedness; therefore, God, your God, has set you above your companions by anointing you with the oil of joy."

How's that for a noble theme? The psalmist says these words of the king, and the writer of Hebrews says these same words of Christ!

I don't know about you, but sometimes I need inspiration. A shot of creativity. Of energy. Sometimes I need a reason even to get out of bed in the morning.

God's character gives us that inspiration. That creativity. That energy. That reason. His character is worthy of our praise. It stirs in us a noble theme. It can make composers of our tongues and pens.

God's character is an inspiration entirely outside of ourselves. It does not depend on our circumstances. It does not depend on our moods.

Whether we are crabby or happy, poor or rich, depressed or euphoric, God's character is one of love. His throne will last forever. He has given us eternal life. His kingdom is just. He loves righteousness and hates wickedness. Christ has been set above all His companions in heaven, and has been anointed with the oil of joy. He is going to be united with us as our bridegroom!

Now *that's* inspiring!

Sometimes there isn't a lot going on around us that is inspiring. Sometimes the things going on inside of our minds and hearts are anything *but* inspiring. But that doesn't matter. We can still be stirred on the inside by a noble theme. We can concentrate with all our minds and hearts and strength on God's character. We can recite our verses for the king.

Dear God, You are loving. You love me even when I am down and uninspired. Your perfect character gives me something to look up to. To set my sights on. You are flawless, God. You are beautiful. You are my bridegroom. You are my King. In Jesus' name, Amen.

Psalm 46 "Therefore we will not fear, though the earth give way and the mountains fall into the heart of the sea, though its waters roar and foam and the mountains quake with their surging. . . Nations are in uproar, kingdoms fall; he lifts his voice, the earth melts" (v. 1-2, 6).

Roar
Foam
Quake
Surge
Uproar
Melts

These words conjure up quite a picture in my mind. I think of earthquakes. Of hurricanes. Of tornadoes. Of natural disasters. Of revelation. Of end times.

What emotions do these words evoke in you?

Terror?

Trembling?

Fear?

Interestingly enough, verse 2 starts out with the words, "Therefore we will *not fear*." This is the very opposite reaction to what these fearful words evoke. That is what the psalmist says we are to feel. *No fear.*

Why?

Why shouldn't we fear?

The reasons are sprinkled throughout Psalm 46.

1. "God is our refuge and strength, an ever-present help in trouble" (v. 1).

"Ever-present" means that God is always there. In the midst of an earthquake, God is there. In the midst of trouble, God is there. We don't have to wait for the disaster to pass before God's presence will return. It never left! God is there in the middle of even our worst circumstances.

2. "The Lord Almighty is with us; the God of Jacob is our fortress" (v. 7 & 11).

We have a fortress. A castle. A stone structure into which we can run. We have a hiding place. We have safety. We have a God who watches over and cares for our bodies, our minds, our souls, and our spirits. When our bodies finally do give in to death, we have an eternal fortress in heaven, where our spirits go to live.

3. "He lifts his voice, the earth melts" (v. 6b).

We have a God who can stop natural disasters. All He has to do is raise his voice. Jesus did it for the disciples. He rebuked the wind. The wind! Think of it! The wind obeyed His voice! (Luke 8: 24-25).

With a God like that, it is no wonder that the psalmist says we need not fear.

I'm not sure how I will react to roaring, foaming, quaking, surging, or melting if it is happening all around me, but I have a feeling that God will take care of it if that time comes. He is bigger than all of those things. His grace will cover us in fearful situations.

Dear God, sometimes I fear the threat of natural disasters. Help me to remember that I don't need to fear. You are an ever-present help in trouble. I know that even death has lost its sting because of Christ. Thank you that during the times we need it most, your grace is always there. Thank you for your perfect love that casts out fear. In Jesus' name, Amen.

Psalm 47 "He chose our inheritance for us, the pride of Jacob, whom he loved" (v. 4).

Have you ever received or chosen an inheritance? Perhaps you've looked around your house and chosen certain items to be left for your children when you die. A special vase. A piece of jewelry. An antique chair or table. Perhaps you have received an inheritance. A sum of money. A tract of land. A house or business.

God chose an inheritance for us. He looked around at all that He owned and said, "I'll give this to my children."

His children are "the pride of Jacob." That's us! Let's look at our ancestry for a moment. Who are our ancestors, and what is our/their inheritance?

Abraham and Sarah had Isaac.

Isaac and Rebekah had Jacob.

Jacob and Rachel had Joseph.

We could go on and on. But we can see that Jacob, "whom God loved," could easily trace his heritage back to his grandfather, Abraham. Abraham and his descendants had been promised an inheritance by God. What is that inheritance?

Genesis 12:2-3 tells us. God said to Abraham, "I will make you into a great nation and I will bless you; I will make your name great, and you will be a blessing. I will bless those who bless you, and whoever curses you I will curse; and all peoples on earth will be blessed through you."

Later on, in the same chapter, God shows Abraham the promised land and says, "To your offspring I will give this land" (v. 7). We know that ultimately, God did bless "all peoples on earth" through Abraham's descendant, Jesus Christ. God also fulfilled His promise to Abraham's offspring by giving them the promised land. Even though there were years of slavery and wandering in between, God came through with His promise. Joseph's bones were carried out of Egypt and were buried in the promised land! (Joshua 24:32).

The promised land of the Old Testament is, of course, a foreshadowing or picture of heaven. Heaven is our *promised* land. It was *promised* to us by God. God has chosen *heaven* as our inheritance!

We don't deserve it. But then, neither did Jacob in our psalm verse. Do you remember Jacob's story?

He had a twin brother, Esau. Esau was the older sibling. Esau had a right to receive Isaac's, his father's, inheritance. Jacob, whose name means "deceiver," was the younger son. He did not deserve his father's inheritance under Old Testament custom. But Jacob tricked his brother. He disguised himself to look like Esau. (See Genesis 27 for the whole story.) He received his father's blessing and inheritance!

We, of course, cannot deceive our way into the kingdom of God. But the story of Jacob is an encouragement in a way. Jacob did not deserve his inheritance. Neither do we. Yet God has chosen to make that inheritance available to all.

Romans 4:13-17 says, "It was not through law that Abraham and his offspring received the promise that he would be heir of the world, but through the righteousness that comes by faith . . . *Therefore, the promise comes by faith, so that it may be by grace and may be guaranteed to all Abraham's offspring, not only those who are of the law, but also to those who are of the faith of Abraham.* He is the father of us all. As it is written: 'I have made you a father of many nations.' He is our father in the sight of God, in whom he believed, the God who gives life to the dead and calls things that are not as though they were."

A true inheritance does not take place until someone dies. In our case, God, or Jesus, had to die in order to put into effect our inheritance.

Hebrews 9:15-18 says, "For this reason Christ is the mediator of a new covenant, *that those who are called may receive the promised eternal inheritance, now that he has died* as a ransom to set them free from the sins committed under the first covenant. In the case of a will, it is necessary to prove the death of the one who made it, because a will is in force only when someone has died; it never takes effect while the one who made it is living. This is why even the first covenant was not put into effect without blood."

If we believe in Jesus Christ as our Savior, we are "of the faith of Abraham." We are "called to receive the eternal inheritance:" life in heaven with God!

Dear God, you are the God of Abraham and Sarah, of Isaac and Rebekah, of Jacob and Rachel, and You are my God. I don't deserve the inheritance You have chosen for me, yet because Jesus died, I can receive it. More than any earthly inheritance I will ever receive, I look forward to the inheritance promised me through faith and grace. In Jesus' name, Amen.

Psalm 48 "Walk about Zion, go around her, count her towers, consider well her ramparts, view her citadels, that you may tell of them to the next generation" (v. 12-13).

And "as we have heard, so we have seen in the city of the Lord Almighty, in the city of our God: God makes her secure forever" (v. 8).

Have you ever seen a ghost town? I grew up near one.

My childhood home was a farm eight miles north of Wheaton, Minnesota. We were about six miles from the South Dakota border, and the town of White Rock, South Dakota. White Rock was a booming town. Well-known. Growing. Bustling. As a prairie town in the early 1900's, White Rock was one of the biggest in the area.

At one time, the town boasted seven grain elevators, five hotels, two banks, a thriving main street, a school, and a theater where live plays were staged.

Most of all, White Rock had a railroad. The railroad was what made prairie towns in those days. Farmers shipped their grain and received supplies via rail. Towns sprang up along the tracks like mushrooms around a bog.

My father even told the story of White Rock's first piano being shipped by railroad car. Most of the townspeople came out to witness the event of a fancy piano being unloaded from the train, purchased for White Rock's dance hall!

Those days are long gone now. You see, the railroad left White Rock. I saw the town's demise. From seven elevators to one. From five hotels to none. I even watched the brick schoolhouse and theater come tumbling down from old age and disuse.

People moved away. They had to. There was no longer any economic base to keep the town alive.

Visitors to White Rock now can drive down its' abandoned streets and see the remnants of the town's main street buildings. Bricks and weeds are all that remain on most lots. A population sign on the ghost town's city limits reads: "White Rock, Population, 2." A large gravestone sits at the edge of town and tells of White Rock's history.

That stone with its message reminds me of Psalm 48.

"Walk about Zion, go around her, count her towers, consider well her ramparts, view her citadels, that you may tell of them to the next generation."

That's what the gravestone is doing for White Rock. It is telling the next generation of that city's past greatness: its seven elevators, its five hotels, its two banks, its main street, its school and its theater.

Towns like White Rock will fade. In fact, one day, all of our cities will be ghost towns, if you will. They will be abandoned. Not because the railroad left or because their economic base gave way. No, our fair cities will be abandoned because their inhabitants will be in a new city, "a city with foundations, whose architect and builder is God" (Hebrews 11:10).

The people of God, we're told in Hebrews 11, lived as "aliens and strangers on earth." They were "longing for a better country, a heavenly one." "Therefore," the Bible tells us, "God is not ashamed to be called their God, for he has prepared a city for them" (Hebrews 11:13,16).

If we feel sometimes that this earth is a ghost town for us, we need not despair! As God's people, this is not our final dwelling! We may have to watch some decay and suffering. Our earthly cities and dwellings, even our bodies, weren't made to last forever. But *God* has prepared a city for us! He is its architect and builder! God's city will *never* become a ghost town!

> "As we have heard,
> so we have seen
> in the city of the Lord Almighty,
> in the city of our God:
> God makes her secure forever."
> Psalm 48:8

It is God's presence that will make our heavenly city secure forever. We will live there for eternity. Our population sign in heaven will never drop down to 2! In fact, it will never drop at all! We will never lose family or friends again. We will not cry. We will not die. Heaven will never become a ghost town, because her foundation and builder is God.

Dear God, prepare me for your holy city. I am a stranger here. When my surroundings feel like a ghost town, remind me that you will not abandon me. You are my foundation. I look forward to living in heaven, God, a place that is secure forever. In Jesus' name, Amen.

Psalm 49 "A man who has riches without understanding is like the beasts that perish" (v. 20).

Do you have understanding about riches?

I'll be the first to admit that I don't. At least not all the understanding I *should* have. But I do have a *desire* to understand, and God honors that. He will increase our understanding when we ask Him.

There are differing degrees of richness, that I know. But to a degree, most of us in America are rich. Most of us have "riches" of some kind.

With riches come responsibilities. One of those responsibilities is to obtain understanding. That's what Psalm 49 says. Let's see what principles or understanding we can gain from Psalm 49's insights. All of its verses deal with wealth.

First of all, verse 2 says that Psalm 49's advice is for *all people*, "both low and high, rich and poor alike."

With that established, verses 5-6 ask, "Why should we fear when evil days come, when wicked deceivers surround us, those who trust in their wealth and boast of their great riches?"

"Don't sweat it," is the message I get from those verses. We all know people who trust in their wealth, people who boast about their money. There is nothing to fear in them. We needn't feel belittled or overwhelmed or jealous or embarrassed. Why? Because "No man can redeem the life of another or give to God a ransom for him; the ransom for a life is costly, no payment is ever enough, that he should live on forever and not see decay" (v. 7-9).

Only Jesus can pay that sort of ransom. Only blood could atone for our sins. No amount of wealth or riches can redeem the life of another. Why is there comfort in that knowledge? Why does that knowledge bring understanding?

Because we needn't trust in our wealth. Because Jesus paid the full price for our greatest need: salvation.

When we see wealthy people who boast or trust in their riches, it needn't bother us at all. We have understanding about riches from Psalm 49.

"You can't take it with you." That's sort of a summary of verses 10-14. People may have "named lands after themselves" (v. 11). They may have "princely mansions" (v. 14). But in the end all wealth is "left to others" (v. 10). Our forms will all "decay in the grave, far from our princely mansion" (v. 14).

Where is the comfort in that? What are we to understand? Well, perhaps such knowledge will give us right perspectives regarding our riches. Perhaps knowing the tentative nature of things on earth will cause us to hang on less tightly to the things that will decay. Perhaps we will strive less, and enjoy more what we are given. Perhaps we will seek to store up treasures in heaven, where moth and rust do not destroy.

The next verses in psalm 49 are my favorites.

"Do not be overawed when a man grows rich, when the splendor of his house increases;" (v. 16) "...Men praise you when you prosper" (v. 18).

Isn't that the truth? We have dear Christian friends who at one time in their lives increased in wealth. They bought land and sold it in lots for new housing developments. They built new houses, moved into them, and then sold them. On a tour through one of their homes, I remarked, "How can you bear to sell this once you've lived in it? It's so beautiful!"

My friend's answer was simple, "It's just a house!"

Her answer was so true! After all, it *is* just a house. People do tend to praise us when we prosper. They fawn all over us and pat us on the back. They talk about us and whisper in tones both of jealousy and admiration. But the fact is that in God's eyes, and in the eyes of one who has understanding, it *is* just a house.

God may bless us with riches.

He may not.

But with whatever we have, we are to gain understanding. We are to seek God's perspective. We are to view wealth, our own, and other people's, through God's eternal eyes.

Lord, I don't want to have riches without understanding. Open my mind to a whole new way of thinking about riches. Your way of thinking. That is what I desire. Throughout my life, whether I have little or much, let me gain understanding about the riches you give. In Jesus' name, Amen.

Psalm 50 "Sacrifice thank offerings to God, fulfill your vows to the Most High, and call upon me in the day of trouble; I will deliver you, and you will honor me" (v. 14-15).

"He who sacrifices thank offerings honors me, and he prepares the way so that I may show him the salvation of God" (v. 23).

Both of the above scriptures speak of "thank offerings." Thank offerings are different from sacrifices. God tells the people of Israel in Psalm 50 that he "has no need of a bull from their stalls or of goats from their pens" (v. 9). Every animal on earth, God says, is already his (v. 10-11). God did require animal sacrifices in the Old Testament. There had to be a shedding of blood to atone for sin until Christ's blood was shed as a sacrifice once for all sin. But sacrifices were not first on God's list of importance. What God desired from his people was a thankful heart.

God still desires that today. Being thankful to God can require sacrifice on our parts. Sometimes when I wake up in the morning, the last thing I'm feeling is thankfulness. Sometimes I wake up with aches and pains. Sometimes I wake up with thoughts from the day before flooding over me. Sometimes those thoughts are depressing. Sometimes I wake up feeling angry about careless words that were spoken to me the previous day. It takes sacrifice on my part to push those thoughts aside and to be thankful.

Sacrifice means "a giving up of one thing for the sake of another." It also means "an offering to a deity." Offering means "to present in worship."

How about it? Can we do that? Can we give up our depression or anger or fear or self-pity in exchange for an attitude of thanksgiving? Can we sacrifice the negative thoughts we sometimes feed on? Can we put them to death on God's altar and instead offer to Him a thankful heart? Can we "present in worship" our attitudes of praise and thanksgiving?

God says that when we do, it honors him. God says that thank offerings "prepare the way" so that He may show us the salvation of God.

Thank offerings prepare the way.

They are a start.

They are a beginning.

Thank offerings are a first step on our way to knowing God's salvation. We may think when we've given thanks that we've done God a favor, or that we've completed our task. No, God says that's just the door-opener. Having an attitude of thanks to God opens the door so that He can show us more! It opens our hearts and puts us in a position to receive from God.

It is hard to receive when we're angry. It is hard to be shown anything or taught anything when our eyes and minds are closed. Thankfulness opens our eyes. It opens our minds. It opens our hearts. It allows us to *see* God's saving acts.

On an eternal scale, God has saved us from sin, from death, from hell.

On a daily scale, thankfulness can save us from selfishness, from apathy, from oblivion.

We can live our whole lives being oblivious to the deep joy around us. We can take life for granted. That is our choice. Or, we can sacrifice thank offerings to God and begin to *really live!* We can be freed up to see His saving acts on a day-to-day basis.

Join me today in thanking God. Who knows what great things He will show us as we do our part to simply "prepare the way?"

O God, I thank you today! Your mercy is everlasting! Your goodness is beyond measure! Your love reaches to the stars! For daily life, I thank you. For saving faith, I thank you. For Jesus Christ, I thank you. In Jesus' name, Amen.

Psalm 51 "Create in me a pure heart, O God, and renew <u>a steadfast spirit</u> within me... Restore to me the joy of your salvation and grant me <u>a willing spirit,</u> to sustain me... The sacrifices of God are <u>a broken spirit</u>; a broken and contrite heart, O God, you will not despise" (v. 10, 12, and 17). (underlining mine)

A steadfast spirit.
A willing spirit.
A broken spirit.

How is your spirit today? We all have one, you know. A spirit. That inner part of us that is eternal. That part of us that senses God. That part of us that is in tune with Him. That part of us that hears His voice.

Our spirits, or our inner person, can be out-of-sorts just as can our bodies, or our outer person. David's spirit was out-of-sorts in this psalm. His spirit was troubled. It hurt. It felt ashamed.

David had just been confronted by Nathan the prophet with his own sin. David had committed adultery with Bathsheba. He had sinned against God, and he knew it.

We've all been there. No matter what our particular sins, we can say as David did in verses 3-4, "For I know my transgressions, and my sin is always before me. Against you, you only, have I sinned and done what is evil in your sight, so that you are proved right when you speak and justified when you judge."

We can hurt people when we sin.
We can hurt God's creation when we sin.

But ultimately, it is God against whom we sin.

It is also God alone who can restore us. David knew that. He knew where to go to receive a clean heart. He knew where to go when His spirit was hurting and in need of restoration.

"Create in me a pure heart, O God, and renew a steadfast spirit within me" (v. 10).

That word "renew" suggests that David had had a steadfast spirit in the past. This was not the prayer of an unbeliever, or of a person who had not walked with God. David's prayer was one of a Christian who had been steadfast towards God, but who had recently fallen into sin. That happens to Christians, you know. We can be faithful and steadfast in following God, and then suddenly, boom! We can fall. If it's happened to you, you're not alone. It certainly has happened to me.

But the good news is, *we can go to God*. He will renew in us the same, steadfast spirit that we had before we sinned. He will restore us to a faithful walk in Him. He will again make our witness for Christ a credible one, perhaps even more credible than before, because only God can restore. Only God can renew. When we've sinned and been restored, people will see and give all the glory to God.

"Restore to me the joy of your salvation and grant me a willing spirit, to sustain me." That's the next verse about David's spirit. It needed to be willing. A willing spirit sustains us. Why? Because without being *willing* to change, there is no hope. Even our willingness is up to God. He will grant it if we ask. We may not have the gumption and internal fortitude to cut loose of sin's hold right away, but if our spirits are *willing*, God will grant a freedom from sin's entanglement. He sees our willingness. I believe, as with Abraham's faith, that God credits even our willingness as righteousness.

If you are caught in sin today, dear reader, please be willing to change. Ask God to grant you a willing spirit to sustain you. Willingness comes first, then comes ability. Willingness will sustain your heart until ability is granted by God. God sees our spirits. He communes with them. And willingness pleases God.

"The sacrifices of God are a broken spirit; a broken and contrite heart, O God, you will not despise."

Have you ever known anyone who likes to fix things? My dad was that way. It didn't matter what was broken; a glass vase, a wooden bowl, a piece of Mom's best china. No matter what the item, Dad wouldn't let it be thrown away. He'd wait until evening for a quiet time, and then get out the glue.

Epoxy.

Resiweld.

Elmer's.

Dad had a type of glue for every emergency.

God does, too.

It doesn't matter what the sin is. God loves to work on broken spirits. He doesn't cast us away like broken garbage. No, instead He tenderly fits the pieces back together. The pieces of our lives. The pieces of our dreams. The pieces of God's plan for our lives. God has a glue for every emergency.

Sexual sin.

Drunkenness.

Envy.

Lying.

Gluttony.

You name it. God has the cure.

He will not despise us when we're broken. He will not say, "That piece is broken. It is no longer pleasing to my eye." No, God will lovingly pick up the pieces and restore us again to working order. We may even be more beautiful in his eyes after he has taken the time to refurbish us. Like a treasured heirloom or priceless antique, God may prize us more in our brokenness. He will once again use us for noble purposes. For beauty. For His delight.

A steadfast spirit.

A willing spirit.

A broken spirit.

May we, like David, pray for these.

O God, please renew in me a steadfast spirit. Please grant that my spirit be willing. I am sorry for my sins, and ask your forgiveness. Thank you for not despising me in my brokenness. Thank you for instead prizing brokenness in people. I await your restoring in me the joy of your salvation. In Jesus' name, Amen.

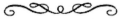

Psalm 52 "But I am like an olive tree flourishing in the house of God; I trust in God's unfailing love for ever and ever" (v. 8).

Olive: "an evergreen tree of S. Europe and the Near East; or, its small oval fruit, eaten as a relish or pressed, when ripe, to extract its light-yellow oil." (Webster's New World Dictionary)

Today I am writing with a jar of Venecia Olive Oil on the book table beside me. I know, it sounds silly, but please don't call the people in white coats to take me away yet. Let me explain! You see, the images of olive trees and olive branches in the Bible have always soothed me. I find them peaceful and comforting. Perhaps that is partly because the olive branch has long been a symbol of peace in the world. I am not sure of the other reasons for this calming effect that olive tree images evoke in me, so today I want to explore them with God.

I have never seen an actual olive tree, so the closest I can get for today is the 100% pure yellowish-colored olive oil in the bottle that my husband uses for cooking. The bottle tells me that this oil is a product of Turkey. It is expensive. My husband loves to cook Italian food, and these dishes often call for olive oil, so we keep some on hand. Even the color of the oil is soothing to me. It is pale and golden and smooth.

An olive tree is called an evergreen. That word, "evergreen," is itself a very beautiful word. It suggests life. It suggests always, forever, eternal. Evergreens do not lose their leaves. They do not turn brown or yellow in the fall. They stay green. They flourish.

That is what the scripture says of us. "I am like an olive tree *flourishing* in the house of God; I trust in God's unfailing love *for ever and ever.*"

For ever and ever.

Evergreen.

That is a picture of our life in God.

On the other hand, those who "boast of evil," (v. 1), and who "love every harmful word" (v. 4), are *not* forever. They are *not* evergreen. They will *not* flourish. The psalmist uses *temporal* words to describe their fate.

"He [God] will *snatch* you up and *tear* you from your tent; he will *uproot* you from the land of the living" (v. 5).

That is quite a warning for us to choose humble and kind words rather than boastful and harmful words. When we choose Godly words and ways, we will flourish like an olive tree.

Remember the story of Noah? He and his family had been in the ark for hundreds of days, waiting for the floodwaters to recede. They needed a sign of hope that dry land would once again appear. They must have been very claustrophobic by this time! So they sent out a dove to see if it could find dry land on which to set its feet. At first the dove came back, unable to find dry ground. But seven days later, when Noah sent the dove out again, it returned with a freshly-plucked olive leaf in its beak! "Then Noah knew that the waters had receded from the earth!" (Genesis 8:11).

What a picture of hope!

What a symbol of life!

Psalm 52 says that we can flourish like that!

We can be a symbol of life to others by our living words, and by our trust in God's unfailing love!

May we be like an olive tree in our Christian walk, flourishing in the house of God!

Living Words

Where do words live
until
they
rest
or
nest
in our thoughts?
Until
they
light like birds
on
our
tongues?
Who
decides
if
they'll
be
spoken or sung?

the tongue?
the brain?
sometimes lips hold words
sometimes hearts
sometimes they escape their oral cage
and fly out,
they thrash their angry wings
against frightened faces
sometimes they perch lightly
and lovingly
on the shoulder of a friend
or stranger.

Are words like you, God?
Homeless, hovering
over the waters
with no dry land in sight?

Dove of God,
fly far
and find your olive branch
in me.

by Linda Winter-Hodgson

Psalm 53 "God looks down from heaven on the sons of men to see if there are any who understand, any who seek God" (v. 2).

Remember Abraham and Lot and the story of Sodom and Gomorrah? In Genesis chapters 18-19 we find the account of how Abraham pleaded with God to spare those cities. An outcry had gone up to God's ears about how wicked the cities had become. God decided to destroy the cities and all of their inhabitants. Because Abraham was God's friend, God let him in on these plans. Abraham's nephew, Lot, and his family lived in Sodom. Abraham didn't want his relatives to be destroyed, so he pleaded with God to spare the cities.

Remember Abraham's bargaining? "What if there are fifty righteous people in the city? Will you really sweep it away and not spare the place for the sake of the fifty righteous people in it?" (Genesis 18:24).

The Lord answers, "If there are fifty righteous people in the city of Sodom, I will spare the whole place for their sake" (Genesis 18:26).

The bargaining between Abraham and God goes on until Abraham finally says, "What if only ten righteous people can be found there?"

And God says, "For the sake of ten, I will not destroy it" (Genesis 18:32).

But do you know what? There must not have been even ten righteous people in Sodom, because God does destroy the city. We see the mercy of God, too, because He does spare Lot and his family by leading them out of town. Every other inhabitant of Sodom and Gomorrah is destroyed.

That story reminds me of Psalm 53. God says, "The fool says in his heart, 'There is no God.' They are corrupt, and their ways are vile; *There is no one who does good*" (v. 1).

And again in v. 3, "Everyone has turned away, they have together become corrupt; *there is no one who does good, not even one.*"

Kind of sounds like Sodom and Gomorrah, doesn't it? God is looking for righteous people, people "who understand," people "who seek God" (v. 2).

I find encouragement in this psalm verse. God is actively looking for people who understand and seek him. He is actually watching us from heaven, just as He watched Abraham in Old Testament times. Those who seek God, can, like Abraham, be considered God's friends. I find great comfort in the picture of God looking down on earth from heaven, taking delight in those who love Him. We may be one of only a handful of Christians in a certain area of the world, but God doesn't miss us.

He looks for us!

He sees us!

There will always be fools who say in their hearts, "There is no God" (Psalm 53:1). Among them, God may find "no one who does good."

But there will also always be those "who understand," "those who seek God" (v. 2). May we be among them.

Dear Lord, when You look down from heaven to see if there are any who understand, any who seek God, may You see me. In Jesus' name, Amen.

Psalm 54 "I will sacrifice a freewill offering to you; I will praise your name, O Lord, for it is good" (v. 6).

I like that word, "freewill." It indicates a willingness. A choice. A voluntary action.

In David's case in this psalm, his choice to sacrifice a "freewill offering" is almost a miracle. It is amazing. It is mind-boggling.

You see, David is being pursued by strangers. Ruthless men are seeking his life. He is in big trouble.

Doesn't seem like a time to be sacrificing freewill offerings, does it?

But that is exactly what David does. In the midst of turmoil, fear, and trouble, he chooses to give an offering to God. In fact, David even takes things one step further in the next verse of Psalm 54. He chooses to *thank* God for delivering him from *all* of his troubles, even when God *hasn't* delivered him yet!

"For he has delivered me from all my troubles, and my eyes have looked in triumph on my foes" (v. 7).

When David wrote those words, he was in hiding from his foes. He was in danger of being discovered at any moment. Yet at that moment of greatest stress, David chose to say with assurance that God *had already* delivered him! He chose to say, in the past tense, "*I have looked* in triumph on my foes."

That is an unnatural way to look at problems! To speak in the past tense when we are in the midst of a crisis is not natural. It is *super*natural! To sacrifice freewill offerings to God when we are in trouble is not a natural response. It, too, is a *super*natural response.

Both are responses which require a choice on our parts. A voluntary response. A using of our free wills. When we have not yet been delivered out of a problem or situation, we can choose to thank God already for His deliverance. We can choose to believe that we will look back in triumph on our foes. We can choose to have faith in God's deliverance so strongly that we view our current problems as past tense!

We can also choose to sacrifice a freewill offering to God even when we don't feel like it. It may be a freewill offering of praise. It may be a freewill offering of money. Sometimes when we are short of money, it can seem very hard to tithe or give to the kingdom of God. But in those times, we can still choose to be faithful with the little we may have been given. We can give the "widow's mite" freely, of our own accord. Any offering given of our own free will, will be multiplied many times over in the work of God's kingdom.

I encourage us all, myself included, to give a *freewill* offering today, and to believe God strongly for deliverance even in the midst of trials.

May we offer God our faith, our offerings of praise, our offerings of money, and our offerings of time *freely,* of our own free will.

Oh Lord, may You be pleased with my offerings and sacrifices and responses today. May they be freewill offerings, even in the midst of struggle. May they be offered to You joyfully, without hesitation or grudge. May they be multiplied for use within Your kingdom. In Jesus' name, Amen.

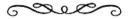

Psalm 55 "I said, 'Oh, that I had the wings of a dove! I would fly away and be at rest I would flee far away and stay in the desert; I would hurry to my place of shelter, far from the tempest and storm" (v. 6-8).

Recently a hailstorm hit our area. It was on July 4th, and our family was having a gathering. We were picnicking and playing croquet outside when suddenly the sky got dark. We picked up everything and headed for the house. No sooner were we inside than the hail started pelting our roof. It sounded like rocks dropping on us from heaven! The roof rattled and banged. Our cars outside were dented and damaged. Hundreds of acres of crops were destroyed within one-half hour's time during that hailstorm. Only those things and people that had made it to shelter were unharmed.

That's how it often is for us in our spiritual lives as well. There are times when we have to *hurry* to a place of shelter. We have to flee far away and stay in the desert for a time.

There are battles being waged against us. Satan would have our very souls if he could. He "prowls about like a roaring lion, seeking whom he may devour" (I Peter 5:8). Sometimes we can sense his presence. Evil may be very near. It prowls. It crouches. Our skies may get suddenly dark.

At those times, we must *hurry* to our place of shelter. We must drop the busyness of whatever we are doing. We must set schedules aside. We must feed our spirits with the pure word of God. We must pray.

God is in those quiet times. He is in our getaways. Our hideaways. Our time-out places. God will meet us there and restore calm. He is our shelter.

Jesus knew that of His Father. When the crowds pressed too closely, Jesus fled to a quiet place. He sought shelter. He sought solitude.

He sought it when he went to the desert. He sought it when he rowed a boat across the lake to escape the crowds. He sought it when he prayed to the Father.

Jesus even prayed, "Lead us not into temptation, but deliver us from evil" (Matthew 6:13). He knew about battles. He knew about evil. He knew that they would come near.

But Jesus also knew that for those who seek shelter in God, there would be safety. Jesus faced the ultimate battle with evil when he died and went to hell for us, but he also knew the safety and shelter of God's right hand through the resurrection. Jesus came through the worst battle of history unharmed!

That is *our* promise, too, from Psalm 55. "He ransoms me *unharmed* from the battle waged against me" (v.18).

Battles will be waged.

Storms will rage.

But like those who hurry to shelter when a hailstorm strikes, we can hurry to our shelter in God. We may be tossed about. We may hear the rocks of battle over our heads. It may even look like we've lost. After all, it looked like Jesus had lost.

He died.

He went down to the grave.

He went to hell.

But three days later He emerged unharmed!

What a shelter!

What a safe place our God is!

He ransoms us *unharmed* from the battle waged against us!

Dear God, please remind me to hurry to You when storms rage. Help me to seek solitude and shelter when evil presses near. Help me to pray and read Your word. Help me to draw close to You. Help me to flee to my hideaway, far from the storm. Thank you that even when it appears that I may have lost a battle, Your promise is to ransom me unharmed. In Jesus' name, Amen.

Psalm 56 "My slanderers pursue me all day long; many are attacking me <u>in their pride</u>" (v. 2). (underlining mine)

What do we attack *in our pride?*

We all do it. We often do it without thinking. We do it so often, that it becomes a habit.

Attacking people in our pride.

For example:

We think that our way of keeping house is good. Therefore we criticize the way others keep their homes.

We feel that our method of raising and disciplining children is best. Therefore we make nasty comments about the way others raise and discipline their children.

We like the way we do our jobs. Therefore we put down our co-workers and bosses for the different ways they approach their jobs.

The list could go on, but you get the idea. All of us, on one level or another, have probably attacked others in our pride.

It may not feel like or seem like pride at the time, but at the root of slander *is* pride. I am guilty, too. David's words strike home. They remind me that I need to repent. To turn away from that kind of talk. That kind of pride.

Pride that is satisfaction is not bad.

Pride in our children's accomplishments.

Pride in our homes.

Pride in our own work well done.

Pride that brings contentment and satisfaction is a good thing.

But pride that brings slander is an entirely different matter.

Pride that says, "My ways are better than yours."

Pride that says, "If only others were like me."

Pride that says, "Your methods are not as good as mine."

That sort of pride "goeth before a fall" (Proverbs 16:18 KJV).

I like Galations 6:4 which says, "Each one should test his own actions. Then he can take pride in himself, without comparing himself to somebody else."

It is in comparing ourselves to somebody else that pride leads to slander. Testing one's own actions, and taking pride in oneself is healthy. Comparing one's actions and oneself to others is not.

Dear Lord, grant me, please, a healthy pride in myself. Help me to test my actions, and to be pleased and proud if they are godly. Forgive me when my pride becomes unhealthy. Forgive me when I compare myself and my actions to someone else. Forgive me when I pursue others with slander. I repent of wrongful pride. Please grant me grace to turn from it. In Jesus' name, Amen.

<hr />

Psalm 57 "Have mercy on me, O God, have mercy on me, for in you my soul takes refuge. I will take refuge in the shadow of your wings until the disaster has passed" (v. 1).

"My heart is steadfast, O God, my heart is steadfast; I will sing and make music" (v. 7).

At first glance, these verses seem unconnected. However, if we put ourselves in David's place at the time he wrote these words, I think we will make the connection.

Imagine yourself in a cave. You are hiding. A man named Saul is after you. He is going to take your life if he finds you. You call out to God to have mercy. You talk with God. You picture yourself covered by the shadow of God's wing. God has always protected you. He has spared your life. He has promised to make you a king one day. He has promised to fulfill His purposes for you.

Suddenly, being hidden in the cave seems safe. You realize that God is there. You can safely rest in the shadow of God's wings until the present disaster has passed. A great relief passes over your heart. You begin to praise God.

That is exactly what David does. He is "in the midst of lions," as he puts it in verse four. His enemies are so close and so ferocious that in his mind, David pictures them as wild beasts. Yet after crying out to God, meditating on God's purposes for his life, and receiving God's love and faithfulness (v. 3), David realizes that his heart no longer feels fearful. Rather, his heart feels *steadfast* (v. 7). It feels *secure*.

Have you ever been gripped by fear or anxiety for a long time, and then suddenly experienced relief from it? Have you ever suddenly realized that your heart is secure?

David says, "My heart is steadfast, O God, my heart is steadfast; I will sing and make music."

For a heart to be steadfast, it must be "firm; fixed; or constant" (Webster's New World Dictionary). It feels secure. Psalm 112 says of the person who fears the Lord, "He will have no fear of bad news; *his heart is steadfast*, trusting in the Lord. *His heart is secure*, he will have no fear" (v. 7-8).

The natural outpouring of a secure heart is praise. David's next step after realizing that his heart is secure in God is to "sing and make music." And what music he makes! We know that David composed many of the psalms! We know that he played the harp and lyre! (Psalm 57:8). We know that he sang! (Psalm 57:9).

Being freed up from fear results in creativity. It releases joy! One minute we can be bound in fear and hiding in a cave, and the next minute we can realize that God is there! He is there with us in our fear and anxiety. He is spreading His wings of safety over us. He is promising to fulfill His purposes for us. He is giving us secure and steadfast hearts.

Out of those hearts can flow praise and creativity of every kind!

A heart at rest produces life.

A heart at rest produces strength.

A heart at rest produces music to God.

David's did.

Ours can, too.

Dear God, I want to make music to You. Grant me a steadfast heart. Give me a heart that is fixed and constant in trusting You. When I feel fearful, remind me that You will fulfill your purposes for me. My heart can feel secure. Out of that security, may creativity bubble forth! In Jesus' name, Amen.

Psalm 58 "Do you rulers indeed speak justly? Do you judge uprightly among men? No, in your heart you devise injustice, and your hands mete out violence on the earth" (v. 1-2).

I would like us to ponder these verses in light of Jesus' trial before the Sanhedrin, as recorded in Matthew 26:57-58. The footnotes in the NIV Study Bible tell us that Psalm 58 was applied by the early church to Jesus' trial. I would like to meditate on that today.

Matthew 26:57 says, "Those who had arrested Jesus took him to Caiaphas, the high priest, where the teachers of the law and the elders had assembled."

Wouldn't you like to ask Psalm 58's question to Caiaphas today?

"Do you rulers indeed speak justly? Do you judge uprightly among men?"

Like most wicked leaders, he would probably answer, "Yes, of course I speak justly. Of course I judge uprightly."

But Jesus knew better. Matthew 26:59 says, "The chief priests and the whole Sanhedrin were looking for false evidence against Jesus so that they could put him to death."

False evidence! They weren't even looking for true evidence. For facts. They wanted false evidence. False witnesses. False testimony.

And they got it. We know the rest of the story. Finally, Jesus is accused of blasphemy, of claiming to be the Son of God. He is condemned both by false witnesses and by his own telling of the truth.

"Look," Caiaphas says, "now you have heard the blasphemy. What do you think?"

"He is worthy of death," comes the reply from the Sanhedrin.

"Then they spit in his face and struck him with their fists" (Matthew 26:65-67).

Sometimes it's good to meditate on what Jesus went through. He stood before men who, "in their hearts devised injustice," and who, "with their hands meted out violence on the earth" (Psalm 58:2).

There has been no greater injustice, no greater violence, than what was done to Jesus.

Both injustice and violence have been committed throughout history. We see and hear of wicked rulers throughout the world both in the past and in the present. Some of us may even have been before such rulers and leaders. Some of us may have to face them in the future.

But Jesus' response in the face of injustice and violence gives us hope. It gives us encouragement. It gives us a guide, should we ever be in similar circumstances.

"He was oppressed and afflicted, yet he did not open his mouth; he was led like a lamb to the slaughter, and as a sheep before her shearers is silent, so he did not open his mouth," says Isaiah 53:7 of the Lamb of God.

And Peter says in I Peter 2:20-23, "If you suffer for doing good and you endure it, this is commendable before God. To this you were called, because Christ suffered for you, leaving you an example, that you should follow in His steps.

'He committed no sin,

and no deceit was found in his mouth;'

When they hurled insults at him, he did not retaliate; when he suffered, he made no threats. Instead, he entrusted himself to him who judges justly."

"Surely the righteous still are rewarded; surely there is a God who judges the earth," ends Psalm 58.

What a reward our Lord received after all his suffering! Jesus sits at the right hand of God! Though his life on earth was cut short, though he had no descendants, Jesus reigns *forever* with *all Christians as his children*!

"Surely the righteous still are rewarded" (Psalm 58:11).

May we be among them by God's grace.

Dear Jesus, Your example is perfect. I need Your help to follow it in the face of injustice and violence. May Your grace be with me should those circumstances arise. Thank you for suffering for me, that I might have an eternal reward. In Your name, Amen.

Psalm 59 "O my Strength, I watch for you; you, O God, are my fortress, my loving God" (v. 9-10a).

Do you watch for God?

He comes sometimes in unexpected ways. Unexpected times. Unexpected places.

Like the manger. Remember that? Not many were watching then.

Mary was.

Joseph was.

The shepherds and wisemen were.

Simeon and Hannah were.

But very few got to see the Son of God at his birth-time.

And the disciples. They got to see the Son of Man firsthand. They watched him on a daily basis. They watched his interactions with the people of his day. They watched Jesus go to people in the least expected circumstances.

Remember Zacchaeus? He wanted to watch Jesus so badly that he climbed a sycamore tree to see Him! When Jesus saw Zacchaeus up in the tree, he said, "Come down immediately. I must stay at your house today" (Luke 19:5).

What an unexpected blessing! A man climbs a tree to watch for a glimpse of Jesus, and ends up entertaining the King of Kings as an overnight houseguest!

And the Blind Beggar. Remember him? He couldn't see, yet he was watching by the roadside for Jesus. "Watching" as the crowd drew near. "Watching" as he asked what was happening (Luke 18:36). "Watching" as he shouted, "Jesus, Son of David, have mercy on me!" (Luke 18:38). "Watching" as he said, "Lord, I want to see" (Luke 18:41).

What an unexpected answer Jesus gave to that watcher! "Receive your sight; your faith has healed you," Jesus said! One minute a blind beggar is watching for Jesus, and the next minute he receives his sight!

God comes that way. He comes into our daily lives, and into our daily circumstances. He comes so subtly and so quickly sometimes that unless we're watching, we might miss Him!

He comes in unexpected people.

He comes in unexpected places.

He comes in unexpected times.

We are to watch and be ready for Jesus' return. For Jesus' second coming (Luke 12:40). But I believe we are also to watch for Him on a daily basis in our everyday, work-a-day lives.

That's how the shepherds got to see Him. By tending their flocks and looking up.

That's how the wisemen got to see Jesus. By taking a trip and watching the stars.

That's how Simeon and Hannah got to see Him. By watching in the temple until they *saw* the salvation of Israel and held Him in their hands!

That's how Zacchaeus got to see Jesus. By climbing a tree to get a better look.

That's how the blind beggar saw Christ. By asking what was going on and asking for his sight!

That's how we can see Jesus, too. By watching for Him in our cars and houses. In our cities and rural areas. In our schools and workplaces. In our children and spouses and friends. In strangers. In ourselves.

In all the least-expected places, we can see Jesus. All we have to do is watch.

Dear Lord, make me a watcher. Help me to see you in unexpected places. I watch for You, O My Strength. In Jesus' name, Amen.

❦

Psalm 60 "But for those who fear you, you have raised a banner to be unfurled against the bow" (v. 4).

When my sister bought a house, she had a housewarming party. In order to bless her new home, a friend led all the houseguests in a Christian liturgy from New Zealand. The liturgy speaks a blessing on each room of a person's new house. As we walked from room to room, all of the guests together carried a twelve-foot banner of beautifully colored cloth. When the blessing was spoken in each room, we raise the colored banner up over our heads. This was a sign of God's blessing over the room.

It was a moving experience to bless a loved one's home in such a manner. We were thankful for the custom of another culture which showed us clearly that "His banner over us is love" (Song of Songs 2:4).

God does raise a banner over those who fear Him.

A banner of protection.

A banner of victory.

A banner of love.

In Exodus 17 we are told that Joshua fought the Amalekites as Moses had ordered. Moses watched the battle from atop a hill. He held in his hands the "staff of God." Verse 11 tells us that "as long as Moses held up his hands, the Israelites were winning, but whenever he lowered his hands, the Amalekites were winning."

When Moses' hands grew tired, Aaron and Hur, "held his hands up, one on one side, one on the other, so that his hands remained steady till sunset. So Joshua overcame the Amalekite army with the sword" (v. 12-13).

Moses then built an altar and called it. *"The Lord is my Banner."* He said, "For hands were lifted up to the throne of the Lord" (v. 15-16).

Isn't that a good picture of God's banner over us?

You wouldn't think that a banner made of cloth would do much in the way of protecting against weapons like a bow and arrows. But the banner is simply a symbol of God's mighty power of protection. It is a colorful reminder that God is our "refuge and fortress" (Psalm 91:2).

"You will not fear the terror of night, nor the arrow that flies by day," says Psalm 91:5. "With God, we will gain the victory, and he will trample down our enemies," says Psalm 60:12.

When we dwell in the shadow of the Almighty, we can rest in safety.

When we dwell under the protection of God's banner, we can enjoy all of the privileges that symbol affords.

Just as the United States' flag or another country's flag symbolizes certain rights and freedoms for those who live under it, so God's banner symbolizes certain privileges for those who live under it.

The privilege of freedom (John 8:36).

The privilege of forgiveness (Col. 1:14).

The privilege of adoption as sons and daughters (Eph. 1:5).

The privilege of eternal life in heaven (John 11:25).

We must fear Him. We must respect His laws and ways. We must obey those laws as much as we can, and repent when we fail. Then, like Moses, we can say, "The Lord is my Banner."

Dear Lord, thank you for raising Your banner over me. In Jesus' name, Amen.

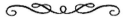

Psalm 61 "Hear my cry, O God; listen to my prayer. From the ends of the earth I call to you, I call as my heart grows faint; lead me to <u>the rock that is higher than I</u>. For you have been my refuge, <u>a strong tower against the foe</u>. I long to dwell in <u>your tent</u> forever and take refuge in <u>the shelter of your wings</u>. Selah" (v. 1-4). (underlining mine)

There are four places mentioned in today's verses where I would like to go. Four places of refuge. Four places of God.

1. The rock that is higher than I
2. A strong tower against the foe
3. Your (God's) tent
4. The shelter of Your (God's) wings

Two of these places are high or suggest height. Two of them are low or on ground level. Sometimes places of refuge on both levels are necessary.

What about height? What sort of refuge does that bring?

I like to remember my cat, Rumplestiltskin. She liked height. Her favorite place to sit during the day was on the top step leading to our upstairs. On every other step I had a stuffed animal of some sort, looking down on the living room below. Rumplestiltskin would position herself smartly between the stuffed goose and the stuffed bear. She would gaze down between the banisters near the top step. From this vantage point she would survey her kingdom.

Rumplestiltskin felt safe up there. It gave her good perspective. Cats are smaller than most of their surroundings, and they sometimes need height to gain a sense of security. That's why windowsills, steps, and the tops of refrigerators seem to be cats' favorite spots!

People, too, need a sense of height. We sometimes need to climb up to more clearly view our circumstances. We need to gain distance on the things that surround us. We are smaller than so much that goes on around us in this world. We need "a rock that is higher that I" in order to gain perspective.

Imagine yourself on a high rock today. Or on your top stair step if that feels safer! A high rocky ledge that is firmly embedded in a mountainside. From there you can look down on the everyday places in which you live. You can see their beauty. You can see their pitfalls. You can see the places that need patching, or fixing, or cleaning. You can see so much more clearly from above, than you could from being in the midst of those low spots.

We live in the low spots. Low spots are not bad. They are the living rooms and kitchens of our lives. They are the valleys and plains beneath the mountains. They are beautiful. But sometimes we need to climb above them and look down in order to appreciate them more. We need God to lead us to "the rock that is higher than I," in order to see what He is doing down below.

God gives us places of refuge in the low places, too. He gives us His "tent." We have churches and sanctuaries as places of worship. In fact, the word "sanctuary" can mean both "a place of worship," and "a refuge or place of protection." Let us not neglect going to church. We can find there a place of refuge.

We have "strong towers" against the foe. We have the Bible, God's word of life, to encourage us. We have the "armor of God" (Ephesians 6) to put on every day to fight off depression and evil.

And lastly, in our low places, we have "the shelter of God's wings." We can curl up anytime, anywhere, under God's wing. He is like a big mother hen, looking down on us, and wanting to give us comfort. "He will cover you with his feathers, and under his wings you will find refuge" (Psalm 91:4).

Let us go often to these four places of refuge mentioned in Psalm 61. Let us go there to gain perspective. To gain shelter. To gain security. To gain comfort.

Dear Lord, thank you for Your places of refuge. Please lead me there by Your gracious hand. In Jesus' name, Amen.

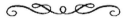

Psalm 62 "Lowborn men are but a breath, the highborn are but a lie; If weighed on a balance, they are nothing; together they are only a breath" (v. 9).

My husband and I have a friend who our society would label as indigent. Our friend's sister recently died. She, too, would be called indigent. She had nothing when she died. No money. No home. No children.

We went to her burial. I can't call it a funeral, because our society doesn't provide funerals for people who can't pay for them. Instead, our culture gives these people something called "immediate burial." That, we learned from the mortician, means that the body is not embalmed. Therefore, it must be put in the ground immediately. No funeral service. No church. No flowers. No gravestone. No memorials. Just a burial.

The coffin is what struck me as the most sad. I remember having picked out a coffin for my father when he died years earlier. We were taken by a mortician to a room in the funeral parlor where there were many coffins to choose from. Most ranged in price from hundreds to thousands of dollars. We chose one in a moderate range. A pretty bronze-colored wood with sheaves of wheat carved on it. There was one casket in that room, though, that caught my eye. It was blue. Instead of wood or bronze, this one looked to be made out of plasterboard. Very thin and flimsy looking. It had a garish paisley design on the outside. To the touch, the outer material felt like suede or cheap velvet. It was tacky. It stuck out in a room of beautifully crafted caskets as an eyesore. Undignified. Unsophisticated.

"Who would ever choose that one?" I asked the mortician.

"Oh, no one *chooses* that one," was his reply. "That's the coffin type we use for indigents. People who can't afford to pay."

That was the coffin I stood looking at now at our friend's immediate burial.

There were six of us gathered there in the cemetery around this blue box, my husband and I, our friend, his sister-in-law, the mortician, and our pastor.

We had asked our pastor to come, even though he had never met the deceased. He agreed to say a few words at the burial. What he said, I will always remember.

He said, "We must never forget the value of a human life. Every human life."

He said, "*People* put different values on different things. People put more value on a Cadillac than they do on a Chevrolet. But what gives those cars different values is their makers." "*People*," he said, "*all* have the same Maker. We *all* have the same value. We are *all* special to God."

"Yes," I said in my heart as I looked at that blue box. "Yes, we *all* have the same Maker."

"Lowborn men are but a breath, the highborn are but a lie; If weighed on a balance, they are nothing; together they are only a breath."

Lowborn or high, rich men or poor, wealthy or indigent, our Maker is the same. Together, we are only a breath. Our time here is so short. We may leave this world in riches or rags, in wealth or in want, in a bronze box or blue.

For both, Jesus died.

For both, Jesus lives.

For both, the value in God's eyes is the same.

Dear Lord, thank you that in Your eyes we are all priceless. Thank you for being our Maker. Thank you for making every human life one of inestimable value. In Jesus' name, Amen.

Psalm 63 "Because you are my help, I sing in the shadow of your wings" (v. 7).

We had a duckling named "Peep-a-lot." That's what she did; she peeped a *lot*! We acquired her through a set of interesting circumstances.

There had been a flood around our town of Morris, Minnesota. The fields and ditches were full of water. Lake Crystal, a small lake near Morris, had flooded its' banks.

A lot of ducks made their home on Lake Crystal, and somehow, we surmise, one duckling from a brood of babies must have gotten lost or washed away from the others. Somehow, this one duckling got carried by the flood waters from Lake Crystal to the culvert system. One of those culverts leads to a drainage system near Morris' main street.

That's where we come in. One hot evening in the summer, my husband and I drove to town to get a Dairy Queen treat. The Dairy Queen in Morris is on Main Street. As we came out of the DQ with our ice cream cones, I spotted a tiny shape moving on the pavement near our vehicle. As we got closer we saw that, sure enough, it was a baby duckling! Tiny, fuzzy, yellow and brown. Peeping up a storm! That was Peep-a-lot.

We searched the area for her mother and other baby ducklings, but neither could be found. Knowing that she would soon get run over in the Dairy Queen parking lot, we brought her home to join the tribe of other lost or abandoned animals who call our place "home."

We fed Peep-a-lot crushed oatmeal, corn, and bread. She swam three times a day in our bathtub. She followed me around the house, peeping. And *pooping*! We could've called her "Poop-a-lot," but "Peep-a-lot" seemed nicer!

Many things endeared her to us, but most of all, I remember Peep-a-lot when it was time for her to sleep. You see, she had no mother duck, and I think at sleeping time, she realized this the most. She would get tired, and her peeping would get louder and faster. She'd walk around the room, almost falling from fatigue, but never able to settle down enough to sleep.

At those times, I would pick her up and cup my hands around her tiny body. I would lie down on the carpet and hold her gently against my neck. She fit perfectly in the hollow between my neck and shoulder.

For a few minutes, the loud peeping would continue. Then, as Peep-a-lot realized that she was safe and warm, and in a dark, quiet place, she would begin to relax. Her peeping would subside into quiet cheeping. Then contented chirps. Quiet breathing. And finally, peaceful, deep sleep. She slept so long and hard that the place on my neck would start to sweat. I could feel her soft, downy fluff against my skin. I felt her breathing, slow and safe. Now and then, a contented chirp, barely heard, as she dreamed.

"Because you are my help, I sing in the shadow of your wings."

That's what our duckling, Peep-a-lot, did. She sang in the shadow of my wings. OK, My neck and shoulder! You see, she thought I was her mother. She felt safe with me. With me she could relax. It made her sing. It made her rest. It made her sleep. All she needed was shelter.

A safe place.

A warm place.

A quiet place.

God is that. He is our Father. He has a place hollowed out in His own right hand. It fits us perfectly. It protects us. It shelters us. It warms us.

God has a place for us to go when we are so tired that all we can do is walk around, almost falling over from fatigue. God has a place for us when we feel lost. God has a place for us when we're abandoned.

In that place we can sing. Not the loud singing (or peeping!) of confusion, but rather, the quiet, contented singing of safety. In that place we can relax. Our breathing can slow down. We can sleep. We can rest. We can dream.

Heavenly Father, bring me often to the place where I can rest. The shadow of your wings is where I want to be. Hide me close to you, tangibly, Lord, that I might feel your warmth and closeness. There let me sing to you. In Jesus' name, Amen.

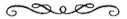

Psalm 64 "Hear me, O God, as I voice my complaint; protect my life from the threat of the enemy" (v. 1).

Depression
Busyness
Overwork
Favors for others

Good Things
Commitments
Ungodly philosophies

Whew! What a list! Some of these things seem contradictory to one another. They don't seem to belong on the same list. But all of them have something in common. They can be our enemies.

I recently spent a weekend on a retreat with sixty-eight members of my husband's college choir. They rented a camp facility and spent three days there singing, playing volleyball, eating, having bonfires, getting to know one another, singing, singing, and singing! It was a great weekend with lots accomplished during choir rehearsals and during social times.

My husband and I get to know these students well, as many of them are in choir for four years during their college experience. We spend much time together rehearsing, traveling, going on tours, and giving concerts. We also have a Bible study in our home for college students who want to come on Sunday evenings.

This, year, however, I had determined not to have the Bible study group. I had decided that what with teaching music at an elementary school, teaching piano lessons at my home, and writing a book, I was just too busy.

That was until I went on this retreat with the college students. Remember how the verse for today says, "protect my life from the threat of the enemy"? Well, at this retreat, I heard lots of things that I would label "threats of the enemy." Oh, they weren't *bad* things. They weren't *terrible* things. They weren't *big* things. But taken together, they struck me as a threat.

I heard college students talking of depression. Of being too busy at school. Of being overworked. I heard them talking of books they were reading. Books that told them to put themselves first. Books that told them there are many gods. Books that told them there is no God. Books that told them sex with a consenting partner at any time is OK.

Now I'm not an alarmist. And I'm never in favor of censorship. I believe that questioning is one of our best tools for finding God. But I also believe that many things in our society can threaten our stability, our sanity, and our peace. They can threaten our walk with God if we know Him, and our search for God if we are seeking Him.

God cares about those things that threaten us. He wants to listen as we voice our complaints about those threats, those enemies.

So, at the retreat, I voiced my complaints to God.

"God," I said, "these students are facing enemies. They are facing busyness, overwork, depression, and ungodly philosophies that lead them away from their quest for peace and for You."

And, I confess, I voiced another complaint.

"God," I said, "I feel too busy to have a Bible study for college students this year. We've got children and jobs, and we're already going to another Bible study. Isn't that too much, God?"

God's answer was clear.

"No. That's not too much. You may have to cut back in other areas. I will help you. But don't cut back in an area that fights my enemies."

So, we're having Bible study! It's only one small thing, I know. But I believe it's one small thing that God is asking me to do. When you feel called by God to do something, you don't say "no!" You say "yes," joyfully!

I often feel so overwhelmed myself by threats of the enemy. I am so glad that God says, "Voice your complaint to me. I'll protect you."

That's God's job. He is our protector. He protects us from threats of the enemy. Threats like:

Busyness

Ungodly philosophies

Overwork

Commitments

Favors for others

He helps us choose those things that we need to say "yes" to, and those things we need to say "no" to. Sometimes good things can threaten us, also. We can say yes to so many good things that we are over-committed. Sometimes we must say "no" to ungodly philosophies that steal our peace or lead us away from our search for God.

When we feel threatened by an enemy of any kind, we can voice our complaint to God. He is our protector.

Dear God, whether I am threatened by "good" things or "bad" things today, please protect me. Let nothing come between You and me. Thank you for letting me voice my complaint to You. I pray today, too, for others who I see being threatened by enemies. Help me to do my part to encourage them. In Jesus' name, Amen.

Psalm 65 "You crown the year with your bounty... the hills are clothed with gladness. The meadows are covered with flocks and the valleys are mantled with grain; they shout for joy and sing" (v. 11a, 12 & 13).

Each year at Christmastime I buy myself a new dress. I get to wear it numerous times for special occasions. There are my husband's Carol Concerts at the college where he directs the choir. There are Christmas Eve services at church and our family celebration at home afterward. There are New Year's Eve services at church and then card-playing and fun and feasting at a New Year's Eve party.

All of these times are special occasions that mark the end of another year. They also mark our celebration of Christ's coming to earth as a little child. For each of these occasions I wear my new dress. It makes me feel special. It makes me feel celebratory. It makes me feel prepared.

I believe that's what the earth does each year. It changes garments. It gets a new dress. It puts on new clothes.

"The hills are *clothed* with gladness. The meadows are *covered* with flocks and the valleys are *mantled* with grain."

This week I drove by a ripe soybean field. The plants had turned a deep red color and were swaying in the wind. I was listening to flute and recorder music on the radio as I drove. As I passed the field, the combination of beautiful, soothing music and richly hung, red, ripe plants was so overwhelming that I stopped the vehicle. I stopped and listened and looked. I even cried.

God's creation is so beautiful! It changes with each season. It puts on new clothes to honor God. It prepares, each year, for Christ's coming.

There are so many seasons in life to prepare for. Some require a change of dress. Some require a change of heart. All require some quiet, reflective time in order to be ready.

There is Advent which prepares us for Christ's coming. There is Lent which prepares us for Christ's dying and rising. There are fall and winter and summer and spring. There are dyings and birthings of all kinds going on each day in individual lives. All of these season changes require preparation. They require time spent with God in order to be ready and to adjust.

May our hearts prepare for each of the seasons we may be entering. May we, like the earth, clothe ourselves with fitting garments with which to honor God. May we welcome change, and welcome God.

Linda Winter-Hodgson

<u>The Earth Is Changing Garments</u>

The earth is changing garments;
She's putting on new clothes;
Each season, one to honor
When Christ came, and died, and rose.

White Winter says the Babe who came
Was pure and innocent;
The branches bare and brown
Received the Savior heaven sent.

In Fall, the milkweed bows to spin
A seedpod filled with fleece
The treetops turn their leaves to gold
To greet the Prince of Peace.

"He's royalty!" the sumac sings,
"I'll wear a bright red gown!"
"He's royalty!" the grapevine sings,
"I'll twine a purple crown!"

"Christ died;" the flowers bow their heads;
The rose begins to wilt;
"Christ died; I'll drop red petals
For each drop of blood He spilt."

Then Spring returns, reminding,
With its vibrant gown of green,
The story did not end in death;
Christ once again was seen!

The earth is changing garments;
Let all the hills be glad!
Let flocks adorn the meadows;

Lowlands with grain be clad!

For Summer says, "My Groom will come,
Although I don't know when;
I'll wear my wedding gown
For when the Bridegroom comes again!"

      by Linda Winter-Hodgson

Psalm 66 "I will come to your temple with burnt offerings and fulfill my vows to you vows my lips promised and my mouth spoke when I was in trouble" (v. 13-14).

When my husband and I got married, I had been reading in the book of Deuteronomy. In chapter 26 it says, "When you have entered the land the Lord your God is giving you as an inheritance and have taken possession of it and settled in it, take some of the firstfruits of all that you produce from the soil of the land the Lord your God is giving you and put them in a basket. Then go to the place the Lord your God will choose as a dwelling for his name and say to the priest in office at the time, 'I declare today to the Lord your God that I have come to the land the Lord swore to our forefathers to give us.' . . . 'Now I bring the firstfruits of the soil that you, O Lord, have given me.' Place the basket before the Lord your God and bow down before him" (Deuteronomy 26:1-4,10).

When I read those verses during the first year of our marriage, the Lord quickened them to my heart. I knew that Ken and I were to do what those verses said after we had "entered the land the Lord was giving us as an inheritance," and after we had "taken possession of it and settled in it." I promised the Lord that when that time came, Ken and I would bring the firstfruits of all that God had given us to the pastor of our church, and present them to the Lord.

During the first year of our marriage, we rented a farmhouse and thirty acres of land. The house and property were not for sale, and so we knew that this was not the land that the Lord would give us to "take possession of and settle in." However, the second year we were married, we prayed about buying a home, and the Lord allowed us to buy the house and property where we now live.

Because of our promise to God that we made when reading Deuteronomy, we knew that the firstfruits of our garden and income after settling in our new home should be brought to the Lord.

We took our promise seriously because we had made it before God. Even though it was almost three years later from the time we had first read in Deuteronomy and made our promise to God, we did bring the firstfruits of our garden and income to our church. We brought a basket of fresh garden vegetables and boxes of canned tomatoes and beets. We brought frozen packages of beans and peas and corn. We presented them to the pastor and told him of our promise to God three years earlier after reading Deuteronomy chapter 26. He took the produce and income and distributed it among needy people in the community. We don't even know where it went, only that we were to fulfill our vow to God.

"I will come to your temple with burnt offerings and fulfill my vows to you, vows my lips promised and my mouth spoke when I was in trouble."

Have you ever made a vow to God? In the New Testament it says that we are not to make an oath. We are to let our "yes be yes," and our "no be no" (Matthew 5:37). But I believe that making a vow or promise to God is different.

I think of Martin Luther, who, before giving his life to God, found himself caught in a terrible thunder and lightning storm. He hung on to a tree for dear life as the winds and rains and lightning raged around him. During that storm he prayed, "Lord, if you spare my life now, I will spend the rest of it serving you."

That was a vow or promise to God. As we know, Martin Luther did spend the rest of his life serving God. He fulfilled his vow or promise.

I believe that we are to do the same. We are not to make vows or promises frequently or flippantly, but if we do make a vow, we should fulfill it. God honors that. He blesses it. He is pleased in it.

Dear God, thank you that You are a keeper of promises. Help me to keep my promises to You and to others. If I have failed, I confess that as sin, and know that You forgive me. Help me in the future to fulfill my vows to You. In Jesus' name, Amen.

Psalm 67 "May God be gracious to us and bless us and make his face shine upon us, Selah, that your ways may be known on earth, your salvation among all nations" (v. 1-2).

Life isn't always a struggle, you know. Sometimes we look around at Christians and we think, "Boy, what an awful life. If that's what it is to be a Christian . . . no thanks!"

Yes, there are struggles and sometimes tremendous sufferings in the Christian life. Yes, I believe we are to be partakers in the sufferings of Christ. And yes, we are to share our burdens in the body of Christ.

But sometimes in Christian churches and circles that's all we see.

The struggles.

The burdens.

The problems.

We forget the prayer of the psalmist when he says, "May God be gracious to us and bless us and make his face shine upon us, Selah."

God's grace and favor can rest on us. We can live a life of graciousness. We can let God's face shine upon us.

Selah.

After thinking about that and letting it happen in our lives, we can see that the *result* of God's face shining on us is "that your ways may be known on earth, your salvation among all nations."

Remember the Lord's Prayer where Jesus prays, "Thy kingdom come, Thy will be done, on earth, as it is in heaven"?

God's will is being done in heaven all the time. Jesus prayed that his Father's will would be done on earth, too. When God is gracious to us, and His face shines upon us, I believe that people can see His will being done on earth. They can see the true Christian life, a life where God shines through ordinary human beings. The result is that people are drawn to Christ.

When people see God's graciousness shining in our lives, they see His ways on earth. They see God's will being done on earth as it is in heaven. They see His salvation and ways being made known on earth and among all nations.

Everyone wants a life where God is gracious to them. Everyone desires God to bless them and to shine upon them. It is our job as Christians to let them see that life of graciousness and to let them be drawn to it.

God wants his ways known on earth. He wants His salvation known among all nations. Only if we allow His graciousness to shine out through our lives, will others see God's ways.

Dear God, forgive me when I let others see only the troubles and problems in my life. Help me to more often let them see your graciousness and blessing. Make your face shine upon me, and through me, that your ways may be known on earth, your salvation among all nations. In Jesus' name, Amen.

Psalm 68 "May God arise, may his enemies be scattered; may his foes flee before him. As smoke is blown away by the wind, may you blow them away; as wax melts before the fire, may the wicked perish before God" (v. 1-2).

To these verses I might add, "As fog is burned away by the morning sun, may the enemies in each day be pushed back; may they evaporate before You, O God."

This morning when I got up, the fog around our house was so thick that I couldn't see our neighbor's fields or house. I felt like I was in a vacuum. Although it was morning, very little light was getting through. It was dark, and felt more like night.

As I had breakfast and went about the morning's chores, I could see the fog starting to recede. The sun poked through and started to burn off the fog from the fields. The fog literally vanished and evaporated before my eyes!

That's how it is with our enemies in each day when we let God arise. Our days may seem clouded or dark. We may be so "fogged in" by problems that little or no light can get through. We may feel stress or pressure so thick that we seem to be living in a vacuum.

But God, like the morning sun, can push back those enemies of stress or pressure or despair. He can burn them away with the warmth of His love. Our enemies literally vanish or evaporate before God!

Fog lifts.

Wax melts.

Enemies scatter.

Foes flee.

That is what Psalm 68 tells us.

We can trust God to scatter our enemies. We may need to sit quietly with God to let the warmth of his love melt our insecurities. We may need to pray and ask God to arise and blow back the problems and fog of the day so that we can see clearly.

God will do it. He will scatter our enemies. Then we can say with the psalmist in the next verse of Psalm 68, "But may the righteous be glad and rejoice before God; may they be happy and joyful."

Dear God, please burn away the fog that often envelopes me; the fog of fear, depression, bitterness, stress, and pressure. You know my enemies, God. Please arise and scatter them. May the warmth of Your love burst through my problems like the morning sun, giving me clear vision and a bright future. In Jesus' name, Amen.

Psalm 69 " ...the insults of those who insult you fall on me" (v. 9b).

Is that how you feel about God? When people insult God, do you feel insulted?

The psalmist felt that way. He felt very close to God; so close that when people's comments about the Lord were negative, the psalmist took it personally.

I think of my own mother and father when they were living, and how I would've felt if someone insulted them. It would have hurt me. I would have felt terrible. I loved and respected my parents. I wanted to honor them. If someone had made fun of them or had spoken disrespectfully of them or to them, it would have been as if the insult had fallen on me, too.

God is our father and our mother. He is our heavenly parent. We are to love and respect God, even more than we do our earthly parents. If someone is disrespectful to God, it should be as if the insults have fallen on us, too.

What are some ways in which people insult God?

They use His name in vain.

They curse.

They swear.

They take God's name lightly.

They make fun of His word and of his principles.

How many times have we heard the names "God," and "Jesus," and "Christ" misused? We hear it every day. If people used our earthly parents' names as curse words, we would be deeply hurt and offended. Imagine if every time someone felt angry, they shouted your name or your parents' names. It would be a hurtful and dishonorable thing.

I believe that we should feel insulted when God is insulted. We should feel bad when people misuse God's name. We should lovingly tell them that when they insult our heavenly parent, the insults fall on us, too.

Many people swear and curse without much thought. They do not always realize how these words directly hurt God. They do not always realize how these words can hurt God's people. If we tell them that God is our best friend, our heavenly parent, and that it is as if they were insulting our own mother or father when they insult God, perhaps they will think twice before cursing again.

Perhaps they will realize that God can be their best friend, too. Perhaps they will ask us how they, too, can feel so close to God.

Dear God, may we all be so close to You, that when others insult You, we take it personally. Help us to lovingly remind others and ourselves, that Your name is the most honorable name. Help us to treat You with the respect and love and honor that you deserve. In Jesus' name, Amen.

Psalm 70 *"...may those who love your salvation always say, 'Let God be exalted!'" (v. 4b)*.

Do you love God's salvation?

It's what God does. He saves.

God's vocation or occupation, if you will, is that of Savior.

We may be farmers or carpenters or homemakers or teachers, but *God* is a *savior*. His work, all day long and all night long, is to save. He works all shifts. Days. Swing shift. Graveyard. Full-time.

He saves us from hell.

He saves us from a sinful life.

He saves us from eternal death.

God also saves us from daily perils and strife. He rescues us from all kinds of pickles and messes that we get into and then can't get out of on our own.

That's why the psalmist starts Psalm 70 with, "Hasten O God, to save me; O Lord, come quickly to help me" (v.1).

He didn't mean, "Quick, God, send a Messiah today to save all Israel from destruction!" No, he meant, "Help, God! I'm in a tight spot! Get me out of here!"

God saves in all sorts of daily struggles and situations. Salvation is His business. He "majored" in it, if you will!

Yes, God has other work. He creates. He sanctifies. He redeems. But most of all, God *saves.*

Luke 2:10 says, "I bring you good news of great joy that will be for all people. Today in the town of David a *Savior* has been born to you; he is Christ the Lord."

It doesn't say "a farmer" has been born to you. It doesn't even say, "a carpenter" has been born to you! Jesus *was* a carpenter by earthly trade! But his main occupation was that of Savior. His main work on earth was *salvation!*

What a work! We are to *love* that work! "Let those who love God's salvation say, 'Let God be exalted!'" Another translation says, "Let those who love Thy salvation say continually, 'Let God be magnified!'"

Wow! That shows excitement! That shows enthusiasm! That shows real love for God's work!

In Genesis 45, we see Joseph as a foreshadowing or type of Christ. He *saves* his brothers, even though they have sold him into Egypt. He says to his brothers, "Come close to me . . . I am your brother Joseph, the one you sold into Egypt. And now, do not be distressed and do not be angry with yourselves for selling me here, *because it was to save lives that God sent me ahead of you.* For two years now there has been famine in the land, and for the next five years there will not be sowing and reaping. But God sent me ahead of you to preserve for you a remnant on earth *and to save your lives by a great deliverance*" (v. 4-7).

Can't you just imagine Jesus saying those words to us? "Come close to me. Don't be distressed or angry with yourselves for selling me to my captors. Don't be angry at yourselves for causing my death on the cross; *because it was to save lives that God sent me ahead of you! God sent me ahead of you to preserve you and to save your lives by a great deliverance!*"

I imagine Jesus saying that to me and to you! That, after all, was his work! That's why he came to earth as a baby. God sent him here to do a saving work!

I think of the works of my dad. He was a farmer. He took his business seriously. He cared for the land. He fought against chemical use. He used old machinery instead of new in order to stay out of debt. Dad did all of that for me and for my sister and for my mother. He did it to provide for us, and to preserve the land for future generations. That was Dad's work.

I loved his work. It warms my heart to this day to think of him on the tractor or on the combine. I can see my dad in my mind's eye, even though he has passed away. I can see him stooping down in the field, handling the black dirt in his hands. He loved the dirt. He loved its smell and its feel. He even loved its taste when it blew in his face! I can still hear Dad saying when we got dirty, "Don't worry about it! There's nothing like good, clean dirt!"

To this day I love the soil because of Dad. Other things can make me feel dirty. I can feel sticky or soiled or in need of a bath. But digging in the garden or feeling black dirt on my hands actually makes me feel clean! It makes me feel clean because I love the work!

That is how God wants us to feel about His work. His work of salvation. He wants us to catch the excitement of it! He wants us to get the feel of "digging into" the work of saving others! We can't save them, but we can tell them about Jesus, who can!

My Dad no longer lives on earth, but he passed on to me the love of his work.

Jesus no longer lives on earth, but I believe that He passed on to us, through His Holy Spirit, the love of His work!

We are to *love* salvation! We are to "dig in" and participate in it! We are to join in God's work of spreading His saving love!

What a privilege! What a joy! What an honor!

Lord, may we carry on your work that you taught us through Jesus, our Savior. May we tell others of your saving work! May we "dig into" the soil of what You are planting and reaping on earth, and may we <u>love</u> the work of your salvation! We love Your salvation, O God! Thank you for saving us through the blood of your Son! Let God be exalted! May we continually say, "Let God be magnified!" In Jesus' name, Amen.

Psalm 71 "Even when I am old and gray, do not forsake me, O God, till I declare your power to the next generation, your might to all who are to come" (v. 18).

I had an uncle named Ray. Ray was a farmer for many years of his life. Before that he had been a janitor. Before that he had run away from home in his teens because his father had physically abused him. Ray had had a rough life in many ways, but to meet him you wouldn't have known it. He treated my sister Lisa and me, and all of his nieces and nephews like gold. He sat with us on the floor of his house and played games. He held us on his lap. He chased us playfully through each room of his house. He served us breakfast on a tray in front of the TV when we stayed overnight. He kept a special tin of mint candies on hand that melted in our mouths when we ate them.

Ray was born in 1899, and he died in 1976. I was born in 1961, so he was old and gray for as long as I knew him. When I was fifteen, Ray developed kidney trouble. It worsened and worsened until finally, he was put on a dialysis machine in a Minneapolis hospital. When that failed to help any more, Ray was brought home to his small town hospital to die near his beloved wife and relatives at home.

All of us took turns watching at Ray's bedside. We spent 6 to 8 hour shifts sitting quietly in his hospital room, just holding his hand.

Ray was in a lot of pain. His kidneys no longer functioned at all, and he was not on a dialysis machine. Nothing was filtering the urine and waste from Ray's body. His skin turned yellow. He literally cried out in pain.

During one of the night shifts I sat with Ray alone. I remember him yelling out with a loud voice over and over, "Lord, why won't you take me? Why won't you take me home?"

He squeezed my hand hard and asked me, "Linda, why has God forsaken me? Why won't he take me home?"

I remember feeling so helpless. I was fifteen years old. I loved my Uncle Ray with all my heart. I didn't know why God wouldn't take him to heaven right away when he was in such pain. But I knew Ray needed to know. I needed to know. So I asked God.

As far as I can remember, I had never before asked God for a direct answer to a question. But I did that night. I prayed, "Dear God, Why won't you let Ray die?"

The answer came so fast and so clear to my mind that I said it out loud immediately to Ray.

"Because some people aren't ready yet for you to die. Some people still need you."

Ray lay still for a minute and then he started to cry. He took my hand gently and he said, "You have a knowledge of things that will never pass away."

That was the last thing Ray said to me. The next day I went to Minneapolis by bus to visit my sister. When I got there, Lisa said Mom had called to say that Ray had died that morning.

"Even when I am old and gray, do not forsake me, O God, till I declare your power to the next generation, your might to all who are to come."

I know Ray felt forsaken by God on his deathbed. It was lonely and painful and confusing. He didn't know why God wouldn't let him die sooner. He was ready for heaven. But God hadn't forsaken him. God had a plan to use Ray to declare His power to the next generation. God knew that a fifteen-year-old girl named Linda needed one more night with her Uncle Ray. She needed to pray and hear God's answer. Maybe Ray needed it, too. Maybe he needed to be reminded that even old and gray and in pain, his life still had purpose until its last breath on earth.

That night had a profound effect on me. I've never forgotten it. I've never forgotten God's words or Ray's. They've reminded me that God speaks through the old and infirm. They've reminded me that God doesn't forsake us even when we feel like He has. They've reminded me that God has a purpose for us on earth from birth until death. They've reminded me that sometimes when God keeps us on earth in pain or old age or suffering, it isn't just our needs He's considering; it's the needs of our loved ones and of others, too.

I hadn't let go of Ray until that night in his hospital room. I couldn't. I wasn't ready. I still needed him. After that experience, it still hurt terribly to hear of his death, but somehow I was ready. God had prepared me.

Oh saints, that we would trust God not to forsake us! He will not!

What a privilege we have, even in suffering, even in old age, to declare God's power to the next generation, His might to those who are to come!

Dear God, may my life, in all its stages, proclaim your love and power to the next generation. Thank you for old age. Thank you for never forsaking us. May our ears and eyes be open to hear and see the declarations of your power through others, especially the old and gray. In Jesus' name, Amen.

Psalm 72 "Endow the king with your justice, O God, the royal son with your righteousness" (v. 1).

"Of Solomon."

That's the title under Psalm 72 in the New International Version (NIV) of the Bible. The study notes in the NIV say that this title means "either by Solomon or for him, of course, both may be true."

Solomon is the king who asked for wisdom. In I Kings 3:5, God appears to Solomon in a dream and says, "Ask for whatever you want me to give you."

Solomon says, in verse 9, "Give your servant a discerning heart to govern your people and to distinguish between right and wrong."

God is pleased with Solomon's request, and says, "I will do what you have asked. I will give you a wise and discerning heart, so that there will never have been anyone like you, nor will there ever be" (I Kings 3:12).

Later on, we see Solomon's wisdom when two women come to him with a baby. They are both claiming to be the baby's mother. One woman has accidentally killed her own baby in the night by laying on him. She then put her dead baby by the breast of her sleeping housemate, and stole her living baby, claiming it as her own (I Kings 3:16-23). Solomon is asked to judge this case, and to determine which woman is the living baby's mother.

He of course does not know the answer, so he orders that a sword be brought to him. He then gives the order: "Cut the living child in two and give half to one and half to the other" (v. 25).

Of course, the real mother has compassion for her child, and screams, "Please, my Lord, give her the living baby! Don't kill him!" (v. 26).

By this response, Solomon knows that she is the real mother and gives the infant to her.

When Israel hears the verdict, they hold the king in awe because they see that "he has wisdom from God to administer justice" (I Kings 3:28).

What a prayer for an official to make! "Endow the king with your justice, O God!" (Psalm 72:1).

We read that Psalm 72 was also used as a prayer by later kings in the line of David. They asked to be endowed with wisdom, and with God's justice and righteousness. Verse 15 of Psalm 72 even says, "may people ever pray for him and bless him all day long!"

Oh, that our governing leaders today would pray that prayer! "Endow me with wisdom and God's justice." "May people ever pray for me."

Some officials today do pray this, I am sure. But many don't. They seek to govern on their own. They ask man's advice, and man's wisdom, but not God's. They are self-seeking, rather than God-seeking. They do not seek God's best for those they govern.

We are to pray for all those in authority over us. Let us pray for God's wisdom and blessing for them. Most of all, let us pray that God will grant all leaders a heart like Solomon's: a heart that *desires* Godly wisdom, justice, and righteousness.

Dear God, thank you for leaders who seek You. Please grant those who don't yet seek You, a heart that desires wisdom. Give them a discerning heart to govern justly and righteously. May we all, like Solomon, ask You for wisdom. May we remember to always pray for our leaders. In Jesus' name, Amen.

Psalm 73 "When I tried to understand all this, it was oppressive to me till I entered the sanctuary of God" (v. 16-17).

"All this."

We all have things that we try to understand but can't. For the psalmist, "all this" was the prosperity of the wicked. It didn't seem fair to him. Why should those who don't follow God seem to have "no struggles?" (v.4). Why should their bodies be "healthy and strong?" (v.4). Why should they be "always carefree," and "increasing in wealth?" (v.12).

The psalmist starts to think that perhaps he has kept his heart pure in vain (v. 13). Every day he feels "plagued" and "punished" (v. 14) for doing nothing but following God.

When we don't understand something, it can become oppressive to us. Lack of understanding oppressed the psalmist *until* he "entered the sanctuary of God" (v. 16).

Then, the Bible says, he "understood their [the wickeds'] final destiny" (v. 17).

I believe that until we enter the sanctuary of God, that place of nearness to Him, we will not gain understanding about what oppresses us.

A sanctuary is a place of protection; a place of refuge; a holy place. It is a place of nearness to God. It doesn't have to be in a church. It can be in our homes; in our place of quiet time with God; in our minds and hearts. In those places of sanctuary, we can gain understanding.

When the psalmist entered the sanctuary of God, he suddenly understood that the final destiny of the wicked was destruction! (v. 19). He realized that though they appear to prosper, they are on slippery ground; ready to be "cast down to ruin" by God (v. 18).

He realized that while he himself felt plagued and punished for doing right, *yet* he was "always with God" (v. 23).

God "held him by his right hand" (v. 23).

God "guided him with His counsel" (v. 24).

God promised, after all his troubles, to "take him into glory" (v. 24).

What a contrast to the slippery ground and ruin of the wicked! Yet until the Psalmist entered the sanctuary of God, he couldn't see this contrast. His situation and his own thoughts had him so entangled that he was oppressed. He couldn't understand.

After entering the sanctuary of God, the psalmist's final thoughts are these: "Those who are far from you will perish; you will destroy all those who are unfaithful to you. But as for me, it is good to be near God" (v. 27-28).

What a statement of faith!

"But as for me, it is good to be near God."

That is enough.

That brings understanding.

That is a good place to be.

Dear God, when I don't understand something, please bring me near to You. Bring me into Your sanctuary, that I may understand. Lift my oppression. May I say with the psalmist, "But as for me, it is good to be near God." In Jesus' name, Amen.

Psalm 74 "Turn your steps towards these everlasting ruins, all this destruction the enemy has brought on the sanctuary" (v. 3).

"Turn your steps toward these everlasting ruins."

That is the cry of the psalmist as he sees the nation of Israel destroyed, and the temple reduced to ruins.

The book of Lamentations in the Bible is also such a cry. It is a lament over the destruction of Jerusalem, her people, and her temple, the sanctuary of God.

Enemies had come into the temple and "behaved like men wielding axes to cut through a thicket of trees" (Psalm 74:5).

"They smashed all the carved paneling with their axes and hatchets. They burned your [God's] sanctuary to the ground; they defiled the dwelling place of your Name" (v. 6-7).

And worst of all, this destruction had come about because God allowed it. God was angry. The book of Lamentations tells us that because of sin and covenant-breaking rebellion, God had destroyed the city and temple through Israel's enemies, the Babylonians.

God loved the city of Jerusalem, its temple, and its people. How it must have hurt Him to destroy it! It was His perfect city; His foreshadowing or archetype of heaven. Yet it was destroyed so thoroughly that Lamentations 2:15 says of Jerusalem, "All who pass your way clap their hands at you; they scoff and shake their heads at the Daughter of Jerusalem: 'Is this the city that was called the perfection of beauty, the joy of the whole earth?'"

Indeed, Jerusalem *had* been called those very names! In Psalm 48:2 we read, "It is beautiful in its loftiness, the joy of the whole earth. Like the utmost heights of Zaphon is Mount Zion, the city of the Great King." Yet now it lay in ruins before the psalmist's eyes.

In a way, we, too, are a city. We are a sanctuary. We are a dwelling place for God. The Bible calls our bodies a "temple of the Holy Spirit" (I Corinthians 6:19). We are to honor God with our bodies. We are to keep them clean and holy as a dwelling place for God.

Like Jerusalem, our bodies can become ruined or destroyed through sin. We can become unclean and unfit for God to dwell within us. And yet, like the psalmist, we can cry out to God, "Turn your steps towards these everlasting ruins."

God will do it! He will turn towards even what He has destroyed in His anger.

He will restore.

He will renew.

He will rebuild.

Revelation 21:1-2 says, "Then I saw a new heaven and a new earth, for the first heaven and the first earth had passed away, and there was no longer any sea. I saw the Holy City, the new Jerusalem, coming down out of heaven from God, prepared as a bride beautifully dressed for her husband."

No more ruins! No more destruction! No more shame!

Jerusalem will be new, and so will we!

Revelation 21 goes on to say of this new Jerusalem, "I did not see a temple in the city, because the Lord Almighty and the Lamb are its' temple. The city does not need the sun or the moon to shine on it, for the glory of God gives it light, and the Lamb is its' lamp . . . Nothing impure will ever enter it, nor will any one who does what is shameful or deceitful, but only those whose names are written in the Lamb's book of life" (22-23, 27).

The Lord will restore His dwelling place! He is in the process of remodeling even now! God *has* turned his steps towards these everlasting ruins! Be they the ruins of His earthly temple in Jerusalem, or the ruins of a sinful human life, God is the Rebuilder! He will make *all things* new! That is His promise to us in the Bible. That is His promise for our future.

Dear Lord, please rebuild the ruins in my life. Turn Your steps towards me. Help me to be a fitting place for You to dwell. I want You to live in my heart, Jesus. Thank you for the promise of a New Jerusalem, a restored Holy City where we will live with all whose names are written in the Lamb's book of life. In Jesus' name, Amen.

Psalm 75 "To the arrogant I say, 'Boast no more, ...do not speak with outstretched neck.' No one from the east or the west or from the desert can exalt a man. But it is God who judges: He brings one down, he exalts another" (v. 4a, 5b, 6-7).

Have you ever spoken with "outstretched neck?"

I have, and afterwards it feels awful. Sometimes it's easy to say too much. We become sarcastic. We become boastful. We become arrogant.

God doesn't like that. It is up to Him to exalt a person. If we've done something well, or done something that has pleased God, He'll let us know! He'll let others know, too, if He wants to.

When Jesus was baptized by John, God was pleased. The Spirit of God descended like a dove on Jesus, and a voice from heaven said, "This is my Son, whom I love; with him I am well-pleased" (Matthew 3:16-17).

There was no doubt of God's pleasure! He made it known! We don't need to exalt ourselves. If God is pleased with us, He'll let us know!

If He is *not* pleased, He'll let us know that, too! Remember the tower of Babel? In Genesis 11:4-9 we read how the whole world had "one language and a common speech. As they moved eastward and settled in new territory, the people said to each other, 'Come, let us build ourselves a city, with a tower that reaches to the heavens, so that we may make a name for ourselves.'"

In the Old Testament, "name" refers to "reputation, fame, or renown." The people wanted to make a reputation for themselves. They sought fame and renown.

Does that sound familiar? Do we do that today? I think so.

God didn't like it then, and He doesn't like it now. God came down to see the city and the tower that men were building in Genesis 11. He was not pleased. In fact, He was so angry that He "confused their language so they would not understand each other" (v. 7). Then He scattered the people over all the earth! (v. 8).

God doesn't want our efforts to exalt ourselves! He wants all that we do to exalt *Him*!

"No one from the east or the west or from the desert can exalt a man" (Psalm 75:6).

It can't be done. Men can try, only to come crashing down like the tower of Babel.

Let us put our reputations in God's hands. If He is pleased with us, we will know it. There is no greater pleasure than to know that we are pleasing God. That brings peace and contentment.

We needn't speak with "outstretched neck." We needn't toot our own horn. If God wants to exalt us, He will. If God wants to humble us, He will. Exalting and humbling are God's jobs, and we can rest knowing that He is in control.

Dear God, please forgive me when I try to exalt myself. Help me not to speak arrogantly on any subject. Help me to keep my head bowed humbly, not "outstretched" boastfully. I trust completely Your judgment, God. It is Your decision to humble or exalt, not mine. In Jesus' name, Amen.

Psalm 76 "Surely your wrath against men brings you praise, and the survivors of your wrath are restrained" (v. 10).

Have you ever been a "survivor" of someone's wrath? It is a subduing experience.

I remember as a kid, staying overnight at the house of a particular girlfriend.

Her father was known for being quite stern. As little children, we sometimes feared him.

One night, my girlfriend had a slumber party. A bunch of giggly, noisy, elementary school girls filled the basement of my friend's house. We laughed, we chattered, we made mountain ranges out of our piles of sleeping bags, we played loud music, and we made *lots* of noise. We got a little out of control, I'm sure. We forgot all about my girlfriend's stern father.

Then, without warning, the basement door opened, and a very loud voice yelled, "That's enough! Quiet down there!"

Needless to say, we were quickly subdued. We were quiet. We were restrained.

People's anger towards others can bring about restraint that is not necessarily positive. Our wrath can be ill-founded, self-seeking, or excessive. It can stifle others and hurt them.

God's wrath is different. It is not ill-founded or self-seeking or excessive. God's wrath against men brings Him praise.

Sometimes we human beings need God's wrath. We need a reminder to quiet down. We need to be told, "You're out of control." We need to hear God say, "That's enough."

"The survivors of God's wrath are restrained" (v. 10). That's not a bad thing: to be restrained.

If, as a little child, I had remembered my girlfriend's father's presence upstairs, I would have behaved differently. I would've had fun, but I would've been mindful of staying in control. Of behaving responsibly. Of being more quiet.

We all have someone watching upstairs, and He is our Heavenly Father. He is not a big, mean, angry figure, but rather a loving God who desires that we are mindful of His presence. God does get angry. And when He does, the anger is justified. It does not hurt us to be mindful of that. It restrains us, and that is good.

Let us do as Ephesians 5:15 says, "See then that ye walk circumspectly, not as fools, but as wise" (KJV).

To walk circumspectly is to walk "carefully, considering all circumstances and possible consequences" (Webster's New Collegiate Dictionary).

If God's wrath brings about the consequence of causing us to be restrained, of causing us to walk circumspectly, then indeed, it is worthy of praise.

Dear God, thank you for Your wrath when it reminds human beings to be restrained. Help us to walk circumspectly, not incurring Your wrath, but rather, Your pleasure. In Jesus' name, Amen.

⚜

Psalm 77 "When I was in distress, I sought the Lord" (v. 2a).

Who do we seek when we are in distress?

A psychic?

A counselor?

A therapist?

A friend?

Some people make telephone calls when they are distressed. They call friends and talk and talk and talk. I do that sometimes! Some people eat. Some people can't eat. Some people take a walk. Some people throw themselves into their work. All of these are active ways of seeking relief from distress.

Some of these methods help and can be healthy. Some of them do not help and can be unhealthy or even sinful.

The psalmist, I think, had the best idea for what to do when in distress: "I sought the Lord," he says.

That's pretty straight forward.

No beating around the bush.

But how do we *do* that? How do we actively *seek* the Lord?

Let's look at more of Psalm 77 for the answer. Let's see what Asaph, the writer of this psalm, did to seek God.

Verse 1: "I cried out to God."

Verse 2: "I stretched out untiring hands."

Verse 3: "I remembered you, O God."
"I groaned."

Verse 4: "I was too troubled to speak."

Verse 5: "I thought about the former days."

Verse 6: "I remembered my songs in the night."
"My heart mused."
"My spirit inquired."

Verse 10: "I will appeal."
Verse 11: "I will remember the deeds of the Lord."
    "I will remember your miracles of long ago."
Verse 12: "I will meditate on all [God's] works."
    "I will consider all [God's] mighty deeds."

All of these steps are part of seeking! They are part of seeking the Lord. They are not easy. They require time and great effort. Prayer requires that, too. Jesus sought the Father's will so hard that He sweat blood on His forehead (Luke 22:44). How much more then, must we mortals seek to know God's will? How much more must we set aside time to cry out, to remember, to muse, to inquire, to appeal, to meditate, and to consider?

Often this process of seeking seems too hard. We give up just when God may be about to reveal more of Himself and of His ways to us. We say, "This is too difficult. God isn't hearing. I'm going to seek help elsewhere. There's got to be a faster answer."

But the psalmist tells us that seeking God *is* worth the effort. It is worth the wait.

The rest of Psalm 77 goes on to tell of God's acts and miracles in the former days. The psalmist meditates on these acts and miracles. He recalls them. He even writes them down! He is comforted in his soul as he takes the time and effort to remember who God is and how He operates.

We can do the same in our lives. We can actively seek the Lord.

It takes effort.

It takes time.

It may even take anguish.

But it is worth it! "God rewards those who earnestly seek Him" (Hebrews 11:6).

Next time we are in distress, let us not seek the easiest or quickest answer. Let us take the time to cry out to God, to inquire, to muse, to meditate, to appeal, to remember, and to consider. Let us even write down what God has done for us and for others in the past. May we be comforted as we remember God's mighty acts and miracles. May we be hopeful as we believe that God is a rewarder of those who earnestly seek Him.

Dear Lord, when I earnestly seek You, it is always worth the effort. Forgive me when I seek an easy way out of distress. Holy Spirit, please prompt me more often to seek God first. May I, like the psalmist, be quick to say, "When I was in distress, I sought the Lord." In Jesus' name, Amen.

Psalm 78 "I will utter hidden things, things from of old - what we have heard and known, what our fathers have told us. We will not hide them from their children; we will tell the next generation the praiseworthy deeds of the Lord, his power, and the wonders he has done" (v. 2b-4).

Without a doubt, my best memory of my father is his story telling. At family gatherings, he and his brothers and sisters would regale us for hours with story after story.

Born between 1899 and 1917, my dad and his seven siblings told stories of mid-western farm life in the early 1900's. They told of threshing with horses, of overturning outhouses, of operating steam engines, of milking cows by hand in the pasture, of going to town for dances, of getting their first radio, first car, and first electric lights. Most of these stories were full of humor and fun. I remember laughing until I couldn't breathe, and then asking for more stories, or for the same ones to be repeated once more.

Along with the stories and humor came wisdom and knowledge, knowledge of a time I had never known personally.

By listening to what our fathers and mothers have told us, we can learn much. The psalmist knew that, as well. He knew the importance of "uttering hidden things, things from of old, what we have heard and known, what our fathers have told us." He knew that by uttering these things from of old, they would be passed on. One generation would learn from another.

As Christians, it is our responsibility to "tell the next generation the praiseworthy deeds of the Lord." If we need some reminders for starters, we can read all of Psalm 78. There are so many praiseworthy deeds of the Lord mentioned there, that in my Bible it takes four pages of small print just to record them!

To name just a few of the wonders God has done for our forefathers, He:

v. 13 divided the sea and led [the Israelites] through.

v. 14 guided them with the cloud by day and with light from the fire all night.

v. 15 split the rocks in the desert and gave them water as abundant as the seas.

v. 24 rained down manna from heaven for the people to eat.

v. 44 turned the rivers to blood [in Egypt].

v. 51-52 struck down all the firstborn of Egypt... but brought his people out like a flock.

It is also our responsibility as Christians to tell of the praiseworthy deeds of the Lord in our lifetimes. What has God done for us? For our parents? For our grandparents? For our great-grandparents?

As we share what we have "heard and known," our stories, too, can spread to the next generation the wonders and power of the Lord.

When I get to heaven, I dream of sitting again at a dining table, surrounded by my dad, my aunts and uncles, and all of our families, as we share the old stories of earth and the new stories of heaven. My spirit waits for that time!

Until then, I repeat the stories they told that I can remember, and I try to tell daily the stories of what God has done for me.

Dear Lord, help us to tell all the stories of what You do for us. Let them not be lost. Help us to pass on what we have heard and known. In Jesus' name, Amen.

I love to tell the story,
For those who know it best
Seem hungering and thirsting
To hear it like the rest.
And when, in scenes of glory,
I sing the new, new song,
'Twill be the old, old story
That I have loved so long.

I love to tell the story,
'Twill be my theme in glory,
To tell the old, old story
Of Jesus and His love.

(Verse four and refrain from *I Love To Tell The Story;* hymn lyrics by Katherine Hankey, 1834-1911; hymn tune by William G. Fischer, 1835-1912.)

Psalm 79 "May your mercy come quickly to meet us" (v. 8b).

I think of the prodigal son when I read this verse. He was met with mercy.

He had squandered his inheritance from his father. Yet when he returned home, repentant, and his father saw him on the road a long way off, his father "was filled with compassion for him; he ran to his son, threw his arms around him and kissed him" (Luke 15:20).

That is being met with mercy.

The angels in heaven rejoice when one sinner repents. There is rejoicing in God's mercy. We too, should rejoice in His mercy. We too, should extend mercy.

It is easier for me to extend mercy to animals sometimes, than it is to feel merciful towards people. I hold people more responsible for their actions. If my dog runs away, I think, "He doesn't know any better." If my cat jumps up on the sofa, I think, "She doesn't know any better." If a person wrongs me, I think, "He or she should know better!"

Why do we think that way of people? God knew better. He called us sheep. Sheep are animals. They screw up. They make poor decisions. They get lost. They wander. They go astray. They get into trouble. They need mercy.

God knew that. Maybe that's one of the reasons He called us sheep.

Psalm 79, verse 13, calls us "God's people, the sheep of His pasture."

Luke 15:1-7 tells of Pharisees and teachers of the law who get angry at Jesus for associating with sinners and tax collectors. Jesus says to them, "Suppose one of you has a hundred sheep and loses one of them. Does he not leave the ninety-nine in the open country and go after the lost sheep until he finds it? And when he finds it, he joyfully puts it on his shoulders and goes home. Then he calls his friends and neighbors together and says, 'Rejoice with me; I have found my lost sheep.'"

That's us! We are the sheep! We go astray every day, and every day Jesus' mercy finds us. His mercy comes out to meet us. It is *new every morning!*" (Lamentations 3:22-23). That's how often we sheep of God need mercy. That's how often we need to extend mercy to our fellow sheep.

Every day.

Every morning.

Every hour.

In His beatitudes Jesus said, "Blessed are the merciful, for they will be shown mercy" (Matthew 5:7).

Oh, that we would show mercy to others as many times in each day as mercy is shown to us by our heavenly Father!

"May your mercy come quickly to meet us."

And may our mercy come quickly to others as we meet them along life's daily roads.

Oh Lord, I want to be among the merciful and also among those who are shown mercy. Help me to be quick to show mercy. Thank you that Yours for me is new every morning. In Jesus' name, Amen.

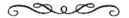

Psalm 80 "Restore us, O God; make your face shine upon us, that we may be saved" (v. 3, 7, & 19).

My dad restored rocking chairs. They all started out looking pretty bad when he got them. They'd be broken or cracked or stripped of their finish. They'd all end up the same. Beautiful. Shining. Restored.

One rocker stands out in my memory more than the rest. It was the biggest chair Dad ever did. High-backed. Long-armed. Pressed-backed. It was the most elegant and beautiful wooden rocker he ever restored. Dad kept that chair for our own family. He sat in it comfortably for most evenings of his life. As children, we sat in his lap in that chair. From there, Dad would read to us the daily paper's comics, or "funnies," as we called them.

That was years ago. The chair now sits in my sister's house. It looks just as elegant and beautiful now as it did when were children. All of that history makes the rocking chair special to me, but what really makes it stand out in my memory is not its shine or elegance or heirloom quality. What makes that chair stand out in my mind is that it used to be purple.

Yes, you read that right. I said, "*purple!*" That elegant, high-backed, long-armed, pressed-backed chair, whose wood grain now gleams with natural beauty, used to be *purple*! That's why Dad kept it, he said. Because of the difference between how it used to be, and how it was after it was restored!

I heard Dad tell the story of how, when he first saw that rocker, it had been painted many times. There were layers and layers of paint to be stripped off, but the top and darkest coat was purple! It took lots and lots of hard work and patience, but Dad got all the layers off. He even got all the paint out of the scroll work. Dad had an eye for what lay underneath. When he was finished with his restoration work, the true beauty of that chair could be seen. It could function as the centerpiece of any living room.

Dad knew that chair could be saved; that's why he restored it.

God knew that we could be saved; that's why He restored us.

He restored us first from sin and eternal separation from Himself. He restored us by redeeming or buying us back with Jesus Christ's blood on the cross. He restored us to Himself as heirs of eternal life in heaven.

But do we remember that secondly, God restores us on a *daily* basis? Every time we sin, we are like that purple chair. Our beauty is covered up with layers of ugliness. Our potential in Christ is hard to see when covered over with sin.

But God sees our potential underneath all of that sin. He sees how beautiful we can be when the sin is removed and we are dressed in a robe of righteousness. He sees how we can look when we are restored.

Jesus was a carpenter. I have a feeling he could both build from scratch and restore. He knew how to work with wood. What better trade or apprenticeship for Jesus' later and higher vocation in life! He showed first in the natural realm how to build and restore, and then brought that work to completion in the supernatural realm when He rebuilt and restored our lost lives on the cross!

Jesus is still in the business of restoring. Each time we hurt one another and then repent, Jesus strips off that layer of sin for us. He sands it down and rubs it away so that the potential beauty of a life in Christ can be seen.

He makes us usable.

He makes us shine.

Just like that chair could function as the beautiful centerpiece of any room, so we, too, can function as the apple of God's eye every day as we are restored by Him!

We don't have to wait! If we have lost our tempers, or spoken words we regret, or been involved in any sin, we can confess that right away! God is right there to restore us! He is right there as the Carpenter of our lives, rebuilding and restoring and saving us every day!

Part of God's business is to make us shine. To make us usable in His kingdom every day. To make us beautiful.

May we go often to the Great Carpenter to be restored.

Dear God, please chip and strip away the layers of sin in my life today. Bring out the natural beauty of Christ in me. Make me usable in Your kingdom each day as You do Your work of restoration. In Jesus' name, Amen.

Psalm 81 "Sing for joy to God our strength; shout aloud to the God of Jacob! Begin the music, strike the tambourine, play the melodious harp and lyre. Sound the ram's horn at the New Moon, and when the moon is full, on the day of our Feast; this is a decree for Israel, an ordinance of the God of Jacob. He established it as a statute for Joseph when he went out against Egypt, where we heard a language we did not understand" (v. 1-5).

Begin the music!

Strike the tambourine!

Play the melodious harp and lyre!

Sound the ram's horn!

Sounds appropriate for a party, doesn't it? Sounds appropriate for a dance or a celebration.

But how about for going to war? How about for living as slaves in oppression? How about for living in confusion where we "hear a language we do not understand?"

These directives from our psalm seem appropriate for times of joy, yet God commanded and ordained them also for times of war, slavery, oppression, and confusion.

I like the scripture song, "*The joy of the Lord is my strength!*" Its melody is light and laughing and full of joy! Just singing it often makes me feel good!

That's what praise does; it changes our outlook.

That's what joy does; it gives us strength.

We need strength when we are at war:

at war with our minds

at war with our enemies

at war with our greatest enemy, the devil

We need strength when we are oppressed and in slavery:

oppressed and in slavery to sin

oppressed and in slavery to depression

oppressed and in slavery to despair

We need strength when we are confused and when we "hear a language we do not understand:"

when we hear voices other than the good, familiar voice of Jesus, Our Good Shepherd

when we are confused about decisions we need to make

when we are in a foreign land of new jobs, new circumstances, or new locations

when we find ourselves in circumstances where we feel we do not belong

All of these situations require strength on our parts, and yet most of these situations do just the opposite: They *sap* our strength! They make us *weak*.

What then, can give us strength?

Joy can!

"Sing for joy to God our strength!" (Psalm 81:1).

"Begin the music!" (Psalm 81:2).

"The joy of the Lord is my strength!" (Nehemiah 8:10).

God felt so strongly about joy that he *decreed* it! He established it as an *ordinance* and as a *statute* for the people of Israel! (Psalm 81:4-5).

In the midst of warfare and slavery and oppression and confusion, God decreed times of feasting and celebrating and singing and playing! It seems incongruous, and yet it works!

The next verses of Psalm 81 tell us, "I removed the burden from their shoulders; their hands were set free from the baskets. In your distress you called and I [God] rescued you" (v. 6-7).

In modern times, we still experience warfare and slavery and oppression and confusion. We still need strength to fight these battles. We still need *joy* to provide that strength!

We may not *feel* joyful, but singing and dancing can help. Listening to good, uplifting music can help. It can give us strength.

Praise always does that. That's why the psalmist often says, "Bless the Lord, O my soul!"

He gives his soul a directive. An ordinance. A decree.

"Bless the Lord!"

Sometimes doing that is all it takes to give us strength.

O Lord, thank you for decreeing joy! Help me to observe and follow your ordinance to sing and celebrate often! Help me to remember that strength begins with joy. In Jesus' name, Amen.

Psalm 82 "God presides in the great assembly; he gives judgment among the gods" (v. 1).

My husband and daughter and I appeared before a judge in order to legalize and make final our daughter's adoption.

Going to court made our daughter nervous. She kept saying to us, "I want to be adopted; I just don't want to go to court."

The idea of entering a courtroom and appearing before a judge can be scary. It is such a formal, somber experience. Most of us associate courtrooms and judges with wrongdoing. We fear consequences. We think of sentencing and punishing.

Not all experiences before a judge need to be scary. We found that out with our oldest daughter, Jessica.

Before our court date arrived, our attorney called us to tell us what to expect. He said the whole procedure shouldn't take more than twenty minutes to a half hour. We would first be sworn in, during which time we would swear to tell the truth. He would then ask us each some questions. We would answer into a microphone. Then the judge would speak and make the adoption legal and final. Our attorney ended the conversation by saying, "Oh, and be sure to bring your camera!"

"Most cases in court," he said, "are not happy. Your time before the judge will be one of the few happy moments that take place in a court room. You'll want to record that moment on camera!"

We did bring our camera to court that day, and it was a happy and memorable time! The judge even invited us up behind the bench afterwards. He offered to be in the picture with our family on this happy occasion! The judge said he had adopted children of his own, and so he had gone through this whole process himself!

His kindness put us at ease. It calmed our daughter's fears and nervousness. It made our adoption day special and memorable for us.

I believe that as Christians, that is how our appearance before God, our Judge, will be. It will be a happy day; a day of final adoption into His kingdom and family.

We are already members of God's family if we know and love Jesus as Savior and Lord. But on that day when we stand before our Judge, we will be ushered behind the bench, into God's private chambers of heaven.

We do not need to fear that day. We do not need to be nervous. In fact, it will be such a happy day, that if we could, I think we'd want to bring a camera! We'd want to record our facial expressions forever on the day when God says, "Well done, thou good and faithful servant . . . Come and share your Master's happiness" (Matthew 25:21).

Not all of our appearances before a judge may be pleasant. If we have done wrong on earth, an earthly judge may require us to pay some consequences. Some earthly judges may even judge us unfairly or unjustly. We may have to suffer injustice.

But in God's court, on the Last Day, there will be cause for rejoicing. If we have received Christ and been born again, we will, on that day, receive full adoption as sons and daughters of God (Romans 8:23). We will receive our full inheritance of heaven and eternal life in the mansion Jesus has prepared for us (John 14:2).

On that day, "*every* knee will bow, and *every* tongue confess that Jesus Christ is Lord" (Philippians 2:10-11).

If you have not yet made that confession, please make it today. Then with all believers on the Last Day, your appearance before the Judge will be cause for great rejoicing!

Dear Lord, I know that all of us will have our "day in court" before You, our Great Judge. My prayer today is that for all of us, that day will be one we want to remember as the day we received our inheritance as Your adopted daughters and sons. In Jesus' name, Amen.

~~~~~

Psalm 83 "O God, do not keep silent; be not quiet, O God, be not still" (v. 1).

We encouraged our children to listen for God's voice during their devotion times. One day I asked our then eleven year old daughter, "Jessica, what did God say to you during your quiet time? Did you hear Him speak any thoughts into your mind?"

She answered, "He said not to say any bad things today, and that He loves me."

God has a lot to say to us if we'll just ask and listen. It takes practice. It takes quiet time. It takes patience.

Waiting for God to speak can be so rewarding! Art Linkletter once wrote a book entitled *Kids Say the Darndest Things!* So does God! What He has to say is often surprising.

Just today I asked God to speak to me what was on His heart. I didn't hear anything for the longest time, and then ever so gently, the thought enveloped me, "Snuggle close to my breast."

That's not what I expected to hear God say! I had all kinds of thoughts of my own going on. I expected God to speak about those. But He didn't. I heard again, "Snuggle close to my breast."

I don't usually think of God snuggling with me, so that sounded kind of funny. But I did it anyway. I closed my eyes and imagined God holding me, with my head and hair nestled against His breast. It seemed I could feel God breathing. I felt warm and peaceful and relaxed, and a verse of scripture came to my mind. "In quietness and confidence shall be your strength" (Isaiah 30:15). That's the last thing I remember, and then I fell asleep.

It may seem rude to have fallen asleep on God, but I think that's what He wanted me to do! I think He wanted to convey healing and warmth and fatherly love to me through letting me sleep on His breast. When I awakened, I knew that I had been with God.

Since God does not often speak audibly, it may be easy to doubt that we are indeed hearing God's voice. It takes faith. The kind of faith mentioned in Hebrews chapter eleven:

"By faith Abel offered God a better sacrifice than Cain did. By faith he was commended as a righteous man, when God spoke well of his offerings. And by faith he still speaks, even though he is dead. By faith Enoch was taken from this life, so that he did not experience death; he could not be found, because God had taken him away. For before he was taken, he was commended as one who pleased God. And without faith it is impossible to please God, because any one who comes to him must believe that He exists and that he rewards those who earnestly seek him" (v. 4-6).

That is the kind of faith it takes to say, "O God, do not keep silent; be not quiet,

O God, be not still."

Faith that God exists.

Faith that God will speak.

Faith that God will answer.

Faith that God will reward those who earnestly seek Him.

May we earnestly desire and seek to hear the voice of God in our daily lives. May we have faith to believe and ears to hear.

"O God, do not keep silent." I desire to hear what You have to say to me always. Please grant me faith to believe and ears to hear. In Jesus' name, Amen.

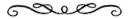

Psalm 84 "Blessed are those whose strength is in you, who have set their hearts on pilgrimage. As they pass through the Valley of Baca, they make it a place of springs; the autumn rains also cover it with pools. They go from strength to strength, till each appears before God in Zion" (v. 5-7).

One of the songs that the University of Minnesota, Morris, Concert Choir has sung under my husband's direction is called *Sing We Merrily Unto God Our Strength* by Martin Shaw. In the song, the phrase "They shall go from strength to strength" is repeated. Then a shorter form of the phrase, "from strength to strength," is repeated over and over. Each time it is sung, it crescendos, louder and louder:

> from strength to strength,
> from strength to strength,
> from strength to strength!

As I have listened to and sung that song, I have truly gotten the feeling that I am gaining strength! It is a powerful song!

These verses are powerful, too. They say that God's people will go from strength to strength. They say that problems and pain and pilgrimage only make us stronger.

The "Valley of Baca" in our psalm text represents an arid place. A dry place. A difficult place. "Baca" literally means "weeping." A place of weeping.

Why then, as God's people pass through this arid place, does our psalm say "they make it a place of springs?"

I believe it is because difficult times make us strong. Not hard. But rather, strong. A "place of springs" does not suggest hardness. Earth that is not watered is hard. But earth that is full of springs and covered with autumn rains is soft. That is how our hearts are to be through struggles. Not hard, but rather, rain-soaked with God's word and with His love.

We are to be vulnerable through hard times. We are to be transparent. We are to be open-hearted and moldable to the Great Potter.

We are, after all, dust, and to dust we will return. That is pilgrimage. We are only passing through. In the meanwhile, the clay of our hearts is to remain soft, well-watered, and moldable. Then, in God's hands, we will go from one beautiful, usable shape of pottery to the next. We will go from "one degree of glory to the next" (II Corinthians 3:18). We will go from strength to strength.

"Blessed are those whose strength is in you, who have set their hearts on pilgrimage."

"Who have set their hearts on pilgrimage" literally means, "in whose hearts are the highways."

Have we thought of our hearts as having highways? The Israelites traveled highways to observe religious festivals in Jerusalem. How much more blessed, then, to travel the highways to Zion (heaven) in our hearts! The roads to worship and to God go through our hearts! The paths to righteousness and peace run through our hearts!

We can travel the roads and streets and sidewalks to church every Sunday. We can travel the same streets to religious festivals and feast days. But where are we traveling in our hearts? Are we allowing God to be our strength? Are we allowing dry, arid places to become springs that feed and water our souls? Are we going from strength to strength?

God says we can. God says we will. That is His promise until we appear before him in heaven.

Lord, may the highways to heaven run through my heart. May the valleys of my life be well-watered places. May they be covered with pools. May they make me strong, yet soft and moldable. May I go from strength to strength. In Jesus' name, Amen.

*Psalm 85 "You showed favor to your land, O Lord; you restored the fortunes of Jacob...
I will listen to what God the Lord will say; he promises peace to his people, his saints,
but let them not return to folly. Surely his salvation is near those who fear him, that his
glory may dwell in our land. Love and faithfulness meet together; righteousness and
peace kiss each other. Faithfulness springs forth from the earth, and righteousness
looks down from heaven. The Lord will indeed give what is good, and our land will yield
its harvest" (v. 1, 8-12). (underlining mine)*

Kathleen Norris, in her book, *Dakota*, often quotes the wisdom of the desert monks: "If a man settles in a certain place and does not bring forth the fruit of that place, the place itself casts him out."

John the Baptist spoke of producing fruit this way: "The ax is already at the root of the trees, and every tree that does not produce good fruit will be cut down and thrown into the fire" (Luke 3:9).

Jesus, too, spoke of the need to produce fruit. He told this parable:

"A man had a fig tree, planted in his vineyard, and he went to look for fruit on it, but did not find any. So he said to the man who took care of the vineyard, 'For three years now I've been coming to look for fruit on this fig tree and haven't found any. Cut it down! Why should it use up the soil?'

'Sir,' the man replied, 'leave it alone for one more year, and I'll dig around it and fertilize it. If it bears fruit next year, fine! If not, then cut if down'" (Luke 13:6-8).

These are all strong words concerning the yields of our lives. We are to produce good fruit. That is one of the reasons we are here.

These words can become burdensome until we see the rest of Luke, chapter three. When John the Baptist spoke of producing good fruit or being cut down, the people asked, "What then, shall we do?"

We might expect John to give some long list of good works in reply. But his answer is quite different. He speaks very practically to each group of people concerning their individual lives and professions.

To the general crowd he says: "The man with two tunics should share with him who has none, and the one who has food should do the same."

To the tax collectors he says: "Don't collect any more than you are required to."

To the soldiers he says: "Don't extort money and don't accuse people falsely; be content with your pay."

Practical advise isn't it? There are simple, easy ways to produce fruit in each of our lives. Remember Jesus' words on burdens?

"My yoke is easy and my burden is light."

"Take my yoke upon you and learn of me" (Matthew 11:29-30).

God has been speaking to my heart about bringing forth the fruit of each place I am in.

In my home, He says: "Be hospitable. Make your home welcoming."

In my family, He says: "Spend time with them. Show them you love them."

In my land, God says: "Plant gardens there. Care for the animals. Be a good steward."

In my job as a music teacher, God says: "Bring out the children's potential. Help them to enjoy music!"

In my spiritual life, God says: "Read the Bible. Meditate on it, and pray to Me. Spend time with Me."

Those are simple, straight forward directives.

They are easy to follow.

They produce fruit.

God has strong words about not producing fruit. If we don't, we will be cut down. If we don't, even the places where we dwell will cast us out.

God has light, simple, easy-to-follow words about producing fruit.

Be honest.

Help the poor.

Be content. (paraphrase, Luke 3:10-14)

Let's ask God today how we can produce fruit in each area of our lives. Each place where we dwell can yield its harvest. Each area of our lives indeed *has* a harvest. We need simply ask God how to make its fruit good.

Dear God, like the fig tree in Your parable, please dig around me and fertilize me. Help me to bring forth the fruit of each place in my life. Thank you that Your burden is light and that Your instructions are practical and easy to follow. I offer back to You the good fruit produced in my life by Your grace. In Jesus' name, Amen.

Psalm 86 "…great is your love toward me" (v. 13).

The psalmist is saying this of God.

"Great is your love toward me."

What a declaration!

To walk through life knowing that we are loved greatly by God is our greatest strength. It is our greatest confidence. We can do anything when we know that we are loved!

Do you know that you are loved today? Jesus said, "Greater love has no one than this, that he lay down his life for his friends" (John 15:13).

Jesus did that! He laid down his life for his friends . . . for us. There is no greater love than that, and it is a love we *all* have from Jesus!

There are people in my life whom I love greatly. I look at them and think, "I never want you to die. I never want to be apart from you."

God loves me that way.

God loves you that way.

He never wanted us to die, so He sent Jesus to take away death's sting.

He never wanted to be apart from us, so He is preparing a mansion for us in heaven, where we can live with Him forever.

That is love, and it is ours from God.

Often before my husband and I go to sleep at night we say to each other, "You are loved . . . by God, and by me."

It is a good feeling to go to sleep with the thought, "I am loved."

We can all go to sleep at night with that as our last waking thought. We can all wake up in the morning with that knowledge: we are loved!

The psalmist knew that it was important to meditate on that knowledge. It is important for us, too.

"I will praise you, O Lord my God, with all my heart; I will glorify your name forever. For great is your love toward me!" (Psalm 86:12-13a).

May the knowledge that we are loved strengthen us today.

Thank you, Lord, that you are a compassionate and gracious God, slow to anger, and abounding in love! (Psalm 86:15). Thank you that I am loved! In Jesus' name, Amen.

Psalm 87 "The Lord will write in the register of the peoples: 'This one was born in Zion'" (v. 8).

Where we come from is important. It establishes us. It says something about who we are.

I hope someday to go back to Germany. I say "go back," but I have never been there. Yet all of my ancestors came from there, and so in my mind, it seems only natural to say "go back." It is where I came from. My origins, my people, are there.

We all have deeper roots than the country or state we came from, though. We have roots or origins in God. We have roots in heaven. We may never have been there before, and yet there is a connection. There is a yearning, a pull, to go back there. After all, there is a book there where our names are recorded. It says, "This one was born in Zion."

Have you ever traced your family tree? It is an interesting process. It involves going to courthouses and churches and cemeteries to check records, books, birth certificates, marriage licenses, and death dates. All of these things are recorded. They are important.

But there is a more important record. It is the record God keeps. In Psalm 87:4, God says, "I will record Rahab and Babylon among those who acknowledge me."

That is the most important record: the record of those who acknowledge God. It is written in heaven. All who look to Jesus, the messiah, as their only source of salvation are on that list. They are recorded in the register of the peoples, and after their names it says, "This one was born in Zion."

That is our ticket back, friends. That is our passport. All of our ancestors are there. All of our connections are there. All of our roots are there.

Adam.

Moses.

Abraham.

Hannah.

Paul.

Mary.

The thief.

You.

Me.

All of our names are there. "This one was born in Zion."

Dear Lord, when we trace our family trees, may we remember to trace them back to You, our Source. Thank you that we have a country to return to, a heavenly country where we will be no longer strangers and pilgrims, but natives, at home with Jesus. In Jesus' name, Amen.

<hr>

Psalm 88 " ...the darkness is my closest friend" (v. 18b).

> Hello, Darkness, my old friend,
> I've come to talk with you again.

So begins a song by Simon and Garfunkel entitled, *Sounds of Silence*.

Dylan Thomas, in his poignant poem, *A Child's Christmas In Wales*, writes: "Looking through my bedroom window, out into the moonlight and the unending smoke-colored snow I could see the lights in the windows of all the other houses on our hill and hear the music rising from them up the long, steadily falling night. I turned the gas down, I got into bed. I said some words to the close and holy darkness, and then I slept."

Writers throughout the ages have written of darkness. Of dark times. Of dark places.

The psalmist in Psalm 88 is in a dark place. Not much good has happened in his life. Even from his youth he has been "afflicted and close to death" (v. 15).

And yet he dares to ask of God, "Are your wonders known in the place of darkness, or your righteous deeds in the land of oblivion?" (v.12). The Psalmist, amidst almost suicidal darkness, dares to call God, "the God who saves me" (v. 1). He dares to say, "But I cry out to you, O Lord; in the morning my prayer comes before you" (v. 13).

The psalmist knows that God is light. Darkness and God cannot co-exist. God's light of truth dispels darkness. And so the psalmist clings tenaciously to God, waiting for light.

"You, O Lord, keep my lamp burning; my God turns my darkness into light" (Psalm 18:28).

We may feel as though our lamps are barely burning. We may feel as though our wicks will be snuffed out. We may feel that darkness is our closest friend. But God says, "No! I will keep your lamp burning!" As Isaiah says of Jesus, quoted in Matthew 12:20, "A bruised reed he will not break, and a smoldering wick he will not snuff out."

I can't imagine anyone's wicks smoldering more dimly than those of the disciples on the days after Jesus was crucified. Their Messiah and Redeemer and Leader and Best Friend had been murdered in cold blood, and their understanding was darkened so that they did not realize that Jesus would rise again. They were in the throes of despair, and two of them were talking about it while walking on the road to Emmaus.

Jesus shows up and walks along side of them, but they do not recognize him.

"What are you discussing together as you walk along?" Jesus says to them.

The disciples' faces are downcast. One of them gets angry.

"Are you only a visitor to Jerusalem and do not know the things that have happened there in these days?" he says to Jesus (Luke 24:18).

He is incredulous and depressed and can't imagine that any one has not heard of the cause of his misery. He tells Jesus all about the crucifixion, still unaware that he is talking to the Crucified Himself.

As they approach a village, Jesus acts as if He is going farther. But they urge him strongly, "Stay with us, for it is nearly evening; the day is almost over." (Luke 24:29)

It is at that point, with day almost over, and darkness setting in, that Jesus does stay.

He stays.

He reveals Himself.

He opens their eyes.

He dispels the darkness.

"Stay with us, for it is nearly evening; the day is almost over."

It is at that point that the writer of a great hymn begins:

> *Abide with me! Fast falls the eventide;*
> *The darkness deepens; Lord, with me abide.*
> *When other helpers fail and comforts flee,*
> *Help of the helpless, oh, abide with me!*
>
> *Swift to its close ebbs out life's little day;*
> *Earth's joys grow dim, its glories pass away;*
> *Change and decay in all around I see.*

O Thou, who changest not, abide with me!

Not a brief glance I beg, a passing word,
But as Thou dwelt with Thy disciples, Lord,
Familiar, condescending, patient, free.
Come not to sojourn, but abide with me.

Hold Thou Thy cross before my closing eyes,
Shine through the gloom, and point me to the skies.
Heaven's morning breaks, and earth's vain shadows flee;
In life, in death, O Lord, abide with me!

(words based on Luke 24:29, by Henry F. Lyte, 1847 music by William H. Monk, 1861)

Earth's shadows are vain, dear friends. For darkness and light are both the same to Jesus. He is the light of the world! That light shines through the gloom, and points us to the skies! Be it in light or darkness, life or death, Jesus abides with us, if we but ask.

Dear Lord, sometimes the darkness seems close. It feels like my only friend. Come to me, then, as you did to your disciples on the road to Emmaus. Reveal Yourself to me. Open my eyes and dispel the darkness with the Light of Your Truth and Your Self. Abide with me, O Lord, I pray. In Jesus' name, Amen.

Psalm 89 "Blessed are those who have learned to acclaim you, who walk in the light of your presence, O Lord. They rejoice in your name all day long; they exult in your righteousness" (v. 15-16).

To acclaim is to give a "loud, eager expression of approval, praise, or assent" (Webster's New Collegiate Dictionary). When we do this to God, we are blessed.

We are not born with the ability to acclaim God. It must be learned. God's ways are not our ways, and his thoughts are higher than our thoughts, so it is not always easy to give a "loud, eager expression of approval, praise, or assent" to God's way of doing things. However, when we do, we are blessed!

We are also blessed when we walk in the light of God's presence. Light changes the appearance of everything it touches. When we go to bed at night, our rooms look dark and shadowy. Images of furniture, lamps, mirrors, etc., are dim and hard to make out. We may trip or stumble over them in the dark. In the morning, when sunlight streams through our window, those images become clear. The light changes them. They are beautiful, many-colored, and pleasing to the eye. They are no longer something to be bumped into or stumbled over in the dark, but rather, they are furnishings that are easily recognized and ready to be used.

When we walk in the light of God's presence, we, too, are easily recognized and ready to be used. Others will see the light of Christ shining on us and in us. God will see that we are ready and available for service in His kingdom. We will be beautiful and useful "furnishings" in God's house! When we have spent time in the presence of God, the light of his presence shines in us!

When we acclaim God and walk in the light of His presence, we can rejoice all day long! We can exult in God's righteousness (v.16). We can put on God's righteousness every morning! We can bathe in it just as we bathe ourselves in water. It can cover us, and leave a sweet-smelling aroma of Christ's mercy and forgiveness and sacrifice wherever we go during the day.

Let us pray to be people who start each day this way:

1. *Acclaiming God* Saying "Yes!" with eagerness and approval to God's way of doing things.
2. *Walking In The Light Of His Presence* Spending time with God and His word, letting His light change our appearance.
3. *Exalting In His Righteousness* Thanking God and reveling in the knowledge that our sinful nature and acts are covered over with the righteousness of Christ, by His death and resurrection for us!

Then, having begun our days this way, we can "rejoice in God's name all day long!"

Dear God, I acclaim You and Your ways of doing things! Your ways are always worthy of approval. I say "Yes" to You today, Lord. May the light of Your presence shine through me! In Jesus' name, Amen.

Psalm 90 "Teach us to number our days aright, that we may gain a heart of wisdom" (v. 12).

I think a paraphrase of this verse might read, "How to live your life without regrets."

As a child, I grew up on a farm place that was located one-quarter mile from the farm places of my aunts and uncles. I had only to walk or ride my bike down our gravel road one-quarter mile, and I had my pick of visiting an uncle and aunt on either side of the road. On the one side was the home of Uncle Ray and Aunt Flo, and on the other was the home of Uncle Bill and Aunt Mae. These dear relatives provided almost second homes to me and to my sister. We visited them daily, and could come and go in their houses just as we could in our own. We could open their refrigerators and have a snack anytime; we could turn on their TVs whenever we felt like watching a program; we could stay for dinner or stay overnight with just a quick phone call home to let our parents know.

The only catch to all of this happiness was that our aunts and uncles were old. They were already in their seventies when my sister and I were in elementary school, and by the time I was in high school, they were in their eighties. My sister and I were very aware, even as children, that these wonderful people in our lives wouldn't be around forever.

This knowledge taught us to number our days.

I remember so many evenings walking home down that gravel road as a child. I would turn around and stand still on the road and just look at the lights in the windows of my uncle's and aunt's farm houses. I could often see Bill sitting in the living room window, reading a book. I could see Flo on her back porch, waving good-bye as I walked down the road. I remember standing still there, watching the lights in their windows, and thinking, "Some day these lights will be dark. Some day these people won't live here. Someday they will be gone."

And do you know what? The lights are dark now. One of the farmhouses is even gone. All of my aunts and uncles who lived there have died. I can no longer walk home on that gravel road and see Bill in his window or Flo on her porch.

But I have no regrets.

I thank God for that, because He taught me as a child to number my days. He taught me to number the days of those I love. God taught me to take every moment that I could to spend with them while they lived on earth. He taught me to stop on the road and to look at them and at their lights burning in their windows, and to be

thankful.

Without that time spent and those moments to pause and be thankful, I would have regrets. I would regret that I didn't get to know them. I would regret that I didn't spend time with them. I would regret that I took these dear people God put in my life for granted.

When we number our days, God gives us a heart of wisdom. He shows us what is important. He shows us how to live without regrets.

Even today, as an adult, those childhood experiences and the awareness of the brevity of life have caused me to ask of myself each day, "Now what is important? If today were my last day on earth, or the last day of one of my loved ones, what would I choose to do?"

Those questions can lead us to leave certain tasks undone, and to choose instead to write a letter, or make a phone call, or pay a visit to someone who may or may not be around tomorrow. Those questions can help us to make wise choices. Numbering our days causes us to gain a heart of wisdom.

Dear God, if I do have regrets in my life, help me to remember that You forgive the reasons and causes for those regrets. Help me to learn from the past, and to number my days, that I may gain a heart of wisdom. Help me to ask wise questions of myself each day ...questions that will guide me in wise living: living, without regrets. In Jesus' name, Amen.

Psalm 91 "He who dwells in the shelter of the Most High will rest in the shadow of the Almighty" (v. 1).

Whose shelter do you rest in?

We had a cat named Blackie. His fur was long and black, (Imagine that!) and literally soaked up the sun. Blackie got so hot outside in the summer that he had to seek shelter. His favorite spot was under our lawn chairs when we were lying out in the sun. Blackie would come and sprawl out underneath us as we sunbathed. Our bodies and our chairs provided a shadow under which he could rest. We took the sun's heat on top, while Blackie rested underneath.

We had another cat named Midnight. (I hope you aren't tired of cat stories yet, because we help the local Humane Society, and so have an unlimited number of cats and cat stories!) Midnight was also long-haired, but he was gray-striped tabby in color. He had different habits than Blackie. Blackie liked to lie down and rest, while Midnight liked to accompany me on long walks.

It was quite a sight when I would take a walk down our country road. On each side of me as I walked along were our two big dogs, Newton and Boswell. They were part Doberman and part German Shepherd, so they were sizable lads. Then, either right behind me, or more often that not, directly *between* my feet, was Midnight, the cat!

Midnight was a faithful walker and companion. The only problem being that cats weren't made to take long walks on hot days. Their legs are short, and they can't sweat easily, so they quickly become exhausted and overheated. Midnight's little legs would go double or triple time compared to Newton's and Boswell's and mine! So, when I walked over a mile on a hot day, Midnight began to pant and puff. I walked more slowly, and even carried him for a while, but that was not Midnight's style. He wanted to be like the big boys, Newton and Boswell. No being carried or special treatment for him! He let me know this by wriggling and clawing his way out of my arms when I tried to carry him!

Eventually, Newton and Boswell and I had no recourse but to stop. We sat along the edge of the gravel road, in the grass of the ditch bank, and rested. Newton and Boswell were not tired yet, so they sat up tall and just patiently waited for Midnight to catch his breath. Midnight appreciated this, because his two big dog companions' bodies created a shadow in which he could rest!

It was the cutest thing to watch how Midnight found the shade created by his friends' big bodies, and would lie down in it! He let Newton and Boswell take the heat for him, and this little guy would just rest in their shelter! When he had quit panting and breathing hard, we would resume our walk, relaxed and rested!

God is like a lawn chair or like those two big dogs, if you will. He is willing to take the heat for us. He is patient to wait while we rest. He is bigger and stronger than we are, and doesn't get tired. He casts a big shadow, and is glad when we lie in it to catch our breath.

That is what God's shadow is for. We are to rest in it. If we are in a tight or hot situation, God invites us to cool off in His shadow. There we can release our anger, our fear, our resentment, our troubles. There we can be refreshed.

Shadows are pleasant places. A shady oak or cottonwood can provide relief for our physical bodies on a hot day. Even greater relief from the burdens of daily spiritual and emotional life can be found in the shadow of the Almighty.

Dear God, thank you for the shade of Your right hand. May I go there often to cool off, to rest, and to be refreshed. In Jesus' name, Amen.

Psalm 92 "It is good to praise the Lord and make music to your name, O Most High, to proclaim your love in the morning and your faithfulness at night, to the music of the ten-stringed lyre and the melody of the harp" (v. 13).

The psalms are among the best poetry and hymns ever written. Their inspiration is the Lord and His name. The psalmist's purpose here is to proclaim God's love in the morning, and His faithfulness at night. What better way to begin and end each day than with a psalm or hymn or poem to the Lord's love and faithfulness?

Poets and scholars and hymn writers through the ages have felt inspired and compelled to begin and end their days with prayers and praise to God. I offer today some of those great yet simple expressions of morning and evening poems and prayers to our God.

Morning

I thank Thee, My Heavenly Father,
through Jesus Christ Thy Dear Son
that Thou hast kept me this night
from all harm and danger;
and I pray Thee
that Thou wouldst keep me
this day also from sin and every evil,
that all my doings and life
may please Thee.
For into Thy hands I commend myself,
my body and soul and all things.
Let Thy angel be with me,

that the wicked foe
may have no power over me. Amen.

(Martin Luther)

Morning Has Broken

Morning has broken, like the first morning;
Blackbird has spoken, like the first bird.
Praise for the singing! Praise for the morning!
Praise for them springing, fresh from the Word!

Sweet the rain's new fall, sunlit from heaven,
Like the first dew fall, on the first grass!
Praise for the sweetness of the wet garden
Sprung in completeness where His feet pass.

Mine is the sunlight! Mine is the morning,
Born of the one light Eden saw play!
Praise with elation, praise every morning,
God's re-creation of the new day!

(Eleanor Farjeon)

Singing Time

I wake in the morning early
And always, the very first thing,
I poke out my head and I sit up in bed
And I sing and I sing and I sing!

(Rose Fyleman)

Evening

At The Close Of Day

O Lord, My God, I thank Thee that Thou has brought
this day to its close. I thank Thee that Thou dost
give rest to body and soul. Thy hand has
been over me, guarding and preserving me.
Forgive my feeble faith and all the wrong I have
done this day, and help me to forgive
all who have wronged me.
Grant that I may sleep in peace beneath Thy care,
and defend me from the temptations of darkness.
Into Thy hands I commend my loved ones.
I commend this household. I commend my body
and soul. O God, Thy holy name be praised. Amen.

(Dietrich Bonhoeffer, 20th cent.
from Letters & Papers from Prison)

For Protection At Night

Dear Jesus, as a hen covers her chicks with her wings
to keep them safe, do Thou this night protect us
under Your golden wings. Amen.
(Traditional: India)

For A Peaceful Night

O God, You have let me pass the day in peace;
Let me pass the night in peace, O Lord who
has no lord.
There is no strength but in you. You alone
have no obligation.

Under your hand I pass the night. You are
my Mother and my Father. Amen

(Traditional prayer of the Boran people)

Now The Day Is Over

Now the day is over,
Night is drawing nigh,
Shadows of the evening
Steal across the sky.

Jesus, give the weary
Calm and sweet repose,
With Thy tend'rest blessing,
May our eyelids close.

When the morning wakens,
Then may we arise
Pure and fresh and sinless
In Thy holy eyes.

Grant to little children
Visions bright of Thee;
Guard the sailor's tossing
On the deep blue sea.

(Sabrine Baring-Gould)

Now The Light Has Gone Away

Now the light has gone away;
Father, listen while I pray,
Asking Thee to watch and keep
And to send me quiet sleep.

Jesus, Savior, wash away
All that has been wrong today;
Help me every day to be
Good and gentle, more like Thee.

Let my near and dear ones be
Always near and dear to Thee;
Oh, bring me and all I love
To Thy happy home above.

Now my evening praise I give;
Thou didst die that I might live.
All my blessings come from Thee;
Oh, how good Thou art to me!

Thou, my best and kindest Friend,
Thou wilt love me to the end.
Let me love Thee more and more,
Always better than before."

(Frances R. Havergal)

May we follow the examples of young and old who have gone before us, proclaiming God's love in the morning, and praising His faithfulness at night. In Jesus' name, Amen.

Psalm 93 "Your statutes stand firm; holiness adorns your house for endless days, O Lord" (v.5).

Can you imagine decorating for eternity?
God did.
He adorned His house with holiness for endless days.

I like to decorate. I love to collect knick-knacks, shop for furniture, pick out wall-paper, choose curtains and drapes, etc. I love antiques - especially things made out of wood - like rocking chairs, benches, and dressers. I like to think that the way my husband and I have decorated our home will never go out of style. But of course it will.

When we moved into our home, it was decorated in 1960's and 1970's styles. Remember those? There were walls painted bright yellow. There was flowered wallpaper in oranges and greens and golds. There was dark paneling on the walls and shag carpeting on the floors. All of those things are gone now, replaced with the styles and colors and tastes that my husband and I prefer.

Our decorating choices won't last forever, though. Only the intangible decorations adorning our home will last forever. Things like love and gentleness and hospitality. Those things will last even through the crucible of God's holy fire.

Paul writes in I Corinthians 3, "By the grace God has given me, I laid a foundation as an expert builder, and someone else is building on it. But each one should be careful how he builds. For no one can lay any foundation other than the one already laid, which is Jesus Christ. If any man builds on this foundation using gold, silver, costly stones, wood, hay, or straw, his work will be shown for what it is, because the Day will bring it to light. It will be revealed with fire, and the fire will test the quality of each man's work. If what he built survives, he will receive his reward. If it is burned up, he will suffer loss; he himself will be saved, but only as one escaping through the flames" (v. 12-15).

Gold and silver and costly stones and wood and hay and straw will not survive God's holy fire. None of our earthly decorations will. But holiness will. Holiness adorns God's house forever.

There is a picture hanging on one of our walls that says, "Within this house may peace be found. In every room may love abound." Long after this house is gone, any peace or love that was given to others here will remain. It remains within us. As Paul also says, "Don't you know that you yourselves are God's temple and that God's Spirit lives in you?" (I Corinthians 3:16).

Only God can put holiness in a home. Only God can put holiness in a human being. Anything holy or righteous in us is of God alone. When we hold firm to God's statutes and to God's ways, it is Jesus in us shining through. When we allow holiness to adorn our homes, it is God who will get the credit and the glory.

My husband and I used to go to a Bible study that met in the home of two bachelor brothers. One was in his seventies and the other was in his late eighties. The older brother was dying of cancer. These brothers loved it when we came to worship and to study God's word in their home. It was not a fancy house. It was a holy house.

The very first time my husband, Ken, and I went there, and were sitting on their couch singing hymns, we looked at each other and at the same time whispered to each other, "This feels like a holy place." There was nothing special about the house itself, but we could _feel_ God's holiness there. It felt sacred. We could sense God's presence.

In the book "*Dear James,*" author Jon Hassler writes of a visit to Lourdes in France: "Such tranquility. And it wasn't the peace of the landscape alone. It was the peace of being among all those pilgrims with their minds on higher things. That's what he meant by holiness. Holiness didn't come down on a beam of light from above. It rose up from the people. All that single-minded devotion, all those prayers directed heavenward, all that sheer *belief*. It produced a sacred aura you could almost see, almost smell, almost reach out and run your hand over, like silk" (*Dear James*, p. 167).

Holiness: "the peace of being among all those pilgrims with their minds on higher things."

Dear Lord, May we be among those pilgrims whose minds are on higher things; the things of God. May holiness be found in our homes as well as in our hearts. And may we look forward to heaven, where Your holiness adorns Your house for endless days. In Jesus' name, Amen

---

Psalm 94 "O Lord, the God who avenges, O God who avenges, shine forth... Judgment will again be founded on righteousness, and all the upright in heart will follow it" (v. 1, 14).

"Avenge" means "to exact satisfaction for a wrong by punishing the wrong doer" (Webster's New Collegiate Dictionary).

Three cases of wrong doing come to my mind which I have little or no hope will be avenged this side of heaven.

One case is that of the murders, years ago, of Nicole Brown Simpson and Ron Goldberg. I have no idea whether O.J. Simpson committed those murders or not, but I do know that his trial seemed to be one of the biggest mockeries of righteousness and justice that I have ever seen. The trial became a media and tabloid event. It seemed to say to the public, "If you have fame and money, righteousness and uprightness are not at issue. Being made a spectacle is all that counts."

Another case involved war in Bosnia. We heard on the news that orphans by the hundreds needed to be evacuated from that country. These children had seen their parents gunned down and murdered. The children themselves needed medical and psychological and spiritual healing and treatment. But the fighting was so fierce that no one could reach them. One fourteen-year-old orphan girl, the news said, had been waiting for two months in a hospital bed to be evacuated to the U.S. for medical treatment. She kept hoping for help, but none ever reached her; she died shortly after the newscast appeared on television.

A third case of injustice that comes to my mind is one of long ago in the country of Scotland. In that country during the 1700's, an honorable way of life of the peasant class was snuffed out unjustly by the ruling class. A movie was made about the injustices suffered by the Scottish Highlanders at the hands of their oppressors. The movie is called *Rob Roy*. While the film is fictional, it chronicles events that were true. The peasants' land was stolen from them; their livestock was slaughtered; their elderly froze to death; their children starved; their women were raped. In the midst of this oppression in the movie, the hero, Rob Roy, fights for his honorable lifestyle and that of his people. He refuses to bear false witness against his neighbor or to treat women dishonorably. In the end, Rob Roy avenges his wife's rape by a brutal upper-class Englishman, by slitting the Englishman's throat during a sword fight. While watching the movie in a theater, one sensed that the audience felt glad when this evildoer received what he deserved.

In all three of these aforementioned cases of wrongdoing, one wonders if those wronged will ever be avenged. The violence and hurt seem too awful. The justice system seems too flawed to exact true justice.

Psalm 94 says, "Judgment will again be founded on righteousness" (v. 14). God is the one who avenges (v.1). We are not to be like the movie character of Rob Roy who takes vengeance into his own hands. God says, "Vengeance is mine" (Deuteronomy 32:35).

Today, in a world of so much violence and so many victims, it is comforting to hear Psalm 94. Of those who oppress God's people, of those who slay the widow and the alien and the fatherless, of those who are full of boasting and who pour out arrogant words (v. 4-7), the Bible says, "Take heed, you senseless ones among the people; you fools, when will you become wise? Does he who implanted the ear not hear? Does he who formed the eye not see? Does he who disciplines nations not punish? Does he who teaches man lack knowledge?" (Psalm 94: 8-10).

God sees and hears all that goes on. For those wrongdoers who repent, He offers full forgiveness. For those who don't, God promises punishment. All of the violence and injustice that we see will not go unheeded by God. It is not up to us to judge or to avenge. In His time, the God who avenges will shine forth, and judgment will again be founded on righteousness.

Dear God, it is a comfort to know that as Psalm 94 says, no corrupt throne can be allied with you; no one that brings on misery is of You (v. 20). You are righteous and holy. In the midst of wickedness You have become our fortress, the God in whom we take refuge (v.22). In Jesus' name, Amen.

Palm 95 "Come let us sing for joy to the Lord; let us shout aloud to the rock of our salvation. Today, if you hear his voice, do not harden your hearts as you did at Meribah, as you did that day at Massah in the desert, where your fathers tested and tried me, though they had seen what I did" (v. 1. 8-9).

"Massah" means "testing," and "Meribah" means "rebellion." The Israelites tested God and rebelled against Him in the desert after Moses led them out of Egypt. At one point, they had no water, and did not trust God to provide it. On two separate occasions, God told Moses to strike a rock or to speak to a rock, and water would flow forth out of the rock. Water from the rock did come forth to quench the thirst of the Israelites both times. God always provided for them. But before he did, the Israelites often hardened their hearts and did not believe. They tested God and rebelled against Him (Exodus 17, Numbers 20).

I find it interesting that the psalmist in Psalm 95 refers to God as "the *Rock* of our salvation." In the same breath, he refers to Massah and Meribah, where God provided for His people out of a rock.

God is our Rock. He is our source of living water. All of our provision flows from Him. We have a choice, as did the Israelites, to either trust in the Rock as our Provider, or to doubt His provision. The psalmist warns, "Today, if you hear his voice, do not harden your hearts as you did at Meribah, as you did that day at Massah in the desert."

We are not to become hard and distrustful toward God. Circumstances may look bleak, but God is still our Rock. Out of Him will flow all that we need. Psalm 145:15-16 says, "The eyes of all look to you, and you give them their food at the proper time. You open your hand and satisfy the desires of every living thing." Philippians 4:19 tells us, "And my God will supply all your needs, according to His riches in glory by Christ Jesus."

We can shout for joy to the Rock of our salvation! He has provided first of all, a sacrificial lamb named Jesus who made a way for us into heaven. He has provided us, also, with His holy word, His living word, on which we can feed and be satisfied. He has provided us, too, with the living water of the Holy Spirit who dwells within us, sanctifies us, and comforts us.

May that Holy Spirit well up within us, overflowing with living water that softens our hearts and provides a satisfying drink of Christ to those around us.

Dear Lord, help me not to harden my heart and distrust You. Thank you for being my Rock and my Provider. May your provision also flow through me to others. In Jesus' name, Amen.

Psalm 96 "Sing to the Lord a new song; sing to the Lord, all the earth. Sing to the Lord, praise his name; proclaim his salvation day after day. For great is the Lord and most worthy of praise" (v. 1-2, 4a).

I'm so glad the Lord has taught me to praise Him. When I was younger, I didn't know a lot about praise. Then I had the opportunity to live with six other women and to travel with them in a Christian ministry team called "Living Water." We traveled across the United States, singing and leading audiences in praise and worship of Jesus Christ.

Until then, I had never abandoned myself to praise. I had never shut everything else out of my mind, and concentrated only on God's worthiness. It is a liberating experience to lay aside all cares of this world, and to think only of things worthy to be praised!

A friend once told me that when God really wants us to take notice of something in His word, He repeats it three times. In verses 1-2 of today's psalm, "Sing to the Lord" is repeated three times! Why are we to sing to the Lord? Verse 4 answers, "For He [the Lord] is great and *most worthy of praise.*"

Very little in life apart from God is worthy of praise. So much of life is *unworthy* of our praise. God knew, then, when He made us, that our minds would need something higher than this world to concentrate on. We are to concentrate on God!

Let's take a break and do that right now! Let's stop reading. I'll stop writing, and think about what makes God great and most worthy of praise. Let's shut out everything else from our minds and praise Him.

this space reserved for praising God

What a gift praise gives us, by putting the rest of our thoughts behind us for a while! God gave this gift of praise to all creation, too. Psalm 96:11-13 says, "Let the heavens rejoice, let the earth be glad; let the sea resound, and all that is in it; let the fields be jubilant, and everything in them. Then all the trees of the forest will sing for joy; they will sing before the Lord, for he comes, he comes to judge the earth."

The heavens, the earth, the sea, the fields, the trees, all of these praise God!

Verse 6 of the same psalm says, "Splendor and majesty are before him; strength and glory are in God's chamber praising him!"

It is a privilege to give God the honor and worship and praise that are due Him. It is also an exercise of the mind and spirit that is required of every Christian.

Paul instructs us in his letter to the Philippians: "Finally, brothers, whatever is true, whatever is noble, whatever is right, whatever is admirable, if anything is excellent or praiseworthy think about such things."

That takes practice! The discipline of praising isn't easy, but it is well worth the effort! It pleases God, and gives us a new perspective! May we practice praising the One who is "most worthy of praise!"

Praise Song

Praise Him in the morning,
when you rise from your bed;
Praise Him all day long.

Praise Him in the evening,
when you're laying down your head;
End each day with a song.

Chorus:
A song of joy;
A song of thank you;
A song of joy welling up
from deep within.
He deserves much more
than we ever give Him
So let us praise Him
forevermore.
Praise and honor
belong to His name.
Love and adoration
to the One who is always the same.
Oh, Holy One!
The Beginning and the End.
What a miracle
That we call Him Friend!
(repeat chorus)

   (by Debbie Amstutz)

Psalm 97 "Let those who love the Lord hate evil..." (v. 10a).

Psalm 97 does not say, "Let those who love the Lord hate *evildoers*." It says, "Let those who love the Lord hate *evil*."

We are not to hate the cheating husband.
We are not to hate the unfaithful wife.
We are not to hate the rebellious teenager.

We are not to hate the disobedient child.

We are not to hate the overbearing boss.

We are not to hate the dishonest employee.

We are not to hate the mistress.

We are not to hate the lover.

We are not to hate the convict.

We are not to hate the political opponent.

We are not to hate the religious fanatic.

We are not the hate the atheist.

We are to hate evil.

Evil is a force. It is not a person. "For our struggle is not against flesh and blood," says Ephesians 6:12, "but against the rulers, against the authorities, against the powers of this dark world and against the spiritual forces of evil in the heavenly realms."

Often our hatred can be misdirected. It can be directed at people instead of at the forces of evil. We are not to fight against the spiritual forces of evil with only human resources. We are to use the spiritual resources provided by God.

What are those spiritual resources with which we can fight evil? Ephesians 6 tells us that they are called the "full armor of God."

"Therefore," says Ephesians 6:13-18, put on the full armor of God, so that when the day of evil comes, you may be able to stand your ground, and after you have done everything, to stand. Stand firm then with the belt of truth buckled around your waist, with the breastplate of righteousness in place, and with your feet fitted with the readiness that comes from the gospel of peace. In addition to all this, take up the shield of faith, with which you can extinguish all the flaming arrows of the evil one. Take the helmet of salvation and the sword of the Spirit, which is the word of God. And pray in the spirit on all occasions with all kinds of prayers and requests. With this in mind, be alert and always keep on praying for all the saints."

These are our spiritual resources with which to fight evil:

The belt of truth.

The breastplate of righteousness.

The shoes of the gospel of peace.

The shield of faith.

The helmet of salvation.

The sword of the Spirit, which is the word of God.

These weapons are not used to fight men or women. They are used to fight the forces of evil. They begin with prayer.

"Lord, help me not to hate that person."
"Lord, help me to forgive."
"Lord, help me to do good to my enemies."
"Lord, help me to hate the sin and not the sinner."

If we are fitted with the full armor of God, then all of these spiritual resources are ours. They are at our disposal. They are there to help us direct our hatred at the forces of evil.

In the face of truth, evil cannot stand.
In the face of righteousness, evil cannot stand.
In the face of the gospel of peace, evil cannot stand.
In the face of faith, evil cannot stand.
In the face of salvation, evil cannot stand.
In the face of the word of God, evil cannot stand.

Oh Lord, may my hatred be directed only at evil and never at people. Forgive me when my hateful feelings become misplaced or misdirected. Help me to remember that my fight is not against flesh and blood, but rather, against the spiritual forces of evil. Teach me about Your armor. Fit me with every piece of it, that evil may not stand. In Jesus' name, Amen.

Psalm 98 "Sing to the Lord a new song, for he has done marvelous things; <u>his right hand and his holy arm</u> have worked salvation for him" (v. 1). [underlining mine]

Our hands and arms do a lot of work. My husband's hands and arms today have scrubbed our kitchen floor, our light fixtures, and the top of our refrigerator. Those are hard jobs for me, and he is gracious and loving enough to volunteer to do those chores for me.

A mother's hands and arms also often do a lot of hard work. There are young children to be held, diapers to be changed, meals to be made, and clothes to be washed.

Construction workers
Piano players
Computer operators
Doctors and nurses
Farmers
Teachers

You name it, almost all occupations require work with our hands and arms.

God's occupation, too, requires hard work with His arms and hands. God's occupation is that of Savior.

Saving is hard work. If you've ever watched a rescue team in action, you've seen arms and hands extended in acts of mercy.

A hand reached out to a drowning victim.

Hands cutting away wreckage from a trapped auto accident victim.

Arms and hands performing CPR on a heart attack victim.

Strong arms of a fireman carrying a victim from a burning building.

All of these acts of rescue require the work of arms and hands.

God's arms and hands have a history of performing daring rescues and saving acts. Psalm 44:2-3 says, "With your hand you drove out the nations and planted our fathers; you crushed the people and made our fathers flourish. It was not by their sword that they won the land, nor did their arm bring them victory; it was your right hand, your arm, and the light of your face, for you loved them."

Those in need of rescue are helpless. They are dependent upon the rescuer. In the Old Testament, the Israelites were slaves to the Egyptians. They were overpowered by Pharaoh. They were helpless and in need of rescue. They depended on their Rescuer, and God did not let them down. His right arm miraculously saved them from slavery and brought them, eventually, to the Promised Land.

In the New Testament, God's people were slaves to sin. They were overpowered by the Devil. They were helpless and in need of rescue. They depended on their rescuer, and God did not let them down. He sent His own arms and hands in the divine person of Jesus Christ to save them from sin, and eventually, to bring them to heaven, the promised land.

God's arms and hands have worked salvation for us. He has reached down from heaven to rescue us, each one of us.

> *See from his hands,*
> *his feet,*
> *his side,*
> *Sorrow and love*
> *flow mingled down.*
> *Did e'er such love and sorrow meet;*
> *Or thorns compose*
> *so rich a crown?*

(from "When I Survey The Wondrous Cross" by Isaac Watts, 1707)

The ultimate picture of God's arms and hands working salvation for us can be seen in the arms and hands of Jesus, outstretched for us on the cross. Palms filled with blood, heart filled with mercy, "for He loved us" (Psalm 44:3).

Oh Jesus, thank you for Your hard work, the hardest work of all, for me. Thank you for rescuing me with Your bare hands. Thank you for extending Your loving arms for me. Amen

The Hands of God

> *One day I'll stand before the Judge,*
> *My Best and Dearest Friend*
> *Who's promised He would love me*
> *and be with me 'til the end.*
>
> *My life on earth will then be past;*
> *I will not miss its ways*
> *For Jesus in His glory*
> *will give Light to all my days.*
>
> *I'll ask Him when I'm standing there*
> *if I can touch his palm*
> *The precious wounds of Gilead*

The Source of healing balm.

I'll ask if I can touch the scars
where Thomas put his hand
I'll look my Savior in the eye,
and then I'll understand

How much the Savior did for me
when nails had pierced Him through
and still He looked out at the crowd,
"they know not what they do."

"Forgive them Lord," He prayed to God,
This God, yet human too.
"Forgive me, Lord," will be my plea;
"I caused this pain for you."

A Judge who bled and died for me,
A God, falsely accused;
A perfect Lamb; A shepherd Man;
A King for sinners bruised.

This is the One who'll judge my fate
One well-informed of grief
Acquainted sore with sorrows deep
My Jesus, my Relief.

I'll take His hands upon that day;
I'll feel their skin and bones;
The Hands of God will welcome me
And gently take me home.

Linda Winter-Hodgson

Psalm 99 "The Lord reigns, ...The King is mighty, ...Exalt the Lord our God and worship at his footstool; he is holy" (v. 1a, 4a, 5).

Have you ever bowed before a king? The chances are that most of us have not. I wish that I had.

I used to travel and sing with a woman who wished for the opportunity to visit a real live king and pay homage or tribute to him. That may sound funny, but she used to say to me, "Linda, I just wish that we had a king or monarch in this country (the U.S.A.), so that we could get a true picture in our minds of what kingship in the Bible is all about."

What is kingship? What does it mean to reign?

Kingship is sovereign power. To reign is to have royal authority. Sovereignty is "supreme excellence or an example of it; supreme power; freedom from external control." (WNCD)

That is our God.

He is King.

He reigns.

He is in control.

We are not in control. It is hard to remember that sometimes, but it is a very freeing revelation. Human beings struggle to be in control of things around them. We try to be in charge.

We were never meant to be in charge. God was. God is.

We need to get a picture in our minds of our Great King.

He "sits enthroned between the cherubim" (Psalm 99:1).

He "is robed in majesty" (Psalm 93:1).

The only person I've ever seen robed in anything kingly was the king at our high school prom. He wore a maroon velvet robe with white fake fur trim. He didn't look very majestic, just kind of silly. I don't mean to be trite, but there just aren't very many living pictures of royalty and majesty who we can look up to. Even the President of the United States is often no longer revered with the respect and honor that office is due.

We can look to the Bible, then, for our picture of kingship and how to approach one in that office. The ultimate king over all the earth is God. We are to "exalt the Lord our God and worship at his footstool."

I don't know if God has an actual footstool in heaven, but I do know that the Bible calls the earth "God's footstool."

Acts 7:48-49 says, "The Most High does not live in houses made by men. As the prophet Isaiah says of the Lord: 'Heaven is my throne, and the earth is my footstool. What kind of house will you build for me?'"

We are living on "God's footstool," our mother earth. We were made by God from its clay. We are to worship here before our King and Maker.

Not a day should go by without our acknowledgment of God's control and kingship over our lives.

Dear God and King, may I receive from You a greater picture of Your kingship and sovereignty over me and over all the nations of Your world. You are in control, Lord. May I rest in that and stop struggling to control my surroundings. I bow humbly today at Your footstool and acknowledge that You alone are worthy to be exalted. I respect You, God, and give You honor. In Jesus' name, Amen.

Psalm 100 "Know that the Lord is God" (v. 3a).

Psalm 100 is listed as "A psalm. For giving thanks."

We can give thanks for what we know. Verse three gives us a command. We are to *know* that the Lord is God. The Bible doesn't say that we *can* know that the Lord is God. It says simply, "Know it."

Rest in it.

It's a fact.

The Lord is God.

There is so much to question in life. There is so much we do not know. Man spends so much time on his quest for knowledge, for more knowing. Writers have written about knowing for centuries. Many have come to the same conclusion: There is little about life we can know for certain, but we can know love; we can know God.

A secular song of the 1980's entitled *Don't Know Much* has these words:

Look at this face

I know the years are showing;

Look at this life
I still don't know where it's going.
I don't know much,
But I know I love you.
And that may be
All I need to know.

Look at these eyes,
They've never seen what mattered;
Look at these dreams,
So beaten and so battered.
I don't know much,
But I know I love you.
And that may be
All I need to know.

(by Barry Mann, Cynthia Weil, Tom Snow,
sung by Linda Rondstadt & Aaron Neville)

The writers of this song found a simple truth: We may not be able to say that we know much for certain in life, but knowing that we love someone may be all we really need to know.

To some that may sound trivial or trite, but knowing that we are loved and that we love in return is sometimes all we have to hold us together. Intellectual knowing and scholarly facts cannot hold us together. Knowing God and love can.

The writer Job, having lost everything dear to him in life without understanding or knowing why, said this: "I know that my Redeemer lives, and that in the end He will stand upon the earth. And after my skin has been destroyed, yet in my flesh will I see God" (Job 19:25-26).

That is knowing!

We are to give thanks for what we know!

In 1775, Samuel Medley paraphrased Job's words and gave thanks for his knowing in this way:

I know that my Redeemer lives;

What comfort this sweet sentence gives!
He lives, He lives, who once was dead,
He lives, my ever-living Head.

He lives and grants me daily breath;
He lives and I shall conquer death;
He lives my mansion to prepare;
He lives to bring me safely there.

He lives, all glory to His name!
He lives, my Jesus, still the same.
Oh, the sweet joy this sentence gives,
'I know that my Redeemer lives!'

The Bible has much to say about knowing.

Of Jesus, Simon Peter says, "We believe and know that You are the Holy One of God" (John 6:69).

Jesus said, "If you hold to my teaching, you are really my disciples. Then you will know the truth, and the truth will set you free" (John 8:31-32).

"My sheep follow me because they know my voice . . . I know my sheep and my sheep know me - just as the Father knows me and I know the Father" (John 10:4, 14-15).

"I will ask the Father, and he will give you another Counselor . . . the spirit of truth. The world cannot accept him, because it neither sees him nor knows him. But you know him, for he lives with you and will be in you" (John 14:16-17).

Of love, John writes in his first letter, "This is how we know what love is: Jesus Christ laid down his life for us" (I John 3:16).

And perhaps Paul, the apostle, has the most to say about knowing: "What is more, I consider everything a loss compared to the surpassing greatness of knowing Christ Jesus my Lord . . . I want to know Christ and the power of his resurrection and the fellowship of sharing in his sufferings, becoming like him in his death, and so, somehow, to attain to the resurrection from the dead" (Philippians 3:8,10).

Of heaven, Paul says, "Now we see but a poor reflection as in a mirror; then we shall see face to face. Now I know in part; then I shall know fully, even as I am fully known" (I Corinthians 13:12).

Until that time, let us give thanks for what we do know: The Lord is God, and

He loves us!

Oh Lord, I close today with words of a song by an unknown author, declaring to You with thanksgiving the things that I know:

Father, You are my Father.
Jesus, You are my Savior.
Holy Spirit, You are my Comforter.
My soul knows it well.

Father, I love You, Father.
Jesus, I love You, Jesus.
Holy Spirit, I love You, Spirit.
My soul knows it well.

Psalm 101 "I will be careful to lead a blameless life, when will you come to me? I will walk in my house with blameless heart. I will set before my eyes no vile thing... he whose walk is blameless will minister to me" (v. 2-3, 6b).

Here we go again with something being repeated three times in scripture! That means God wants us to take note. It means there's something important here!
Blameless.
Blameless.
Blameless.
There it is in Psalm 101, three times.
Fault.
Guilt.
Culpability.
Three synonyms for blame.
Wouldn't it be great to be without these things? To be without fault. To be without guilt. To be without culpability or blame.
God says we can be blameless. He said to Abraham in Genesis 17:1, "I am God Almighty; walk before me and be blameless." He said of Nathaniel in John 1:47,

"Here is a true Israelite, in whom there is nothing false." (or KJV, "in whom there is no guile.")

How do we go about being blameless? Psalm 101 says it involves being *careful*. "I will be *careful* to lead a blameless life" (v. 2). Of what should we be careful? What should we avoid? Here's the list from Psalm 101.

In order to be blameless we must:

Set before our eyes no vile thing (v. 3).
Hate the deeds of faithless men (v. 3).
Keep men of perverse heart far from us (v. 4).
Have nothing to do with evil (v. 4).
Put to silence whoever slanders his neighbor in secret (v. 5).
Endure not anyone who has haughty eyes and a proud heart (v. 5).
Allow no one to dwell in our house who practices deceit (v. 7).
Allow no one who speaks falsely to stand in our presence (v. 7).
Silence the wicked (v. 8).
Cut off evildoers (v. 8).

If we are to set before our eyes no vile thing, what then, should we set our eyes on? Verse six says that our eyes should be on the *faithful* in the land. It says that those whose walk is blameless can minister to us. The above list may be hard to follow, but what an encouragement it is to us to set our eyes on those around us and those who have gone before us who are *faithful!* There *are* those dear souls among us, who, like Abraham and Nathaniel, through God's grace, are already walking blameless before God! That doesn't mean that they are sinless; it means that they are trying, and that when they fail, they are repentant and forgiven. Their sins are covered by the blood of Jesus, their Savior.

Like Abraham and Nathaniel, our first step towards a blameless walk must be that of *faith*. Abraham had faith in God's promise and covenant. Nathaniel had faith that Jesus was the promised Messiah. We, too, must have faith in God as our Lord and Savior, and as our only source of forgiveness and strength in leading a blameless life.

We are still sinful.

But we can sin *less*.

We can be *careful* to lead a blameless life.

And when we fail, we can praise God for His grace and for His words, "Blessed is he whose transgressions are forgiven, whose sins are covered. Blessed is the man whose sin the Lord does not count against him and in whose spirit is no deceit" (Psalm 32:1-2, and Romans 4:7-8).

Dear God, I want to be careful to lead a blameless life. I want You to say of me, as You did of Nathaniel, "Here is a true believer, in whom there is nothing false." Help me as I mature as a Christian, to become one whose walk is blameless. In Jesus' name, Amen.

Psalm 102 "Let this be written for a future generation, that a people not yet created may praise the Lord. 'The Lord looked down from his sanctuary on high, from heaven He viewed the earth, to hear the groans of the prisoners and release those condemned to death'" (v. 18-20).

The "people not yet created" mentioned by the psalmist are *us!* When this psalm was written, we were as yet unborn; we were a mere thought in God's mind! And yet for all future generations, these words were recorded so that we might "praise the Lord!"

What written words could be so great as to cause future generations of people not yet created to praise the Lord?

"The Lord looked down from his sanctuary on high, from heaven he viewed the earth, to hear the groans of the prisoners and release those condemned to death."

We were those prisoners! We were condemned to death! We had a death penalty sentence from God, even before we were born. "*All* have sinned and fall short of the glory of God" (Romans 3:23). "The wages of sin is death" (Romans 6:23). Since Adam and Eve's sin, all people have been born condemned to death.

The good news is that God looked down from his sanctuary on high. He heard the groans of all those condemned to death, and He released us!

How did God do that? He did it through Christ, who, Paul says in Ephesians 4:8, "When he ascended on high, led captivity captive and gave good gifts to men." Jesus took even death and captivity captive! He took them as prisoners so that we could be released! We who look to Jesus as Savior will not die forever! We are no longer prisoners of death!

Romans 8: 18-21 says, "I consider that our present sufferings are not worth comparing with the glory that will be revealed in us. The creation waits in eager expectation for the sons of God to be revealed. For the creation was subjected to frustration, not by its own choice, but by the will of the one who subjected it, in hope that the creation itself will be liberated from its bondage to decay and brought into the glorious freedom of the children of God."

Creation itself will be liberated from its bondage to decay! God has heard the groans of the prisoners of earth, and has responded with a message of redemption!

That is why the psalmist wrote that a future generation, a people not yet created, may praise the Lord! Those who come after us and those who came before us all have the same opportunity: to believe in the promise of Jesus and so to be released from the prison of death and condemnation.

"There is now no condemnation for those who are in Christ Jesus, because through Christ Jesus the law of the Spirit of life set me free from the law of sin and death" (Romans 8: 1-2).

A favorite story passed on through oral tradition is one I'd like to share regarding a prisoner's release.

There were two boyhood friends who spent a lot of time together and loved each other very much. As they grew older, the two boys went their separate ways and lost contact with one another. One went to college and eventually became a well-respected judge in a court of law. The other fell in with bad company and led a life of crime. One day his crimes caught up with him, and he was brought to court. The judge for his case was none other than his old boyhood friend.

After hearing the case, the jury found the accused man guilty of the crimes he had committed. He stood before his old friend, the judge, and waited for his sentence.

The judge, an honest man, looked long at his old friend. Then he said, "I must sentence you to the full penalty for your crimes. You are to pay the full fine."

The prisoner had nothing, and could never pay such a fine. He looked at the floor, defeated.

Then, the judge stepped down from his chambers, hugged his old friend, and said, "I will pay the fine for you."

The prisoner was free because the judge had paid the penalty for him.

That is what our Jesus did for us.

Dear Jesus, thank you for taking captivity captive for me. Thank you for taking my death penalty on yourself. Thank you that I can live not as a prisoner to death or sin, but as a free person in all areas of my life! Amen.

⟬⟬⟬⟬⟬⟬⟬⟬⟬

Psalm 103 "As a father has compassion on his children, so the Lord has compassion on those who fear him; for he knows how we are formed, he remembers that we are dust" (v. 13-14).

"He remembers that we are dust" (v. 14b).

Do *we* remember that we are dust? It is easy for humans to forget. We like to look at our bodies and think that we are skin, or bones, or fingernails, or hair, or DNA, or blood, or muscle. But we are not. We are dust.

God remembers that because He formed us. He remembers and it gives Him compassion towards us.

"The Lord God formed the man from the dust of the ground and breathed into his nostrils the breath of life, and the man became a living being" (Genesis 2:7).

What do earthly fathers and mothers have in common with God the father? Both are creators. Both know what it is to have created a child. Creators tend to have special compassion towards what they have created. Even creations such as a poem or a piece of art work are often treated specially and tenderly and gently by their creators.

We are God's creation. He remembers forming us. He remembers the material he used. Dust. He remembers that we are fragile beings. Fragile creations. He remembers that to dust we will return.

In Genesis 3:19, God says to Adam, "By the sweat of your brow you will eat your food until you return to the ground, since from it you were taken; for dust you are and to dust you will return."

Have you ever seen anyone return to the dust? Every time we bury a person or an animal, they are returning to dust. Some burial customs include a special ceremony at the graveside, whereby each loved one of the deceased takes a handful of dirt and throws it lovingly into the grave. This covering with earth symbolizes the loved one returning to dust.

Paul says in I Corinthians 15: 47-49, "The first man was of the dust of the earth, the second man from heaven. As was the earthly man, so are those who are of the earth; and as is the man from heaven, so also are those who are of heaven. And just as we have borne the likeness of the earthly man, so shall we bear the likeness of the man from heaven."

We have all borne the likeness of the first man, Adam, and we will all bear the likeness of the second man, Jesus. Our flesh and blood cannot inherit the kingdom of God. Our perishable, fragile, dust-like bodies cannot inherit the imperishable kingdom of heaven (I Corinthians 15:50). But, Paul says, "Listen, I tell you a mystery: . . . we will all be changed, in a flash, in the twinkling of an eye, at the last trumpet. For . . . the dead will be raised imperishable, and we will be changed. For the perishable must clothe itself with the imperishable, and the mortal with immortality. When the perishable has been clothed with the imperishable, and the mortal with immortality, then the saying that is written will come true: 'Death has been swallowed up in victory'" (I Corinthians 15: 51-54).

Every time we see the open grave of a believer, ready to swallow them up in the dust of the earth, we can remember, as Paul did, that really, our dusty, perishable graves are a picture of death being swallowed up in victory! We will be raised imperishable! It is okay to return to dust in the meantime, while we wait for the trumpet to sound!

I think farmers have a special grasp of that truth. My dad was a farmer who loved the land. He liked to take the rich, black topsoil and crumble its lumps in his hand.

He liked the dirt.

He liked the dust.

Dad had a couple of sayings about dirt and dust that showed how much he liked them. During rock picking, or cultivating, or harvesting, Dad would come in from the field and say, "I ate a tablespoon of dust today! But that's okay. I figure every farmer eats about a pint of dirt per year!"

Or, when my sister and I would complain about how dirty we were after helping in the garden or field, he'd say, "That's all right. It's just clean dirt!"

Dirt and dust were clean to Dad because he understood them. He understood that our living comes from dirt. Our food is grown there. Our lives were formed there. Dust is our Maker's chosen material for creating us!

Perhaps that is why I like the idea of being buried in a wheat field, or a garden, or a cemetery, but not in a cold, stone vault. Perhaps it is the farmer in me that hopes the dirt will fall on me when I am dead. Not some fancy, bronze coffin with pink satin pillows for my body. Just dirt. Just dust. Just waiting for the trumpet to sound.

When I die
let the wheat
blow over me

let it swirl and sway
the way it did tonight
while I stood
hip-deep in gold.

no vault or cold container, please.

just let me seep back
into the earth
the warm dust
from whence I came.

until these clay nostrils
sown in mortality,
reap immortality,
and breathe again
the breath of God.

by Linda Winter-Hodgson

Psalm 104 *"How many are your works, O Lord! In wisdom you made them all; the earth is full of your creatures. There is the sea, vast and spacious, teaming with creatures beyond number - living things both large and small. There the ships go to and fro, and the leviathan, which you formed to frolic there" (v. 24-26)*.

Water
The Sea
The Deep
Creatures

Animals
Beasts

These are the themes of Psalm 104. They bring to mind the beloved stories of the author and veterinarian, James Herriot. James titled one of his books about animals, *All Creatures Great and Small*. The author of Psalm 104 spoke similar words: "There is the sea, vast and spacious, teaming with creatures beyond number - living things both large and small."

I offer here some poems and verse written by others to help us as we pray with the psalmist: "May my meditation be pleasing to him, as I rejoice in the Lord" (Psalm 104:34).

All Things Bright and Beautiful

All things bright and beautiful,
all creatures great and small,
all things wise and wonderful,
the Lord God made them all.

(Cecil Frances Alexander, 1848)

Many and Great, O God

Many and great, O God, are Thy things,
Maker of earth and sky.
Thy hands have set the heavens with stars;
Thy fingers spread the mountains and plains.
Lo, at Thy word the waters were formed;
Deep seas obey Thy voice.
Grant unto us communion with thee,
Thou star abiding one;
Come unto us and dwell with us;
With thee are found the gifts of life.
Bless us with life that has no end,
Eternal life with thee."

(Joseph R. Renville c. 1846, paraphrased by Philip Frazier 1929, based on Psalm 104: 24-30)

Dear Father, Hear and Bless

Dear Father,
     hear and bless
Thy beasts
     and singing birds:
And guard
     with tenderness
Small things
     that have no words."

(Little Golden Book, *Prayers For Children*)

Travelers

Eternal Father, strong to save,
Whose arm doth bind the restless wave,
Who bidd'st the mighty ocean deep
Its own appointed limits keep:
O hear us when we cry to Thee
For those in peril on the sea.

O Saviour, whose almighty word
The winds and waves submissive heard,
Who walkedst on the foaming deep
And calm amid its rage didst sleep:
O hear us when we cry to Thee
For those in peril on the sea.

O sacred Spirit, who didst brood
Upon the chaos dark and rude,
Who bad'st its angry tumult cease,

And gavest light and life and peace:
O hear us when we cry to Thee
For those in peril on the sea.

O Trinity of love and power,
Our brethren shield in danger's hour;
From rock and tempest, fire and foe,
Protect them whersoe'er they go:
And ever let there rise to Thee
Glad hymns of praise from land and sea."

(William Whiting 1860, Rev. John B Dykes, 1861)

A Great Gray Elephant

A great gray elephant,
A little yellow bee,
A tiny purple violet,
A tall green tree,
A red and white sailboat
 On a blue sea
 All these things
 You gave to me,
 When you made
 My eyes to see
Thank you, God!

(a Little Golden Book, Prayers For Children,
National Society For the Prevention of Blindness)

He Prayeth Well, Who Loveth Well

He prayeth well
 Who loveth well
Both man and bird and beast.

He prayeth best
　　Who loveth best
All things both great and small;
　　For the dear God
　　Who loveth us,
He made and loveth all.

　　(Samuel Taylor Coleridge, from *The Ancient
　　Mariner)*

Dear God, may I remember that while You are my Maker, You are also the Maker of all. May I treat Your creatures and Your creation with love and goodness. May I be among those who "prayeth best," and "loveth best all things both great and small." In Jesus' name, Amen.

Psalm 105 "When they [the Israelites] were but few in number, few indeed, and strangers in it, [the promised land,] they wandered from nation to nation, from one kingdom to another. He allowed no one to oppress them; for their sake he rebuked kings: 'Do not touch my anointed ones; do my prophets no harm.'" (v. 12-15) ...and "Give thanks to the Lord, call on his name; make known among the nations what he has done" (v. 1).

　　A nation is "a community of people composed of one or more nationalities and possessing a more or less defined territory and government" (Webster's New Collegiate Dictionary).

　　The nation of Israel was given God's promise of a land in which they could settle and have rest on every side; a land in which not one of their enemies could withstand them (Joshua 21:43-44). That land was Canaan, or "the promised land."

　　Before reaching that land, the nation of Israel first had to endure 430 years of oppression and slavery in the land of Egypt. Then God, through Moses, led them out of captivity. He sent plagues and signs and miracles to show His power and love to the Israelite nation.

　　After leaving Egypt, God's people wandered for 40 years in the desert. But even there, God provided for them daily, with manna, quail, and water. He led them with a pillar of cloud by day, and with a pillar of fire by night.

The Israelite nation entered the Promised Land where "Not one of the Lord's good promises to the house of Israel failed; every one was fulfilled" (Joshua 21:45).

We, too, are awaiting a promised land. Our promised land is heaven. There, we will have rest on every side. There, none of our enemies will withstand us. Not sickness. Not sorrow. Not sin.

Before reaching heaven, we must endure this life on earth. Some of it is joyful and abundant, but some of it is oppressive and sad. But even here, God provides daily for us. He gives us "manna:" food, drink, and direction from His word. He leads us and sustains us as we await entrance to the Promised Land.

All nations are invited to God's promised land. Our job as Christians is to "make known among the nations what he has done" (Psalm 105:1).

We can make known what God has done among the nations in many ways.

We can pray.

We can support missions and missionaries.

We can be missionaries.

We can tell our neighbors the Good News.

We can use technology to reach unreached nations with the Gospel.

Only when we do these things will the "gospel of the kingdom be preached in the whole world, as a testimony to all nations," and only then "the end will come" (Matthew 24:14).

Let us pray, as Jesus did, "Our Father, who art in heaven, hallowed be Thy name. Thy kingdom come; Thy will be done, on earth, as it is in heaven." May we hasten the coming of Your kingdom, Jesus, as we make known among the nations what You have done. In Jesus' name, Amen.

Psalm 106 "But they soon forgot what he had done and did not wait for his counsel. In the desert they gave in to their craving; in the wasteland they put God to the test" (v. 13-14).

"Elephants never forget." So goes an old saying. People do forget. We have all kinds of methods to help us remember.

We tie strings around our fingers.

We make lists and notes.

We ask others to remind us.

Still, the people of Israel forgot. They forgot what God had done for them.

Verses 21-22 of our psalm say, "They forgot the God who saved them, who had done great things in Egypt, miracles in the land of Ham and awesome deeds by the Red Sea."

Has God done awesome deeds for us? Do we forget about them? Do we ever forget the God who saves us?

Of course we do. We're human. We're just like the Israelites. We forget and do not wait for God's counsel. We give in to our cravings and put God to the test (v. 13-14).

It is hard to remember to wait for God's counsel when we are craving something.

We crave more money.

We crave a promotion.

We crave a boyfriend or girlfriend.

We crave having a spouse.

We crave having a child.

We crave food or alcohol.

We crave excitement.

The more we crave, the more important it is to remember to wait for God's counsel. He will instruct us. He will hear our prayers. His timing is perfect.

Verse 44 of Psalm 106 says, "But He [God] took note of their distress when He heard their cry; for their sake he remembered His covenant."

God remembers.

We may forget God, but He does not forget us.

Has God ever spoken a word to you or made a promise to you that is as yet unfulfilled? If it was of God, *it will be fulfilled.*

Paul says, "I thank my God every time I remember you. In all my prayers for all of you, I always pray with joy because of your partnership in the gospel from the first day until now, being confident of this, that he who began a good work in you will carry it on to completion until the day of Christ Jesus" (Philippians 1:3-6).

God will not forget the work He has begun in us. He will bring it to completion.

God forgets only one thing: our sin. When we live under God's new covenant, trusting in the shed blood of Jesus, God says, "I will forgive their wickedness and will remember their sins no more" (Hebrews 8:12).

May we, too, forget our sins after confessing them. May we forget the wrongs others have committed against us. May we remember, instead, God's new and lasting covenant with us in Christ. May we remember all that God has done for us and be thankful!

I Want To Be Remembered As One Who Forgets

When someone wrongs me, Lord,
I
want
to
be
quick to forgive.
I do not want to be
one
who
sleeps
on my anger
one
who
tosses and turns
on
it.

When someone hurts me, O God,
let
me
not
make them pay
for
their
sins.

Linda Winter-Hodgson

You already did that, Jesus.
You
paid
once
for
all.

When someone offends me, dear, Lord,
let
me
forget it.
as far as
East
is
from
West,
Let it be removed
from
my
memory.
I do not want to remember
those
things.
I want to remember
Jesus,
and that He paid
for
every situation
sin
puts us in.
Every
awful, painful, tearful, gut-wrenching,
place
has been covered
and

paid for
by
Jesus.
That's what I want to remember.
I want to forget
all
the
rest.
When I am wronged, O God,
let
me
show
mercy.
Let me be remembered
as
one
who quickly forgets.

   (by Linda Winter-Hodgson)

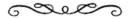

Psalm 107 "Then they cried out to the Lord in their trouble, and he delivered them from their distress" (v. 6, 13, 19, 28).

   Four different times, in four different verses, the author of Psalm 107 says this same thing. Let us look together at what circumstances brought the people to cry out to God, and how God delivered them.

Circumstance #1, Verse 6:
   In this instance, "Some wandered in desert wastelands, finding no way to a city where they could settle. They were hungry and thirsty, and their lives ebbed away." God's response:
   "He led them by a straight way to a city where they could settle" (v. 7).

Circumstance #2, Verse 13:

In this case, "Some sat in darkness and the deepest gloom, prisoners suffering in iron chains, for they had rebelled against the words of God and despised the counsel of the Most High" (v. 10-11).

God's response:

"He brought them out of darkness and the deepest gloom and broke away their chains" (v. 14).

Circumstance #3, Verse 19:

Here, "Some became fools through their rebellious ways and suffered affliction because of their iniquities. They loathed all food and drew near the gates of death" (v. 17-18).

God's response:

"He sent forth his word and healed them; he rescued them from the grave" (v. 20).

Circumstance #4, Verse 28:

"Others went out on the sea in ships; they were merchants on the mighty waters ...he [God] spoke and stirred up a tempest that lifted high the waves . in their peril their courage melted away. They reeled and staggered like drunken men; they were at their wits' end" (v. 23-27).

God's response:

"He stilled the storm to a whisper; the waves of the sea were hushed" (v. 29).

Each time God saved them from their particular distress, the peoples' response was the same: they gave thanks to the Lord for his goodness.

Our response, too, should be one of thanks when God rescues us out of our modern day distresses and dilemmas.

We may not wander in desert wastelands, but some of us may wander in the wastelands of alcoholism, drug abuse, gambling, and pornography, hungering and thirsting, while our lives ebb away.

Let us cry out to God. He will lead us by a straight way, to a place where we can settle. He "satisfies the thirsty and fills the hungry with good things" (v. 9).

We may not be in darkness and gloom, sitting in iron chains, but some of us may be in literal modern day prisons. Many of us may be in figurative chains of bondage because we have rebelled against God or our earthly authorities. We may have rejected the counsel of our parents and teachers and pastors.

"Let us cry out to God. He will break our chains. He breaks down gates of bronze and cuts through bars of iron" (v. 16).

We may not be fools, suffering because of our iniquities, loathing all food and drawing near the gates of death. Then again, plenty of us in modern day America suffer from eating disorders such as anorexia and bulimia. We may indeed feel that we are "drawing near the gates of death," as a result of our physical and psychological disorders.

Let us cry out to God. He will "send forth his word and heal us." He will "rescue us from the grave" (v. 20).

We may not be out on the sea in ships, at our wits' end fighting the storms and high waves. Then again, some of us may be at our wits' end, fighting the storms and high waves of life. We may be reeling and staggering from natural disasters such as tornadoes, hurricanes, earthquakes, and floods. We may be reeling from man-made disasters such as divorce, separation, abuse, and isolation.

Let us cry out to God. He will cause our storms to grow calm. He will guide us to our desired haven (v. 30). "He will still the storms to a whisper; the waves of the sea will be hushed" (v. 29).

Whatever our circumstances, let us cry out to God. Then let our response to His deliverance be one of thanks.

Dear Lord, I cry out to You. I tell you my troubles. I trust that you will deliver me from my distress. I thank You for your unfailing love and for Your wonderful deeds. In Jesus' name. Amen.

Psalm 108 "Awake, harp and lyre! I will awaken the dawn" (v. 2).

One has to get up early to "awaken the dawn!" I'll admit, I'm not often one to awaken the dawn or anything else for that matter. I'm a go-to-bed-later and sleep-a-little-later type person. However, when I do get up bright and early, the Lord always has special rewards.

I like to walk on our gravel road in the country. The ditches on either side of the road are filled with delights. Wild asparagus. Milkweed. Clover. Wild roses. Further on past the ditches I am surrounded on all sides by the most beautifully flat farmland one has ever seen. The eye's vision is limitless out here. As far as one can see are lush fields of corn and soybeans and wheat. Only an occasional grove or silo breaks the landscape. It is here on early morning walks that God quietly speaks.

I remember one morning in particular when the dawn was breaking. Misty. Foggy. Cool. I walked with sunlight just breaking through patches of mist and fog. My two dogs and one of our cats walked along the road with me. We all stopped to examine God's beauty. In the ditch was a spiderweb with sunlight spraying through it. It was anchored with four strong strands to pieces of prairie grass. The web's middle was an intricate circle design that reminded me of geometric spirograph patterns I had done as a kid. Dew clung to each strand of web, each blade of grass.

"Awake harp and lyre! I will awaken the dawn."

Such beauty asks for music.

Asks for poetry.

Asks for praise.

I come to the garden alone,
while the dew is still on the roses.
And the voice I hear,
falling on my ear,
the Son of God discloses.
And He walks with me;
And He talks with me;
And He tells me I am His own.
And the joy we share
As we tarry there,
None other has ever known.

[In The Garden, by C. Austin Miles, 1913] A Hymn
(based on Psalm 108:2, Genesis 2:2-3, Exodus 20:8-11, Hebrews 4:9-10)

<u>Gentle Sabbath Morning</u>

Gentle Sabbath morning
that leads to Sabbath rest
We gather with believers
at Christ our Lord's behest.

Watch Him in the dawning,
In sun and rain and mist
Thank Him for the Sabbath,
With blessing lightly kissed.

Day to cease from labor;
A day when work is done.
Waken, harp and lyre!
Praise Father, Spirit, Son!

Work and toil mounting;
since Abel and since Cain
but for all God's people,
a Sabbath rest remains.

Day of rest and blessing;
A day of quiet peace
Day when, at God's urging,
we from our labors cease.

Come into communion
with God and fellow man
to keep the Sabbath holy;
to follow God's command.

God, our Great Creator,
Himself found time for rest
And for His dear creation

deemed what he knew was best.

Gentle Sabbath morning,
begins each seventh day
Waken, harp and lyre!
Sing and praise and pray.

by Linda Winter-Hodgson

May we praise You, O God, with music and poems and praise as we awaken the
dawn! In Jesus' name, Amen.

Psalm 109 "In return for my friendship they accuse me, but I am a man of prayer. They
repay me evil for good, and hatred for my friendship" (v. 4-5).

These words make me think of Jesus. David wrote them about himself, but how
well they apply to our Lord!

Jesus offered friendship to all the people of His day. Instead of receiving his
friendship, they accused Him. Jesus offered them only good, and they repaid Him
with evil and hatred. In the face of accusation, evil, and hatred, Jesus responded with
prayer.

On the Mount of Olives, Jesus knew that His accusers were about to overtake
Him. He responded with prayer.

"Pray that you will not fall into temptation," Jesus says to his disciples (Luke
22:40). "He withdrew about a stone's throw beyond them, knelt down and prayed,
'Father, if you are willing, take this cup from me; yet not my will, but yours be done.'
An angel from heaven appeared to him and strengthened him. And being in anguish,
he prayed more earnestly, and his sweat was like drops of blood falling to the
ground" (Luke 22:41-44).

In the face of accusation, evil, and hatred, Jesus was a man of prayer.

Still later, Jesus' betrayer, Judas Iscariot, approaches Jesus on the Mount of
Olives. He kisses Jesus to let the soldiers know that this is their man. One of Jesus'
disciples reacts in fear and anger by drawing his sword and cutting off the ear of the

high priest's servant. Jesus responds by saying, "No more of this!" and He touches the man's ear and heals him (Luke 22:51).

Jesus repays evil with good; hatred with friendship.

On the cross, in pain and agony, Jesus hangs over his accusers and prays, "Father, forgive them, for they do not know what they are doing" (Luke 23:34).

Jesus is a man of prayer.

We are to follow Jesus' example.

In return for accusation, we are to offer friendship.

In return for evil, we are to offer good.

In return for hatred, we are to offer love.

Like Jesus, we are to be people of prayer.

Dear Lord, help me when I am weak like the disciples, who, in the midst of evil on the Mount of Olives, fell asleep and did not pray. Help me to be like Jesus, who, in the midst of hatred and accusation, remained a man of prayer. In Jesus' name, Amen.

Psalm 110 "The Lord says to my Lord: 'Sit at my right hand until I make your enemies a footstool for your feet.'" And "...you will rule in the midst of your enemies" (v. 2b).

The Bible has a lot to say about enemies.

Proverbs 16:7 says, "When a man's ways are pleasing to the Lord, he makes even his enemies live at peace with him."

Psalm 23:5 says, "You prepare a table before me in the presence of my enemies."

Of the good king Asa, Chronicles 14:6-7 says, "He built up the fortified cities of Judah, since the land was at peace. No one was at war with him during those years, for the Lord gave him rest. 'Let us build up these towns,' he said to Judah, 'and put walls around them with towers, gates and bars. The land is still ours, because we have sought the Lord our God; we sought him and he has given us rest on every side.' So they built and prospered."

Growing up as a little girl, I never thought about enemies. In fact, I didn't think they existed. To me, everyone was a friend.

That is a nice way of thinking, but not realistic. God says that we will have enemies. When David wrote Psalm 110, he knew prophetically that "my Lord," Jesus, the Messiah, would have enemies. He knew that eventually, all of Jesus' enemies would be under His feet, subservient to Him as His footstool.

If our Great Leader and Lord, Jesus, has enemies, we may know that we, His disciples and followers, too, will have enemies.

In Luke 6:22 and 26 Jesus says, "Blessed are you when men hate you, when they exclude you and insult you and reject your name as evil, because of the Son of Man." "Woe to you when all men speak well of you, for that is how their fathers treated the false prophets."

Being a Christian does not always mean being well liked! We may be hated for certain political views, for certain social views, for certain religious views. We may have enemies because we have hurt people and offended them. Our offense against others may be intentional or unintentional. Either way, we may have made enemies.

Modern day enemies may include men and women who were married but are now divorced. They may be divorced parents engaged in custody battles over their children. They may be abortion proponents versus abortion opponents. They may be neighbors who have had angry words. They may be bosses versus employees. They may be Democrats versus Republicans. They may be Christians versus non-Christians.

In any case, God says that we can live *at peace* with our enemies.

"But I tell you who hear me:" Jesus says, "Love your enemies, do good to those who hate you, bless those who curse you, pray for those who mistreat you" (Luke 6:27).

Ultimately, the true enemies of Jesus will all be made a footstool for His feet. Jesus Christ has conquered sin, death, and the devil by dying on the cross and rising victorious from the grave to reign forever in heaven. But until we all live in heaven with Jesus, we will have enemies.

Some of our enemies are the result of our own sin and wrong thinking and wrong doing. Some of our enemies are the result of our living a godly life and standing up for Christ in our daily lives.

Either way, we can take great comfort in God's promise that, "When a man's ways are pleasing to the Lord, he makes even his enemies live at peace with him" (Proverbs 16:7).

Dear Jesus, I thank you that you rule in the midst of your enemies. I don't want enemies, Lord, but if I have made any, please help me to live at peace with them. Help me to love them and do good to them. Help me to pray for them. In Jesus' name, Amen.

Psalm 111 "Great are the works of the Lord; they are pondered by all who delight in them" (v. 2).

Two scenes come to mind as I read this verse.

One is of a big, fat, happy cat lounging on his favorite front porch step in the hot summer sun. The cat is totally relaxed, and is fully engaged in enjoying the day. His eyes take in the grass around him, the butterflies, the sunshine, and the flowers. He is pondering God's great works. He is *delighting* in them.

The second scene that comes to mind is a memory. It is of a day when, as a child, my parents took me to a plot of land near our Minnesota home known as virgin prairie. The grasses and flowers there had never been cut down. The soil had never been plowed or tilled. The vegetation was original, planted by nature, and undisturbed by man. We looked at the delicate flowers and prairie grasses there. We pondered them.

Our little neighbor girl, Jill, was along with us. She was three years old. She picked one tiny yellow flower and put it gently in my dad's back pants pocket. Then she took Dad's hand and walked with him through the field of flowers. It is a day and a scene I will not forget. A tiny girl's hand clutching a big farmer's hand, while a little yellow blossom bobs in his back pocket.

They are pondering.

They are delighting.

Delighting in the works of the Lord.

God's works are great. They are worth pondering. They are created for His delight and ours. May we, and all of God's creation *delight* in His works!

Dear Lord, thank you for all you have given to delight us! May we be like a happy cat on a warm porch today, and like a little girl roaming blissfully through virgin prairie, pondering Your wonders. In Jesus' name, Amen.

Psalm 112 "He will have no fear of bad news; his heart is steadfast, trusting in the Lord. His heart is secure, he will have no fear" (v. 7-8a).

Since I was a little girl, I have had a fear of certain phone calls: phone calls of bad news. Phone calls saying a relative has died. Phone calls saying there's been an accident. Phone calls saying there's an emergency.

Psalm 112 says that I don't need to fear bad news. My heart can be steadfast, trusting in the Lord.

There is only one thing we are to fear, and that is God. "Blessed is the man," Psalm 112:1 says, "who fears the Lord." A healthy fear of God promotes wisdom. Not a shaking, quaking, trembling fear, but a healthy reverence and fear of the God who has all things, even our eternal destiny, under his control. That fear of God is desirable. All other fears are not.

There is not one fear, other than the fear of God, that is necessary or healthy for us.

I John 4:18 says, "There is no fear in love. But perfect love drives out fear, because fear has to do with punishment. The one who fears is not made perfect in love."

Proverbs 29:25 says, "Fear of man will prove to be a snare, but whoever trusts in the Lord is kept safe."

Psalm 23:4 says, "I will fear no evil, for you are with me."

We don't even need to fear *evil!* There is *nothing* we need fear! Our hearts can remain *steadfast*; that means, "firmly fixed in place, immovable, not subject to change."

The year that my father and my aunt Flo died, my heart had trouble remaining steadfast. It felt to me as though my foundations were moving and shaking.

During that year, my pastor's wife spoke to me about a vision she had from God concerning me. She said she had seen in the vision a railroad bridge with the trestle and foundations crumbling. Then she had seen the trestle being rebuilt with new foundations. She told me that the railroad bridge was my life, and that part of my trestle and foundation had been made up of people. When some of those people died, my life started to crumble. She told me that the new foundation being built was God; God would be my foundation; and my foundation would never be shaken again.

That is not to say that people are not foundational in our lives. Our loved ones are, of course, foundational for us. We will mourn their passing with unspeakable grief and loss. But the very foundation of our lives, if it is God, will not move or shake or crumble. Our hearts can remain steadfast, without fear.

I am not there in my life yet. I admit to still having fears. It is a *process* in life to replace crumbling foundations with secure ones.

It is a building process.

A remodeling project.

God is the designer and builder.

He will do it if we but ask.

O Lord, I want to be in the place of the psalmist, where I have no fear of bad news. Whatever my deepest and most secret fears are, I lay them before You today. Bring me, I pray, to a place in my life of no fear. Make my heart secure and steadfast, trusting in You. In Jesus' name I pray, Amen.

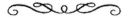

Psalm 113 "He settles the barren woman in her home as a happy mother of children" (v. 9).

God did this for me.

My husband and I were unable to have children together. After eight years of waiting on the adoption list, we were granted the miracle of adopting a ten-year-old girl, our daughter, Jessica. Two years later, a second daughter, eleven-year-old Colleen, was adopted into our family, and two years after that, an eleven-year-old boy, Daniel, became our third adopted child.

God, Romans 4:17 says, is "the God who gives life to the dead and calls things that are not as though they were."

Hanna put it another way in I Samuel 2:4-5: "The bows of the warriors are broken, but those who stumbled are armed with strength. Those who were full hire themselves out for food, but those who were hungry hunger no more."

"Those who stumbled are armed with strength."

"Those who were hungry hunger no more."

"Those who are first will be last, and the last first" (Mark 10:31).

They all have the same ring to them, don't they? These verses all speak of the same truth. God is a God of reversals.

I think Mary Magdalene understood this truth best. One minute her Lord was dead. Jesus was crucified and buried in a tomb. Even his body was missing when Mary came to the tomb, crying.

"They have taken my Lord away," she wails, "and I don't know where they have put him" (John 20:13).

There is nothing but death for Mary to see. Nothing but sad days, hopeless nights, crushed dreams.

The next minute, one word is spoken to her by a man she does not recognize, a man she thinks is the gardener: "Mary," the man says. And instantly, she knows it is Jesus! He is alive!

Happy days.

Hopeful nights.

Renewed dreams.

Reversals.

That is our God. The God who calls things that are not as though they were.

We all have "things that are not" in our lives. Places that are empty. Places where we hunger. Places where we are unfulfilled. But God calls these things "as though they were."

Like Mary, there may be nothing but death for us to see. Nothing but hunger. Nothing but weakness. Nothing but longing.

Like Mary, we may not recognize the One standing next to us. We may think He is the gardener, or some other unfamiliar stranger. Until He speaks our name! Until we recognize Jesus! Until we see reversal!

O Lord, You give strength to the stumbling, food to the hungry, children to the barren, life to the dead. I praise You! May I, like Mary, hear my name on Your lips. May I recognize You as the God of reversals. In Jesus' name, Amen.

⚬⚭⚬

Psalm 114 "Why was it, O sea, that you fled, O Jordan, that you turned back, you mountains, that you skipped like rams, you hills, like lambs?" (v. 5-6).

Let's stretch our imaginations just a little. Do we really believe that the sea fled? Do we really believe that the Jordan turned back? The Bible says it did.

Why?

Why does the Bible give accounts of inanimate objects moving? Why do objects of nature like mountains and hills and seas and rocks and the sun do miraculous, hard-to-believe things in Biblical accounts?

I believe that in every such incident mentioned in the Bible, there was one simple reason for the miraculous feats of nature to occur: The special presence of the Lord.

Let's look at some examples:

1. Joshua chapters 3 and 4: The Lord turns back the Jordan river so that the Israelites can cross over. Why? Joshua says in chapter 3 verses 9-10, "Come here and listen to the words of the Lord your God. This is how you will know that the living God is among you."

    The living God is among you.
    The special presence of the Lord.

2. Joshua chapter 10: The sun stands still over Gibeon. The moon stops, while Joshua and his army fight the Amorites and win the battle. Why? Joshua 10:13-14 says, "The sun stopped in the middle of the sky and delayed going down about a full day. There has never been a day like it before or since, a day when the Lord listened to a man. Surely the Lord was fighting for Israel!"

    The Lord was there, fighting for Israel.
    The special presence of the Lord.

3. Luke chapter 23: The sun stops shining and darkness comes over the whole land in the middle of the day when Jesus dies on the cross. Why? Luke 23:44-47 says, "It was now about the sixth hour, and darkness came over the whole land until the ninth hour (noon to three in the afternoon by the Jewish method of designating time), for the sun stopped shining. And the curtain of the temple was torn in two. Jesus called out in a loud voice, 'Father, into your hands I commit my spirit.' When he had said this, he breathed his last. The centurion, seeing what had happened, praised God and said, 'Surely this was a righteous man.'"

    Surely this was a righteous man.
    The special presence of the Lord.

Psalm 114:7 says, "Tremble, O earth, at the presence of the Lord, at the presence of the God of Jacob, who turned the rock into a pool, the hard rock into springs of water."

God is a miraculous God. His presence brings about supernatural occurrences. The mountains and the hills "burst into song" before Him! The trees of the field "clap their hands!" (Isaiah 55:12). If people don't praise him, the very stones will "cry out!" (Luke 19:40).

We need only enter God's presence for these miracle-working, life-changing powers to be at work in us!

O Lord, I believe that Your special presence can change anything. Thank you for Your miraculous signs that remind me of Your power. Please be at work in my heart and life, making Your special presence known. In Jesus' name, Amen.

Psalm 115 "Not to us, O Lord, not to us but to your name be the glory" (v. 1a).

"Not to us" means getting our eyes off of ourselves and onto God.

"Not to us" means giving credit to someone else.

"Not to us" means humility and humbleness of heart.

"Not to us" attitudes bring about restfulness without striving.

Jesus says of himself, "Take my yoke upon you, and learn of me, for I am gentle and humble in heart, and you will find rest for your souls" (Matthew 11:29).

I believe that humility has a lot to do with rest. When we are proud, we are striving to get glory. We are working. We are exerting effort. Even our minds are never at rest. They are thinking, "What can we do next to receive recognition or attention or glory?" There is no rest in that sort of attitude.

Humility says, "I don't need to prove anything. All I have and am depends on God. He deserves all glory." There is rest in that attitude. Rest for our souls.

There are so many unrested souls among people. People's souls are overworked. Our souls weren't designed to be at work or to strive. Our souls were designed by God to be at rest. That's why Jesus says, "I am gentle and humble in heart . . . learn this, and you will find rest for your souls."

Sometimes people in high places cannot find rest. People who want glory are too busy to rest. There is too much introspection in pride. Our eyes are on ourselves, and that is not restful.

Putting our eyes on Jesus is restful.

Closing our eyes in prayer is restful.

Taking our eyes off of ourselves is restful.

A visiting speaker at our church once said, "Think about mountains and valleys. Which are greener? The valleys are greener because water seeks the low places. Refreshment does not seek the high places."

That is an encouraging word about humility. Water seeks out the low places. It is in the low places of our lives that we can most receive refreshment from God. Our souls are humble. We are repentant. We are sorry. We are eager to say, "Not to us, O Lord, not to us but to your name be the glory" (Psalm 115:1a).

In that place there is rest. There is dependence on God. There is humbleness of heart. In that place we can receive refreshment.

Isaiah 42:3 says of Jesus, "A bruised reed he will not break, and a smoldering wick he will not snuff out."

When we are fragile before God, He will not break us. He will encourage us. He will refresh us. He will lift us up.

"Whoever humbles himself, "Matthew 14:11 says, "will be exalted."

We can be lifted up when we are humble. When we are proud, there is nowhere to go but down. We have set ourselves up for a fall.

Dear Lord, rather than set ourselves up for a fall, may we instead set ourselves up to be refreshed. May we say with the psalmist, "Not to us, O Lord, not to us but to your name be the glory." May our valleys and low places in life be green and well-watered as we learn of Jesus to be humble. May we find rest for our souls. In Jesus' name, Amen.

⁓◦◦⁓

Psalm 116 "I love the Lord, for he heard my voice; he heard my cry for mercy. Because he turned his ear to me, I will call on him as long as I live" (v. 1-2).

What a good reason for loving someone: "He heard my voice!" (v. 1).

One of our primary needs as human beings is to be heard. Toddlers want their parents' attention. Teenagers want their opinions to be heard and considered. Parents want their children to listen to advice and wisdom. Friends want to be heard and understood by other friends.

God knows of this primary need of human beings to be heard, and so He listens. He hears our cries. He turns His ear to us.

We can take a cue from God, and follow His example. We can listen to others.

We can listen to people whose opinions are different from our own.

We can listen to our children.

We can listen to our parents.

We can listen to our pastors.

We can listen to our spouses.

We can listen to our friends.

We can listen to our brothers and sisters.

In my immediate family, we have a little joke: Whenever someone starts saying something the other person doesn't want to hear, we put our hands up to our ears and pretend to turn off an imaginary hearing aid. We pretend to tune out the other person's voice. Of course, we can still hear them and our action is only a joke. But in reality, we do sometimes tune others out. We hear their voices, but we don't really listen.

God never does that. He does not tune us out. In fact, He encourages us to pray and communicate with Him *unceasingly!*

"Pray continually!" is the Bible's admonition in I Thessalonians 5:17. God *always* hears us! That is one of the many reasons the psalmist found to love Him!

"I love the Lord, for he heard my voice" (Psalm 116:1).

When someone hears us, we tend to go back to them to talk again. We like being heard. Verse two of our psalm says, "Because he turned his ear to me, I will call on him as long as I live."

We have a built-in listener in God for as long as we live!

In childhood.

In youth.

In adulthood.

In middle age.

In old age.

God hears us at all times!

Even when our prayers are breathed, or sighed, or whispered, or inaudible, God hears. He hears our thoughts. He hears our heart cries.

We have a listening ear in God.

We have reason to love Him for that listening ear.

Whisper a prayer in the morning;
Whisper a prayer at noon;
Whisper a prayer in the evening;
'Twill keep your heart in tune.

God answers prayer in the morning;
God answers prayer at noon;
God answers prayer in the evening;
He'll keep your heart in tune.

(From the song, Whisper A Prayer, composer unknown)

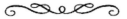

Psalm 117 "Praise the Lord, <u>all you nations</u>; extol him, <u>all you peoples</u>" (v. 1).
(underlining mine)

All nations and all peoples are to be blessed through Israel.

In Genesis 12:3, God says to Abraham, our father in the faith, "I will bless those who bless you, and whoever curses you I will curse; and all people on earth will be blessed through you."

I have always had a special love in my heart for Jewish people. I can't explain it exactly, except to say that from a young age, I have understood that they are God's chosen people. From their race, Jesus came. And of course, I, too, am now among them, grafted in to become one of Abraham's descendants, by faith in Christ.

I am a Gentile, yet I am as much Abraham's child as a person of Jewish descent. We Gentile believers are grafted in to the main tree trunk of Christ. We are not foreigners, but rather, natives, whose homeland is heaven. All believers in Christ are of one body, Jew and Gentile alike.

Isaiah 56:3-8 says: "Let no foreigner who has bound himself to the Lord say, 'The Lord will surely exclude me from his people.' And let not any eunuch complain, 'I am only a dry tree.' For this is what the Lord says: 'To the eunuchs who keep my Sabbaths, who choose what pleases me and hold fast to my covenant, to them I will give within my temple and its walls a memorial and a name better than sons and daughters; I will give them an everlasting name that will not be cut off. And foreigners who bind themselves to the Lord to serve him, to love the name of the Lord, and to worship him, all who keep the Sabbath without desecrating it and who hold fast to my covenant, these will I bring to my holy mountain and give them joy in my house of prayer. Their burnt offerings and sacrifices will be accepted on my altar; for my house will be called a house of prayer for all nations.'

The sovereign Lord declares, he who gathers the exiles of Israel: 'I will gather still others to them besides those already gathered.'"

That's us! We who have been gathered who were not born Jewish! We who have "bound ourselves to the Lord!" (Isaiah 56:3). We are among those who God will bring "to his holy mountain," (v. 7) and among those to whom he will give "joy in his house of prayer" (v. 7).

God's house is called "a house of prayer for *all nations!"* (Isaiah 56:7).

That is inclusive language! Some people think that Christianity is not inclusive. They say it is exclusive. It is true that "the gate is narrow" (Matthew 7:13-14). It is true that only those who love Jesus as Messiah and Savior will inherit the promise. In that sense, Christianity is narrow and exclusive. Jehovah-God is a jealous God (Exodus 20:5). He allows worship of no other gods or religions in His kingdom.

But Jesus died for *all* (John 3:16). God's house is a house of prayer for *all nations*. God loves those of every skin color and of every nationality. His love crosses all boundaries. In that sense, Christianity is inclusive of all.

The choice is still ours.

Gentile or Jew.

Red, white, yellow, brown, or black.

Female or male.

We must choose whom we will serve.

Life or death.

Curse or blessing.

Jesus or another god.

The Bible makes that choice clear. Once that choice is made, we have bound ourselves to the Lord, and are no longer foreigners, but rather, natives in the kingdom of God, headed for the same homeland: heaven.

Dear God, may my love for others, like Yours, be inclusive of all. Remove my prejudices, please Lord. Thank you for grafting all believers into the same vine: Jesus Christ. May we, as branches of that Vine, draw in and love the peoples of all nations. In Jesus' name, Amen.

Psalm 118 "Open for me the gates of righteousness; I will enter and give thanks to the Lord. This is the gate of the Lord through which the righteous may enter. I will give you thanks, for you answered me; you have become my salvation" (v. 19-21).

Gates provide entrances.

They are a means of passage.

In Old Testament times, the Jewish people often had liturgical processions during which the people would march up to the inner court of the temple. A king or leader would approach the gates leading to the temple court first, ahead of the other worshipers. The "gates of righteousness" may be referring to the temple court gates in our psalm, or, they may be referring to the gates of Jerusalem, the city of God.

Isaiah 26:1-2 says, "We have a strong city; God makes salvation its walls and ramparts. Open the gates that the righteous nation may enter, the nation that keeps faith."

"We have a strong city."

I like that line. It makes me think of heaven.

"God makes salvation its walls and ramparts."

Salvation is a sturdy wall. It is the building material of our eternal city; our eternal home with Jesus.

"Open the gates that the righteous nation may enter, the nation that keeps faith."

Christians are a righteous nation. Those who keep the faith and are redeemed and forgiven by Jesus' blood will see the gates of heaven opened.

Jesus says of Himself, "I am the gate; whoever enters through me will be saved. He will come in and go out, and find pasture" (John 10:9).

I believe that as Christians, we need to get a glimpse, or a picture, of heaven in our minds. I believe that we need to see Jerusalem in the Bible as a foreshadowing of heaven, and that we need to see Jesus, with His arms open wide, as her eternal gate.

Jesus is our entrance.

He is our means of passage.

We can go through Him into heaven.

Once we are there, the Bible says, "On no day will its [heaven's] gates ever be shut, for there will be no night there" (Revelation 21:25).

That is a gate worth entering!

That is a gate through which we can come in and go out, and find pasture.

That gate is Jesus.

Open now Thy gates of beauty,
Zion, let me enter there,
Where my soul in joyful duty
Waits for Him who answers prayer.
Oh, how blessed is this place,
Filled with solace, light, and grace!

> *(From the hymn, "Open Now Thy Gates Of Beauty"*
> *by Benjamin Schmolck, 1732, translated by Catherine Winkworth, 1863)*

Psalm 119 "Your statutes are my delight; they are my counselors" (v. 24), and "I will not neglect your word" (v. 16b).

Psalm 119 was my initial inspiration for writing this book of meditations. It made me aware of how much a person can *love* God's word! It also reminded me that God's words are *words of life*. They are our daily bread and butter. Without them we suffer, and eventually, we starve.

The NIV text notes describe Psalm 119's author as, "an Israelite . . . who was passionately devoted to the word of God as the word of life."

God's words were this person's delight!

God's words were this person's counselors!

Oh, the joy and fulfillment when this can be said of us!

Today there are many counselors in the world. There are therapists, analysts, psychologists, and psychiatrists. All of these have their place in helping others, and in giving wise counsel. But to know God's statutes is to know the world's greatest counselors! There is no more trustworthy word than God's!

Psalm 119:140 says of God's words, "Your promises have been thoroughly tested, and your servant loves them." God's word has been tested and tried! It works! We can apply God's statutes and commands to every area of our lives, and they will help us!

My challenge to myself and to you today, is to apply God's commands to every hurting or failing or needing situation in our lives. His word does not fail. His words speak life to every situation.

Our job, like the psalmist's, is to not neglect God's word. When we neglect God's words of life, they cannot help us. If we are not reading our Bibles daily, we are not getting our daily supply of *life*. Areas of our lives will be dead without the nourishing words of God.

What if we have not been reading God's word daily? Are we condemned? No!

Psalm 119:176 says, "I have strayed like a lost sheep. Seek your servant, for I have not forgotten your commands."

It is that simple to get back on track with God! We need only say, "Seek me, God. Come and find me. I'm lost. I've strayed."

And God comes! He seeks lost sheep! He carries us back to the safe pasture and says, "Eat. Be filled. My words are words of life."

Oh Lord, may Your words be my counselors daily! If I have neglected Your word, forgive me! Seek me, I pray. Let me not starve myself, but rather, be filled and delighted by Your words. In Jesus' name, Amen.

Psalm 120 "Too long have I lived among those who hate peace. I am a man of peace; but when I speak, they are for war" (v. 6-7).

How about our neighborhoods? Are we living among those who hate peace?

Jesus did.

He was a man of peace, the Prince of Peace, but those around Him wanted to stir up trouble. They wanted political upheaval. They wanted rebellion. They wanted revolt.

Jesus was an innocent man, innocent of any wrongdoing. Yet His life was taken violently from Him.

There are those in every generation who hate peace. People of peace may speak their minds, but those around them may be for war.

How about us?

Are we living in neighborhoods where racial prejudice exists? Are there gangs and gang activities around us? Are there political differences between us and our neighbors? Is there unforgiveness in our families? Are there those among us who look down on the poor and on those who receive welfare benefits? Are we among those who have hateful attitudes?

The psalmist was a man of peace.

Jesus was a man of peace.

We are to be people of peace.

If we have lived too long among those who hate peace, let us pray for them. Let us forgive them.

Jesus did.

If we have spoken out for peace in our neighborhoods, but others have spoken out for war or violence, let us pray for them. Let us show by our example that we are peacemakers.

Jesus did.

He turned the other cheek.

He forgave.

He loved all.

Let us follow His example as we pray and work for peace among our neighbors.

Dear Jesus, may Your example be the one I follow in being a peacemaker. Please bring peace between those who hate one another. Come into our hearts, Lord Jesus. Amen.

Psalm 121 "I lift up my eyes to the hills, where does my help come from? My help comes from the Lord, the Maker of heaven and earth" (v. 1).

I offer today for meditational reading an essay I wrote based on Kathleen Norris' book, *Dakota: A Spiritual Geography*. (My thoughts after reading about our "inner geography," and our "inner landscape," in Kathleen Norris' book).

The Mountains Of My Soul

The mountains of my soul are a difficult lot: full of valleys and drop-offs and sharp rocks that hurt the climber. And yet, climber I will be, and love it most of the time. The vantage points these mountains afford me are not to be equaled. Not in nature's greatest climb. For their pinnacle is wisdom, and their peak is Heaven's Height.

Not much of life is lived on the pinnacles, but then, pinnacles, by their very nature, do not invite settling in. They are pointed, narrow, good for perspective. Pinnacles are high points; like the high points of life. They are not meant for moving in. For putting in stakes. For permanent dwellings.

Pinnacles, I believe, are meant to be climbed. To be reached. To give us a good view of where we came from and of where we are going. We view our valleys from there.

Valleys have been given a bad name over the years. The Valley of the Shadow of Death. Low points. Valleys are these. But they are more. They are the places of everyday life. They are fertile. They are wide. Wide enough to be lived in. Full of rivers and streams and well-watered places. Valleys are green, signifying life.

We tire of valleys. They are low, and offer no view. No perspective. We tire of life, sometimes. It leads to blind crossings. Cross roads. Lack of vision.

We need then, to start climbing. To reach a place of wisdom; a place of view. Only on the high places do we remember that we have, indeed, "a future and a hope" (Jeremiah 29:11). That future, if only glimpsed, takes us back down the mountain for more valley living; *green* living, mind you, for life, whether lived out in the flat or on the mountaintop, is always *green*. That future, when lived out as a child of God, takes us on to more climbs, more pinnacles, more hopes, and finally, heaven's heights.

Perhaps that is part of what is meant in the words "How beautiful on the mountains are the feet of those who bring good news" (Isaiah 52:7). In Christ, good news comes to the mountains each of us tread. The mountains that rise and fall within the chest of every human being. The mountains of the soul.

Dear Lord, I know that not every day of my life can be a high point. Help me, please, in the low points of life to lift up my eyes to the hills. Thank you for all the pinnacles and mountaintop experiences that You give me. Help me to take my bearings from those times and to remember them. Help me to lift my eyes up often, to receive Your help. In Jesus' name, Amen.

Psalm 122 "Our feet are standing in your gates, O Jerusalem" (v. 2).

Feet symbolize pilgrimage. In order for many Jewish people to go to Jerusalem, pilgrimage was required. They had to travel. They had to walk.

Pilgrimage denotes travel to a shrine or holy place. In pilgrimage, destination is of utmost importance. That is why verse two of our psalm is such a firm declaration. "Our feet are standing in your gates, O Jerusalem." The destination had been reached! The pilgrims had reached their goal!

I had an aunt, who, at the age of eighty years, journeyed to the Holy Land of Israel. She set her feet in the gates of Jerusalem. She stood in the city of God. She walked where Jesus Christ had walked.

I, too, have a dream of one day going to the Holy Land. Not because I have to, but because Jerusalem is a symbol to me of my ultimate destination, heaven.

I want to set my feet in the city of God and declare with my Aunt Mabel, and with the Israelites, and with all the people of God, "Our feet are standing in your gates, O Jerusalem."

I want to be like the pilgrims of the Old Testament of whom Psalm 122 says, "They rejoiced when someone said 'Let us go to the house of the Lord!'" (v. 1).

I want to see the city about which the Bible says, "That is where the tribes go up, the tribes of the Lord, to praise the name of the Lord!" (v. 4).

The tribes of the Lord.

We Christians are members of that tribe! My tribe is the tribe of the Lord. Your tribe is the tribe of the Lord. We belong there! Our ultimate destination is the New Jerusalem, the heavenly city of God!

In order to get there we need to travel.

We need to walk.

We need to make a pilgrimage.

That pilgrimage is our life on earth. Our feet are making that journey now.

Sometimes the road is long. The way is dusty. The path is not level.

But God says, "I will lead them beside streams of water on a level path where they will not stumble" (Jeremiah 31:9).

We can look to God on this journey. We can rejoice with those who say to us, "Let us go to the house of the Lord" (Psalm 122:1). We are all on our way to the same place! One day we will say together, "Our feet are standing in your gates, O Jerusalem!"

Dear Lord, my feet long for the day when they will stand in Your courts. I will look down at my feet and marvel on that day, Lord, that they have traveled earth and have finally reached their destination. Thank you for holy ground, Lord: the holy ground of heaven, where one day I will stand. In Jesus' name, Amen.

Psalm 123 "I lift up my eyes to you, to you whose throne is in heaven. As the eyes of slaves look to the hand of their master, as the eyes of a maid look to the hand of her mistress, so our eyes look to the Lord our God, till he shows us his mercy" (v. 1-2).

Eyes looking up.
Eyes lifted.
Eyes inquiring.
These are the eyes of a slave to a master.
These are the eyes of a maid to a mistress.
These are the eyes of a person to God.

Have you ever seen a loving dog with a loving owner? I had a dog named Boswell. He was the most needy dog I have ever met. Boswell needed love and attention and petting and patting and scratching every few minutes. Or so it seemed! If these attentions were not given to Boswell, he would begin to whine, to whimper, to make almost human talking noises, and to turn his big, brown, moist, pleading eyes on me.

He looked into my face.
He blinked.
He batted his eyelashes.
He raised his eyebrows.

I always gave in. Eventually, I gave him one more pat. One more hug. One more kiss on the top of his head. He knew that I would. He knew that I was his loving owner and friend.

God is our loving Owner and Friend. He is our Master. He is our Mistress. We can look to His hand for all that we need.

Psalm 123 presupposes that masters and mistresses are kind and generous. We know that human beings are not always that way. Some have treated others inhumanely and cruelly. But that is not what our psalmist is thinking. He is comparing God to the kindest of masters. To the most generous of mistresses. He is showing us the relationship of healthy dependence.

"The eyes of all look to You, and You give them their food at the proper time. You open your hand and satisfy the desires of every living thing" (Psalm 145:15-16).

The hand of God gives us all that we need. We need only lift our eyes to Him. He is moved by our eyes looking up at His face. Just as I was moved with compassion every time Boswell looked to me for love, so God is moved with compassion every time we lift up our eyes to Him for mercy.

Hebrews 4:16 says, "Let us then approach the throne of grace with confidence, so that we may receive mercy and find grace to help us in our time of need."

The throne of grace is higher than we are. The position of master is higher than slave. The place of mistress is over that of maid. We need to look *up* to receive attention. We need to get our eyes off of ourselves, and onto the hand from which we can receive. We need to recognize that we are needy, and that our help comes from above.

Acknowledging that is the first step to receiving mercy. We can then approach the throne of grace with *confidence*. We can then "receive mercy and find grace to help us in our time of need."

Oh God, I lift up my eyes to Your face. See my need with Your loving eyes. Meet me in my place of weakness. Generous Master, Kindest Mistress, shower me with Your mercy. I am glad to depend on You. In Jesus' name, Amen.

Psalm 124 "If the Lord had not been on our side, let Israel say, if the Lord had not been on our side when men attacked us, ...the flood would have engulfed us, the torrent would have swept over us, the raging waters would have swept us away... We have escaped like a bird out of the fowler's snare; the snare has been broken, and we have escaped" (v. 1-2, 4-5, 7).

Let's put our names in these verses.
"If the Lord had not been on my side, let *Linda* say..."
"If the Lord had not been on my side, let _____ say..."
If the Lord had not been on our side, what would've happened?
It's not a good thought.
We would not have escaped.
Escaped what?

Psalm 124:7 says, "We have escaped like a bird out of the fowler's snare; the snare has been broken, and we have escaped."

We have escaped capture. Capture by the devil. The devil is real. Evil is real. Satan "prowls around like a roaring lion, seeking whom he may devour" (I Peter 5:8). His three purposes on earth are "to steal, to kill, and to destroy" (John 10:10).

We have escaped sin. We are no longer slaves to sin, but are free in Christ (Romans 6:6).

We have escaped death. "The wages of sin is death, but the gift of God is eternal life in Christ Jesus our Lord" (Romans 6:23). Do we feel like "escapees" today? We should! We are! All of us were literally "ensnared" when we were born. We were born into sin in a sinful world. We could not escape. Without God on our side, and Jesus as our Rescuer, our doom was sealed.

Just like the Israelites at the Red Sea, we had no way out short of a miracle. The Egyptians were behind us (sin and evil), and the raging waters were before us (death and punishment). We had no way to escape.

Unless the Lord had been on our side.

Unless Jesus had come to our rescue.

Unless a plan of escape had been formulated by our God.

The sea opened up!
Israel went through on dry ground!
The Egyptians were defeated and destroyed!
The promised land awaited the people of God!
God had a miraculous plan for their escape!

Jesus Christ opened up our way to God!
We can pass through death to life!
Sin and death and Satan will be forever defeated and destroyed!
The promised land of heaven awaits the people of God!
God had a miraculous plan for our escape!

"If the Lord had not been on our side, let _____ say . . . "
I shudder to think of it.
I shudder to think of getting what I deserve at the end of my life.
I shudder to think of receiving the true wages for all my sins.

But God *is* on our side!
He has given us the *victory* through our Lord Jesus Christ!
(I Corinthians 15:57).
He has provided a means of escape!

Dear Lord, truly, I am an escapee. I should feel as exhilaratingly free as a pardoned convict every day of my life! I can fly as free as a bird who once was captured, but has now escaped the fowler's snare! Oh Jesus, thank you for being my Rescuer. Oh Holy Spirit, thank you for leading me to Christ. Oh God, thank you for being on my side. In Jesus' name, Amen.

Psalm 125 "Those who trust in the Lord are like Mount Zion, which cannot be shaken but endures forever" (v. 1).

I offer today a letter that I wrote to my mother in 1993, and added to after adopting children of my own. My mother was one of those who trusted in the Lord, and was for me like Mount Zion.

Dear Mom,

I know it's been hard for you since Daddy died. So many nights, like tonight, I think of you sitting in your chair at home alone. I wonder what you're doing, and what you're thinking, and if you're feeling contented and strong and happy, or if you're feeling lonely and sad and a little afraid. I imagine that most days and nights hold a little of both.

Life is like that, even for me. I'm much younger that you, but I've already tasted quite a bit of happy and sad, contented and lonely, strong and a little afraid.

I've never lost a husband, but I know what it's like to fear that day if it comes. I've lost a father, and aunts, and uncles, and some friends, and each one has left my heart empty in some ways, and more full in others.

I've had days, many days, when I've felt happy and contented and strong. In fact, most days are like that, and I know that it is God's grace alone that gives us those days. He alone "makes my mountain stand firm" (Psalm 30:7).

Some days my mountain doesn't stand firm. Some days it wobbles. Some day it shakes. I imagine yours does, too, Mom.

But you, Mom, have shown me how to plant my feet on solid ground. You're not unshakeable. Neither am I. But you've shown me who is. I've watched you look to God when your mountain is shaking. I've watched Him make your feet firm. I've watched you, Mom, and I've learned.

I've learned that no matter how shaky I may feel, it will pass. I've learned that in young age or in old age, it is God alone who makes us strong. I've learned that life itself is a series of standing firm and being shaken, standing firm and being shaken, until we realize that all other ground is sinking sand, and that only on Christ, the solid rock, we stand.

I've learned that even when bad times come, they will always give way to good. Like when Dad had his accident, and you were left alone with two little girls. I imagine your mountain shook then. But you did it. You handled it. And bad times gave way to good. Dad recovered. And Lisa and I were blessed with two parents who were healthy and strong.

Parents who played softball with us by the garage. Parents who fielded hits that flew into the garden. Parents who played games like Drop The Hanky, Button-Button, I Spy, and Riddledy-Riddledy-Ree with us. Parents who sacrificed to take their girls on vacation to the lake every year right after harvest.

You and Dad must have been so tired. Dad combining and hauling grain late every night. You making meals, packing lunches, delivering them to the fields. Then dropping everything and packing food and clothes to take to the lake the minute harvest was done.

I didn't think about it then. But I do now. All that work and all that play. That's what parents are all about. Teaching their children to work and play. To enjoy being together. To make the most of being together. That was Dad. And that was you, Mom.

It still is. You still teach me how to work and how to play. How to enjoy being together. How to cook soup and bring it to the neighbors. How to teach Sunday school. How to visit the Nursing home. How to maintain friendships. How to laugh. How to joke. How to send cartoons in the mail to brighten people's days. How to be friends with people of all ages, from age seven to ninety-seven. How to help your children when they move. When they go to college. When they marry. All this time I've watched you, Mom. And all this time I've learned.

(A few years later, I added this note:)

Now that I have children, I hope that they can learn from me as I have learned from you. I hope that through all the times of being shaken, and through all the times of standing firm, that they can look to me and see me standing; sometimes wobbling, but always standing, on the solid rock of Christ.

I hope that through God's grace, they will someday feel towards me, as I do towards you, because:

The compliment I prize
Much more that any other
Is the one when people say,
"You're so much like your mother."
I love you, Mom.
Linda

Dear Lord, may I be among those who trust in the Lord, and are like Mount Zion which cannot be shaken but endures forever. Thank you for my mother, and for all those who, like her, have been wonderful examples among the believers. In Jesus' name, Amen.

Psalm 126 "He who goes out weeping, carrying seed to sow, will return with songs of joy, carrying sheaves with him" (v. 6).

Weeping	Singing
Going out	Returning
Sowing seed	Carrying sheaves

Psalm 126 is a psalm of contrasts. Contrasts give me hope because they show that life can change.

We can be in a time of weeping, and it can change to a time of singing.

We can be in a time of going out, and it can change to a time of returning.

We can be in a time of life where we are sowing seed, and that can change to a time of harvesting and carrying sheaves.

These verses remind me of the time, years ago, when we went to the funeral of a dear relative of ours named Carolyn. She left behind a husband, and four adopted children who were already grown. There was weeping and mourning at this funeral. There was weeping and mourning for days and months to come for the loss of this dear relative.

But although we went out weeping, we also carried seed to sow. Our dear relative left many seeds behind when she died. She was a Christian who had planted seeds all her life. She talked about Jesus. She talked about her faith. She talked about worship.

The last thing Carolyn said to me before she died was during a telephone conversation. "Remember to pray for my children," she said.

That is a seed. It was planted in my heart, and though I wept over Carolyn's death, I will not forget the seed. I will not forget to pray. Who knows what sheaves will be gathered in by our prayers?

We can pray for people's salvation.

We can pray for people's healing.

We can pray for people's protection.

All of these are seeds. We can see nothing of results sometimes until time passes. But then there is change.

Seeds become sheaves.

Tears become joy.

Going out becomes returning.

Jesus knew that in His death on the cross. That was a seed. He knew that, "What you sow does not come to life unless it dies" (I Corinthians 15:36). Jesus died, and then His body was buried or sown in the ground. Three days later, a change occurred, and His body was resurrected, a glorious body! He was the first fruits of those who sleep! We *all* will be changed!

There is hope in change.

We may be in a time of weeping, but it will change. We must let time pass. We must wait.

The writer of psalm 126 had waited. He had been in exile. He had been captured and removed from his own country. He had been in mourning for his homeland. Then the Lord brought the captives back. They were returned to their home. Their fortunes were restored.

There was waiting.

There was mourning.

There was change.

If we are in a time of weeping, of going out, or of sowing seed, let us wait. Let us hope. Change will come. Weeping will turn to singing. Going out will change to returning. Sowing seed will result in carrying beautiful sheaves.

Dear Lord, thank you for contrasts. In contrasts, let us find hope. For all those who are weeping, Lord, I pray for hope to wait for joy. For all those who are going out, I pray for safe returning. For all those who are sowing seed, I pray for a bountiful harvest. In Jesus' name, Amen.

Psalm 127 "Unless the Lord watches over the city, the watchmen stand guard in vain" (v. 1b).

We like to give ourselves too much credit.

We lie in our beds at night and make plans for the following day. We make imaginary blueprints for houses we are going to build. We dream of remodeling projects to improve our homes. We plan trips and tours and vacations. We decide how our money will be spent. We say to ourselves, "I will have this career or that job." We think, "When I am old, or when I retire, I will do this or that."

None of this dreaming and planning is bad unless we forget to begin with one little word: if.

James 4:15 says, "We ought to say, 'If it is the Lord's will, we will live and do this or that.'"

If it is the Lord's will.

That is giving credit where it is due. What we do and succeed at is up to God. It is not up to us. We may be watchmen, guarding a city at night to protect it from intruders. But unless the Lord is watching over the city, our guarding is in vain.

We may be making plans to build a new house. But unless it is the Lord's will, our building will be in vain.

Beginning each plan in life with "If it is God's will," is a comforting perspective for the Christian. If it is *not* God's will and does not succeed, it was not meant to be. God is in perfect control. *We* are not at the helm. God is.

Proverbs 16:9 says, "A man's heart plans his way, but the Lord directs his steps." (NKJV)

We may make all sorts of plans, but if we die or become ill, what good are they? It is better for us to say, "*If it is the Lord's will*, we will live, or do this or that."

I like the children's prayer, *Now I Lay Me Down To Sleep*. I like the old-fashioned version of that prayer:

> Now I lay me down to sleep;
> I pray the Lord my soul to keep.
> If I should die before I wake,
> I pray the Lord my soul to take,
> For Jesus' sake.
> But if I live for other days,
> I pray the Lord would guide my ways.

"If" is used twice in that prayer.

"*If* I should die before I wake," and "*If* I live for other days."

There is no presupposing in that prayer. There is no assuming of control. All is left up to God.

In recent years, this prayer has been often changed and edited. I have heard a number of adults, say, "I don't want my child to pray, 'If I should die before I wake;' that sounds too scary for a child to say."

No. That is not scary. That is realistic. That is admitting that we do not know the future. Not for one year. Not for one night. Not for one day. Not for one moment.

God knows the future. It is His. All plans are His. Let us submit our plans to Him, knowing that we do all else in vain.

Dear Lord, I submit all the plans of my heart to You. Please direct my steps. Let me say every day with James, "If it is Your will, I will live and do this or that." Let me say with the children's prayer, "If I should die before I wake, I pray the Lord my soul to take; If I should live for other days, I pray the Lord would guide my ways." In Jesus' name. Amen.

❧❧❧

Psalm 128 "Blessed is every one who fears the Lord, who walks in His ways. When you eat the labor of your hands, you shall be happy, and it shall be well with you" (v. 1-2).

These verses speak to me of contentment. How many people do we know who "eat the labor of their hands," but are not happy? How many times do we, as Christians, "eat the labor of our hands," yet worry about money, or about tomorrow, or about having enough?

The Bible says that if we "fear the Lord," and "walk in His ways," we can "be happy," and it will "be well with us" (Psalm 128: 1-2).

We may have to take these verses in faith. We may be behind in some payments. We may have incurred unexpected expenses. We may have been good stewards with what God has given us, yet have fallen short of what we need monetarily or materially.

Paul the apostle knew what that was like. In Philippians 4:12-13 he writes, "I know what it is to be in need, and I know what it is to have plenty. I have learned the secret of being content in any and every situation, whether well fed or hungry, whether living in plenty or in want. I can do everything through him who gives me strength."

Are we in need today?

Do we have plenty?

Either way, we can be content.

Ecclesiastes says it this way:

"A man can do nothing better than to eat and drink and find satisfaction in his work. This too, I see, is from the hand of God, for without Him, who can eat or find enjoyment? To the man who pleases Him, God gives wisdom, knowledge, and happiness, but to the sinner he gives the task of gathering and storing up wealth to hand it over to the one who pleases God" (Ecclesiastes 2:24-26).

Contentment, then, comes "from the hand of God" (v. 24). Contentment does not come from having plenty, or from being in need. Our circumstances, whether easy or hard, do not bring true contentment. True contentment comes as a gift, from the hand of God. True contentment comes in realizing that even in want, we can do everything through Him who gives us strength. If we fear the Lord, as our psalm says today, and if we walk in His ways, we can be happy, and it will be well with us.

Let us place our want before God today.

Let us place our plenty before God today.

Let us learn, in both situations, to be content.

Oh Lord, I place my situation before You today. Whether I am in need, or having plenty, I ask to learn contentment. I fear You, and I walk in Your ways, so I know that the gift of contentment is mine as a gift from Your hands. Thank you for this gift. In Jesus' name, Amen.

Psalm 129 "They have greatly oppressed me from my youth, let Israel say, they have greatly oppressed me from my youth, but they have not gained the victory over me. Plowmen have plowed my back and made their furrows long. But the Lord is righteous; he has cut me free from the cords of the wicked" (v. 1-4).

Let us think today of people who have been oppressed from their youth.

Black people.

Jewish people.

Poor people.

Plowmen (oppressors) have "plowed these peoples' backs" and made life hard and miserable for them. There has been slavery, holocaust, and hunger. Those who have truly suffered oppression know what the Bible means when it says, "Plowmen have plowed my back and made their furrows long."

The furrows of hatred and oppression run deep. But the Bible says that even though *people's* actions towards one another can be hateful and sinful, "the *Lord* is righteous." The Lord is the one who cuts people free from "the cords of the wicked" (v. 4).

Let us never confuse God's actions and attitudes with those of the wicked. Some wicked oppressor groups would even use God's name in their cause of hatred. They would say that the Bible says this or that in defense of their oppressive attitudes. But the Bible *never* speaks in defense of oppression or wickedness. Jesus came to set all captives free! Jesus speaks of compassion. Of mercy. Of love for all. Jesus died *for all*.

Let us pray today the prayer of Psalm 129, verses 5-7. Let us pray it before any more hatred can grow:

"May all who hate Zion (or anyone) be turned back in shame. May they be like grass on the roof, which withers before it can grow; with it the reaper cannot fill his hands, nor the one who gathers fill his arms."

Dear Lord, please wither hatred and oppression before it can grow. Let those who sow seeds of hatred have nothing to reap or gather; no followers, no acts of violence, no victories. We pray in Jesus' name, Amen.

Psalm 130 "If you, O Lord, kept a record of sins, O Lord, who could stand? But with you there is forgiveness; therefore you are feared" (v. 3-4).

Why would anyone who is full of forgiveness be feared?

I believe it is because forgiveness is different. Forgiveness is unexpected. Forgiveness is not the norm.

We are caught off guard when someone says, "I forgive you." We are ready for revenge. For get-even. For carrying a grudge. That is the norm among people.

God is different.

God says, "I keep no record of wrongs. Forget it. Your sins are history."

The NIV text notes interpret these verses this way: "But with you there is forgiveness; therefore you are *honored, worshipped, trusted,* and *served.*"

That is our response to One who forgives. God is worthy of our honor, our worship, our trust, and our service. He is worthy because He forgives.

In our society, we often wrongly honor revenge and unforgiveness. We laugh at movies where tough guys say:

"I don't get mad; I get even."

"I don't make threats; I make promises."

"Go ahead; make my day."

But do we really want to honor these people and their attitudes? Are they worthy of our honor, worship, trust, and service? No. Only an all-forgiving God is worthy of such things. Only an all-forgiving God can work forgiveness in our lives towards others.

It is God living inside of people like Corrie ten Boom that allowed her to say to the concentration camp prison guard who had tortured her and killed her sister, "I forgive you."

Only God inside of us can create that attitude and ability to forgive.

That attitude and ability is worthy of fear. It is worthy of honor.

We have come to expect revenge in our society. We have come to expect grudges. We have come to expect unforgiveness. Let us surprise people instead. Let us give them the unexpected. Let us give them God inside of us. Let us give them forgiveness.

Dear God, I fear You because with You there is forgiveness. I honor You. I revere You. Thank you that in a world of unforgiveness, You unexpectedly offer forgiveness. Help me to do the same. In Jesus' name, Amen.

❧

Psalm 131 "But I have stilled and quieted my soul; like a weaned child with its mother, like a weaned child is my soul within me" (v. 2).

This verse always confused me when I'd read it. I used to skip over it when I read the psalms. But after meditating on it, and asking God for understanding, I'd like to share these thoughts about a weaned child:

1. A weaned child is one who no longer breast-feeds. He no longer needs only milk, either from a bottle, or from his mother. Therefore, a weaned child is less demanding of that need from his caregiver.
2. A weaned child has had something taken away. He has had to go on to more mature, solid food. He has had to learn to try something new and different that is good for him.
3. A weaned child has had a nutritious, filling beginning. He has been supplied by his mother or caregiver, and has been filled. His first, basic needs have been met. He has known security at his mother's breast.
4. A weaned child is still a child. He no longer breast feeds or drinks only milk, but he is not yet an adult.

Our *soul*, Psalm 131 says, can be like a weaned child within us. We who have come to know Jesus and have given our hearts to Him can be like that weaned child with his mother:

1. We can come to God with no demands. We can simply spend time with Him. We can enjoy His company.
2. We may have matured enough to have had something taken away in our

Christian life. The weaned child does not like giving up the breast, but it is the only way he will grow up. As weaned children with God, we can go on to more mature, solid foods. We can try new and different things that are good for us.

leading others to Christ
asking God for gifts of the Spirit (I Corinthians 12 & 14)
leading Bible studies

These are just a few examples of things that weaned children, maturing Christians, can go on to as we grow in our faith.

3. As weaned children, our souls have already experienced a nutritious, filling beginning. We have received Christ. We have been baptized. We have known fellowship with God and other Christians. Our basic needs have been met. We have tasted the security of knowing that God loves us. Security is the basis for giving. No one can give to others unless he first has known some degree of security. A weaned child has been close to her mother and nursed at her breast. Our souls within us can be stilled and quieted because we have known closeness with God and the security it brings.

4. As weaned children before God, we are still children. Jesus says, "Unless you become like a little child, you will never enter the kingdom of heaven" (Matthew 18:3). We may have gone on to more solid food, but in God's kingdom, we are still children. We never know it all. We never arrive. We never have all the answers. Not till heaven. Knowing it all is God's job, not ours. Only He has all of the answers. That's why the psalmist says, "My heart is not proud, O Lord, my eyes are not haughty; I do not concern myself with great matters or things too wonderful for me. But I have stilled and quieted my soul; like a weaned child with its mother, like a weaned child is my soul within me" (Psalm 131:1-2).

May we today be like a weaned child with God. May we still and quiet our souls.

Dear God, I come to You today with no demands. I just want to be close to You. Thank you that although we are always growing up as Christians, we are still always children in Your sight. In Jesus' name, Amen.

Psalm 132 "We heard it in Ephrathah, we came upon it in the fields of Jaar: 'Let us go to his dwelling place; let us worship at his footstool, arise, O Lord, and come to your resting place, you and your ark of might'" (v. 6-8).

My Aunt Flo had a great lap. She had many other things about her that I loved, too, like her homemade chocolate-drop cookies, and her pure white hair. It was puffy and white like a giant dandelion puff, or a cumulus cloud in summer. But what I liked best about Flo was her lap.

It was a great resting place. I rested there better than anywhere else. As a small child, I sat on Flo's lap almost every day, as she lived just down the road from my own house. As I got older, Flo had to undergo knee surgery, so for a few years I had to sit lightly on her lap so as not to bother her knee. Then as a teenager and as an adult, I became too big for lap-sitting, so instead, I knelt by Aunt Flo's chair and put my head in her lap. She would touch my cheek and my hair, and we would talk and talk. I can still feel her crisp dress and fresh apron under my face.

Those were close times. Times of love. Times of relaxation. Times of rest.

Flo was eighty-six years old when she died, and right up until that time, I still rested my head on her lap.

In our psalm today, God and His people need a resting place. The Israelites had been wandering in the desert. They needed a place to rest, so God gave them the promised land. God had been wandering, too. His presence had been traveling through the desert with the Israelites, and had been dwelling in tents. God wanted a place to settle. He wanted a more permanent dwelling on earth. So, He chose Zion.

Verses 13-14 of our psalm say, "For the Lord has chosen Zion, he has desired it for his dwelling: 'This is my resting place for ever and ever; here will I sit enthroned, for I have desired it.'"

God found a resting place. The Israelites did, too.

Everyone needs a place of rest. We may not all have a lap to sit on, but we can all find or make a special resting place.

David thought this was so important that he said, "I will allow no sleep to my eyes, no slumber to my eyelids, till I find a place for the Lord, a dwelling for the Mighty One of Jacob" (Psalm 132:4-5).

We may have to search.

We may have to seek.

We may have to make time.

But we *can* find a resting place.

Our resting place should include God. He should feel comfortable there. His presence should be able to rest there. He should be worshipped there. For only *with God* are we truly at rest.

Dear Lord, bring me to a resting place. Let me hear each day, as the Israelites did, Your call to worship and rest: "Let us go to His dwelling place; let us worship at His footstool, arise, O Lord, and come to Your resting place" (v. 7-8). In Jesus name, Amen.

My Homeless God

My homeless God,
where do you lodge
when hearts
have closed the door?

Where do you wander,
Spirit Ghost,
when I
do not implore

You to come in,
indwell my being,
prepare Your
holy place

Make of my heart
Your throne room,
Your lamp make light
my face.

By Linda Winter-Hodgson

Psalm 133 "How good and pleasant it is when brothers live together in unity!" (v. 1).

My husband and I are in love.

That may sound like a ridiculously obvious statement. If we weren't in love why would we be married? But the fact is, we know many married couples who are not in love with each other. In fact, we have dear friends, married couples, who have made statements like this to us:

"We're married, but we go our own ways and each do our own thing." "Divorce is expensive and embarrassing; it's easier to just grin and bear it."

That is not unity!

I am in no way bragging about my marriage. *Only God* can get credit when a couple is truly in love. I thank Him *every day* for the *gift* of being in a marriage where both husband and wife are in love with each other.

My husband and I have fights. Sometimes we have disagreements. But on the big issues we agree. On the big matters, our hearts and spirits are in unity. On life's biggest issue of all, loving Jesus and living to serve Him, my husband and I are one.

Unity and oneness are like oil and dew. That's what Psalm 133 says.

"It [unity] is like precious oil poured on the head, running down on the beard, running down on Aaron's beard, down upon the collar of his robes" (v. 2).

"It is as if the dew of Hermon were falling on Mount Zion" (v. 3).

Unity and oneness pour out and spill over. They spill over into the lives of our children. Children know when their parents are faking it. They also know when Mom and Dad are truly living in unity. Unity spills over and gives children security.

Oil and dew imagery gives us a picture of what unity can do. Oil renews old, dry things. Water gives life and helps things to grow. Unity, when it flows between people, does the same things. It spills over to others and renews parched ground.

It renews.

It offers hope.

It helps bring growth.

Where else can we find and work for unity?

Between husband and wife.

Between parents and children.

Between sisters and brothers.

Between neighbors and friends.

Between one church and another.

Between us and creation.

Between us and our Creator.

Between us and our enemies.

All of these relationships need unity. Unity requires hard work. It requires trying hard to understand someone else. It requires communicating. It requires reaching out. When we fail, it means trying again. And again. And again.

I firmly believe that *all people* were created to live together in unity. That sounds idealistic, but I believe it is God's plan, and that with God, nothing is impossible.

We live in a sinful world, so some of our attempts at unity will fail. But unity is God's best. It is His purpose and plan for us. It was His desire in the Garden of Eden, and it is His desire today.

Whenever we can, let us work for unity. Where we are living in disunity, let us try again, and work harder. Only then will we know, as David did, "How good and pleasant it is when brothers live together in unity!"

Dear God,
  Knit our hearts together
  like Jonathan and David.
  Knit our hearts together
  like Ruth and Naomi.
  Make us one; make us one,
  like the Father and the Son.
  Hide the scars of division
  beneath Your love.
    In Jesus' name, Amen.

(Scripture song; author/composer unknown)

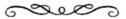

Psalm 134 "Praise the Lord, all you servants of the Lord who minister by night in the house of the Lord" (v. 1).

Last night we had a bonfire. The people from our church came, and we roasted wieners and marshmallows. Then we sat on tree stumps and chairs around the fire, played guitars and recorders and harmonicas, and sang worship songs to the Lord. We sang and danced and praised. We laughed and talked and enjoyed fellowship. The children played games around the fire and in the yard. When it was dark and late and the mosquitoes had bitten every exposed part of us twice, our church friends and family went home.

We had "ministered by night." I appreciated the way our pastor had announced the bonfire in church on Sunday morning. He said, "Next Sunday there is a special speaker coming to our church, and this Sunday night there is a bonfire at Hodgson's. Neither one is more spiritual than the other. We can minister at both."

We can minister by night. As long as God is being praised and worshipped, and prayer concerns for others are on our hearts, ministry is taking place.

Ministry by night holds a special place in God's heart. In Old Testament times, the Levites, a group of priests, were to keep watch in the temple all night. They were to pray and praise. They were to serve the Lord and minister by night in His house.

Years ago, I had the privilege of being one of those who regularly ministered by night in the house of the Lord. I traveled with a Christian ministry team of five women who sang praise and worship to God during evening concerts and church services all across the United States. Our leader, Priscilla, often led us in singing a certain scripture song as we traveled in our van, "Fearless," from town to town. The song's words go like this: "Come bless the Lord; all ye servants of the Lord; who stand by night, in the house of the Lord. Lift up your hands, in the holy place; And bless the Lord; and bless the Lord."

We would sing these lines over and over, and Priscilla would remind us that, even though we might be tired, and might have traveled many miles, it was always a privilege to be among those who "stand by night in the house of the Lord."

Ministering by night is a privilege that many share, but do not often get credit for. As many of us sleep at night, there are those faithful people who continue to hold vigil with God. There are monks in abbeys and nuns in convents. There are singers and speakers holding services nightly in town after town. There are those sick in hospitals and at home who pray all night to God. There are the sleepless, who spend quiet nights with the Lord, and who converse with God on their beds. There are nurses on night shifts and workers of all sorts who use their quiet hours to intercede in prayer for others and to commune with God.

All night, every night, there are those who are awake, serving God.

Isn't that comforting?

Isn't it nice to know?

Maybe we are at times among those who are up all night, ministering to the Lord and praying for others.

Maybe we are at times among those being prayed for by others.

Maybe at times of the night, our prayers and praises are joining with thousands of others who are also ministering or standing by night.

Let us be thankful either way, and let us be comforted:

Day and night, God's people are praying.

Day and night, God's people are praising.

Day and night, God's people are ministering.

Dear Lord, please bless those who minister by night everywhere in the world. Thank you for their prayers. Please give me strength when it is my turn to stay up at night to minister to others and to You. "Let my prayers be set forth before Thee as incense; And the lifting up of my hands as the evening sacrifice" (From The Order Of Vespers, Lutheran Hymnal, p. 42). In Jesus' name, Amen.

❧❧❧

Psalm 135 "For the Lord has chosen Jacob to be his own, Israel to be his treasured possession" (v. 4).

My sister has a little black rock. It is shiny and smooth and small enough to fit in her hand. She found it in one of our dad's fields when we were rock picking there as children. Lisa has kept that rock all these years. It is a treasured possession to her.

She used to kid me about that rock. We used to find lots of pretty stones in Dad's fields. We would keep them in a bucket until the end of the rock-picking day, and then we would dump them out on the floor at home. Then the picking really began! We would take turns picking or choosing who would get to keep each rock. Mind you, we were small children, to whom broken bits of granite and limestone can be real treasures!

When the choosing was over, Lisa would always hold up her little black rock. That one was not up for grabs. That one was hers alone. No little sister was ever going to get her hands on that prized possession!

"If I die," Lisa would say to me, "I want you to put this little black rock in my coffin."

Then we would laugh and giggle and go back to our other "rocky" treasures.

God has treasures, too.

He has possessions.

God's treasures and possessions are us.

"For the Lord has chosen Jacob to be his own, Israel to be his treasured possession" (Psalm 135:4).

God has chosen us to be His own.

I Peter 2:9a says, "But you are a chosen people, a royal priesthood, a holy nation, a people belonging to God."

God's possessions are precious to Him. He will not allow them (us) to be plucked out of His hands.

God the Father even chose Jesus as His precious possession. He chose Jesus as the cornerstone of our faith, and exalted Him high above all else. God then gave us, as His possessions, the choice to choose Jesus as our most dear possession, or to reject Him.

I Peter 2:4-7 puts it this way: "As you come to him, the Living Stone, rejected by men but chosen by God and precious to him, you also, like living stones, are being built into a spiritual house to be a holy priesthood, offering spiritual sacrifices acceptable to God through Jesus Christ. For in Scripture it says:

'See, I lay a stone in Zion,

a chosen and precious cornerstone,

and the one who trusts in him

will never be put to shame.'

Now to you who believe, this stone is precious. But to those who do not believe,

'The stone the builders rejected

has become the capstone,'

  and,

'A stone that causes men

to stumble

and a rock that makes

them fall.'"

Dear God, You own me. You possess me. You treasure me. I am Yours. Thank you, Jesus, for being the precious cornerstone of my faith. Thank you, God, for making me Your treasured possession. Help those who have rejected You to come to trust You as their Rock of salvation. In Jesus' name, Amen.

∽∾₰₰∾∽

Psalm 136 "Give thanks to the Lord of lords: . . . who made the great lights, the sun to govern the day, ...the moon and stars to govern the night" (v. 3, 7-9).

I offer today a meditation in verse, hymn, song, and scripture on the great lights which God made to govern the day and night. May God be praised for His greatness!

"Once for all, I have sworn by my holiness, and I will not lie to David, that his line will continue forever and his throne endure before me like the sun; it will be established forever like the moon, the faithful witness in the sky" (Psalm 89:35-37).

"May they who love you, O Lord, be like the sun when it rises in its strength" (Judges 5:31).

"From the rising of the sun, to the going down of the same, the Lord's name is to be praised" (Psalm 113:3 KJV).

Summer and winter and spring-time and harvest,
sun, moon, and stars in their courses above
join with all nature in manifold witness
to Thy great faithfulness, mercy, and love.
Great is Thy faithfulness!
Great is Thy faithfulness!
Morning by morning new mercies I see;
All I have needed Thy hand hath provided;
Great is Thy faithfulness,
Lord, unto me!
(from *Great Is Thy Faithfulness,* hymn words by Thomas O. Chisholm, 1923, music by William M. Runyan, 1923, based on Lamentations 3:22-23.)

Sun of my soul, Thou Savior dear,
It is not night if Thou be near.
Oh, may no earthborn cloud arise
To hide Thee from Thy servant's eyes.
(from *Sun Of My Soul,* hymn words by John Kelbe, 1820, music from "Allgemeines Gesangbuch," Vienna, 1775)

O God,
When my heart pounds,
When mother laughs,
When it thunders,
When the sun is shining,
Help me think of You.

MOON
THE MOON IS BEAUTIFUL, JESUS.
Bless the moon.
Bless the people who visit the moon.
Bless all the moons,
and stars and skies.
BLESS, O JESUS,
all things
UP HIGH.
(both poems above from *Small Prayers for Small Children about big and little things.*)

"Be glad of life
because it gives you the chance
to love and to work
and to play and to
look up at the stars."
(Henry Van Dyke)

"This is what was spoken by the prophet Joel: 'In the last days, God says, I will pour out my Spirit on all people. Your sons and daughters will prophesy; Your young men will see visions; Your old men will dream dreams. Even on my servants, both men and women, I will pour out my Spirit in those days, and they will prophesy. I will show wonders in the heaven above and signs on earth below, blood and fire and billows of smoke. The sun will be turned to darkness and the moon to blood before the coming of the great and glorious day of the Lord. And everyone who calls on the name of the Lord will be saved'" (from Peter's address to the crowd in Acts 2:16-21).

"Then I saw a new heaven and a new earth, for the first heaven and the first earth had passed away, and there was no longer any sea. I saw the Holy City, the new Jerusalem, coming down out of heaven from God, prepared as a bride beautifully dressed for her husband. And I heard a loud voice from the throne saying, 'Now the dwelling of God is with men, and he will live with them. They will be his people, and God himself will be with them and be their God. He will wipe away every tear from their eyes. There will be no more death or mourning or crying or pain, for the old order of things has passed away.' . . . I did not see a temple in the city, because the Lord God Almighty and the Lamb are its temple. The city does not need the sun or the moon to shine on it, for the glory of God gives it light, and the Lamb is its lamp" (Revelation 21: 1-4, 22-23).

Dear God, thank you for the sun, moon, and stars! In Jesus' name, Amen.

Psalm 137 "By the rivers of Babylon we sat and wept when we remembered Zion. There on the poplars we hung our harps, for there our captors asked us for songs, our tormentors demanded songs of joy; they said, 'Sing us one of the songs of Zion!'" (v. 1-3).

God's timing is everything.

We cannot demand songs of joy from others if the time is not right. We cannot demand things of ourselves if the time is not right. We cannot demand things of God if the time is not right.

The Israelites were in exile. They were captives in Babylon. They were foreigners whose homeland had been taken from them. Now was not the time for joy. Now was not the time for songs. Now was not the time for harps.

Now was a time for mourning for God's people. Now was a time for weeping.

Now was a time for the "joyful harp to be silent" (Isaiah 23:8).

I have a harp. That is why this particular passage interests me so much. My harp has taught me much about God's timing.

Four years before getting the harp I now have, I began to take lessons on a rented harp. After renting for one year, I decided to buy an instrument for myself. To make a long story short, I sent a substantial down payment to a reputable harp builder, who subsequently had many personal problems and took my money but did not build my harp.

I was financially unable to keep renting a harp, so I had to put playing the instrument on hold for four years. That was hard for me, because I enjoyed playing, and believed that God wanted me to use the music for His glory.

However, I did not give up. In my heart, I knew that I would play the harp again, in God's timing. That timing came after four years of waiting!

A woman living near me decided at age eighty-two, to give up playing her harp. She called me and offered to sell hers to me! I jumped at the opportunity, and now have a lovely, thirty-six-string harp sitting in my living room!

God's timing is everything.

God's timing is perfect.

We don't always understand God's timing, but we can trust it.

It is reliable.

It is right.

When the Israelites returned to their homeland after the exile, it was time to sing again!

Psalm 126 says, "When the Lord brought back the captives to Zion, we were like men who dreamed. Our mouths were filled with laughter, our tongues with songs of joy. Then it was said among the nations, 'The Lord had done great things for them.' The Lord has done great things for us, and we are filled with joy!"

For a time, the Lord took writing away from me. Since the fourth grade, I have loved to write.

Poems.

Journals.

Essays.

Letters.

Then, for some reason, all that stopped. I don't know why. It was frustrating. It was sad. It was disheartening. For eight years, I wrote almost nothing. I wanted to, but no inspiration would come. I had previously written volumes of over three hundred poems, and suddenly, no more would come.

I cried out to God, but it was not in His timing then. I had to wait.

Then, after eight years, the poems and essays and inspiration started coming again! They came so fast and often that I have notebooks full of poems and stories and essays. I have file cabinets brimming with writing again!

I don't know why the writing ability and inspiration left me and came back again, but I am learning not to question God's timing.

We cannot demand, like the Israelite's captors did, "songs of joy" when it is not God's time. We cannot *make* others or ourselves or God perform on demand.

We can ask.

We can pray.

We can wait.

Most of all, we can *trust* God's timing.

Dear Lord, when we are waiting for You to restore or bring something in our lives, help us to trust You. Help us to trust Your timing. Help us to pray as Psalm 126 does, "Restore our fortunes, O Lord, like streams in the Negev. Those who sow in tears will reap with songs of joy. He who goes out weeping, carrying seeds to sow, will return with songs of joy, carrying sheaves with him" (v. 4-6). Help us also to trust Your word in Ecclesiastes 3:11 which says, "He has made everything beautiful in its time." In Jesus' name, Amen.

∽✥∼

Psalm 138 "The Lord will fulfill his purpose for me; your love, O Lord, endures forever, do not abandon the works of Your hand" (v. 8).

There is an abandoned farmhouse a few miles from my home. Years ago, my husband and I watched with delight as someone bought this old house and began to restore it. Every time we drove down the gravel road past this house, we remarked on its progress.

First, a coat of white paint.

Second, new black window shutters.

Third, a new front door.

Fourth, new shingles on the roof.

But alas, at this point, to our disappointment, the project stopped. Halfway through the shingling process, the remodeling was ended. One half of the roof was new and shiny, the other half lay old and full of holes. The project was abandoned.

To this day, when I drive by that house, it makes me sad. I never knew the reason for the abandonment of the house. Rumor had it that the couple who bought it got divorced. Some said they simply ran out of money to finish the project. The half-finished farmhouse stands as a reminder of man's unfinished business. Man's abandoned projects. Man's unfulfilled purposes.

God promises us in Psalm 138 that He does not operate that way. God does not abandon the works of His hands. God does not let His purposes go unfulfilled.

"The Lord *will fulfill* his purpose for me" (Psalm 138:8) [emphasis mine].

That promise is comforting to me. Sometimes I feel like there won't be enough time in my life to fulfill all of my plans. Sometimes I feel like I'll never get an important project finished. Sometimes I feel like my dreams won't come true. Sometimes I feel like someone in my life might be taken from me prematurely.

This verse contradicts all that. Psalm 138:8 says, "The Lord *will fulfill* his purpose for me."

We must, of course, seek what *God's* purposes are in our lives. Proverbs 19:21 says, "Many are the plans in a man's heart, but it is the Lord's purpose that prevails." After all, God's plans for us are infinitely better than those we plan on our own. If we submit our lives to His divine plan, we can trust that His purposes will be fulfilled.

To us, it may seem that some people's lives and works have been cut short. But the Bible says, "No." God *will fulfill* his purposes for us.

Even Jesus' life seemed to be cut short. Think of all that Christ could have done on earth, had He lived longer than thirty-three years! But God's purposes for Jesus were fulfilled at age thirty-three. Dying on the cross and rising again was Jesus' ultimate purpose. When that was finished, God said it was time for Jesus to go.

We don't have to worry that God the Father took God the Son home too early. God fulfills His purposes!

We have all the time we need to complete the good works that God has prepared in advance for each of us to do!

Ephesians 2:10 says, "For we are God's workmanship, created in Christ Jesus to do good works, which God prepared in advance for us to do."

And in Isaiah 55:11, God says, "My word that goes out from my mouth . . . will not return to me empty, but will accomplish what I desire and achieve that purpose for which I sent it."

Let us seek God for His purposes for our lives. Let us not worry that His purposes will be left unaccomplished or unfulfilled.

God will fulfill His purposes for us.

We have His word on it.

Dear God, thank you for never abandoning Your work in me. Let me rest in the promise that You will fulfill Your purposes in my life. Everything that You want to get done will be done. In Jesus' name, Amen.

Psalm 139 "For you created my inmost being; you knit me together in my mother's womb. I praise you because I am fearfully and wonderfully made; your works are wonderful, I know that full well" (v. 13-14).

Until I read these verses, I had never imagined my mother pregnant. I am the youngest child in my family, so of course I never saw my mom when she was pregnant. Now, years later, it is hard to imagine what Mom would've looked like carrying my sister or me inside of her body.

She would've looked younger, of course. Younger than I picture her today. She wouldn't have had gray hair yet. Or any wrinkles.

What did *I* look like inside her? Was I really that tiny? So tiny that I lived inside her womb? Were my fingers ever *partially* formed? It is hard to imagine myself unborn. It is hard to imagine my mother carrying me inside her belly.

It is not hard for God to imagine these things. God knit us together in our mother's wombs. We are fearfully and wonderfully made by God. We are *works of God!* We are *wonderful!*

"Your works are wonderful!" says our Psalm. "I know that full well!"

Do we know that we are wonderful? God's works are wonderful, and *we* are among His works! All babies are! All people are!

I heard a speaker at a church once who told about a certain woman's special experience with God. She became filled with the Holy Spirit and saw a vision or dream from God. In the dream, a little girl was in heaven. The little girl was happy and smiling. She took Jesus' hand and pointed down to earth at the woman who was having the dream.

"Look, Jesus!" said the little girl, "That lady was my mommy on earth!"

This woman had had an abortion years earlier. When she awoke from her dream or vision, God had healed her of all her past guilt and pain over having the abortion.

That was a beautiful story to me of how God works. He loves us. He heals us. He forgives us. He has compassion on us.

God knits each of us together in our mother's womb. He creates our inmost being. His "eyes see our unformed bodies" (Psalm 139:15b). "Our frame is not hidden from Him when we are made in the secret place" (v.15a).

May we know full well that we are God's works, and that we are wonderful! May we praise Him because we are "fearfully and wonderfully made!"

O God, I praise You for knitting me together in my mother's womb! I can't imagine it, but I like to try! The way You create life is fearful and wonderful to me! No one but You could do it. Thank you, God. In Jesus' name, Amen.

Psalm 140 "O Sovereign Lord, my strong deliverer, who shields my head in the day of battle, do not grant the wicked their desires, O Lord; do not let their plans succeed, or they will become proud" (v. 7-8).

There are traps and snares set for us each and every day. Psalm 140 says, "Keep me, O Lord, from the hands of the wicked; protect me from men of violence who plan to trip my feet. Proud men have hidden a snare for me; they have spread out the cords of their net and have set traps for me along my path" (v. 4-5).

What trips your feet?

What trips my feet?

The answer is different for each of us. Each of us falls into different traps and snares.

Some of us fall into the trap of busyness. Some of us fall into the snare of pornography. Some of us fall into the trap of gossip. Some of us fall into the snare of jealousy. Some of us fall into the trap of greed. Some of us fall into the snare of worry. Some of us fall into the trap of lust. Some of us fall into the snare of laziness.

Satan knows where to lay traps for us each day. He knows our weak spots. He has a strategy to defeat us in our Christian walk. That is why the psalmist refers to our walk as *a battle* sometimes.

"O Sovereign Lord, my strong deliverer, who shields my head in the day of *battle*," says verse seven of our psalm.

We are in a battle for purity and holiness and Godliness and goodness in our lives every day. And *God* is our strong deliverer! He shields our heads. I like to paraphrase that line to read, "O Sovereign Lord, my strong deliverer, who shields my *mind* in the day of battle."

Our minds are in our heads. God shields our *minds*. He gives us *clear thinking*. He gives us the mind of Christ. He helps us to "take captive every thought to make it obedient to Christ" (II Corinthians 10:5).

Only then will the enemy be routed. Only then will we avoid the snares and traps set for us each day. The potential to fall off the path of holiness is there. But we have a strong deliverer! We have a God who shields our heads and our minds in the day of battle!

Dear God, there are traps and snares set for us each day. Lord, make us alert and clearheaded, that we may avoid the snares of today, and be single minded in doing Your will. May we not be distracted by the days' snares; may we not waver to the right or to the left of the path You have set for us today. In Jesus' name, Amen.

Psalm 141 "My eyes are fixed on You, O Sovereign Lord" (v. 8a).

What are our eyes fixed on?
Are they fixed on failure?
Are they fixed on sickness?
Are they fixed on financial problems?
Are they fixed on ourselves?
Hebrews 12:2a says that we are to "fix our eyes on Jesus, the author and finisher of our faith." Earlier, the verses in Hebrews speak of our life as a race. They say that a

runner must keep his eyes on the finish line, or he will become discouraged. If we focus on our aches and pains, we will not finish the race. If we spend our time watching the other runners, we will become distracted from our goal.

Jesus had His goal in mind. His goal was "the joy set before Him" (Hebrews 12:2b). His goal was victory over Satan and sin and death! His goal was resurrection!

Jesus, "for the joy set before Him, endured the cross, scorning its shame, and sat down at the right hand of the throne of God" (Hebrews 12:2b).

"Consider Him who endured such opposition from sinful men, so that you will not grow weary and lose heart" (Hebrews 12:3).

Jesus had His goal in mind, and so must we! With our eyes on the goal, we can endure anything!

What are our goals?

Eternal life in heaven!

A closer walk with God on earth!

To share the love of Christ with others!

To see Jesus!

The only way to attain these goals is to keep our eyes on Jesus. When we get distracted, we fall short of our goals. We see failure. We see defeat. We see our own problems. We become discouraged. We lose heart. We become short-sighted.

Let us pray today for God to open our eyes. Let us ask Him to fix our eyes on Jesus, the Author and finisher of our faith!

Open our eyes, Lord,
We want to see Jesus;
to reach out and touch Him,
and say that we love Him.
Open our ears, Lord,
and help us to listen.
Open our eyes, Lord.
We want to see Jesus.

(from the hymn: "Open Our Eyes," by Bob Cull)

Turn your eyes upon Jesus.
Look full in His wonderful face.

And the things of earth
will grow strangely dim,
in the light of His glory and grace.

(from the hymn: "Turn Your Eyes Upon Jesus," words and music by Helen
Howarth Lemmel, copyright 1922)

Psalm 142 "Look to my right and see; no one is concerned for me. I have no refuge; no
one cares for my life" (v. 4).

Does this sound familiar? Is anyone you know feeling this way? Are you?

David, the psalm writer felt this way when he was hiding in a cave. Saul was after him to take his life. David felt alone and afraid.

In the Hebrew, "no one is concerned for me" can also be translated, "no one knows me," or "no one notices me."

I know some teenagers and children who feel this way. Sometimes they forget that the adults around them were once children and teenagers, too. They feel misunderstood, unknown, and unnoticed.

I know some adults who feel this way, too. We all feel unnoticed at times. We feel that no one is concerned for us. We feel, like David, that no one cares for our lives.

At its worst, this feeling can lead to depression, withdrawal, and even suicide. It is not a feeling to be taken lightly.

David knew that this feeling was not to be ignored when he cried out to God.

"I cry aloud to the Lord . . . I pour out my complaint before him; before him I tell my trouble" (v. 1-2).

David wasn't quiet about his feelings or his troubles. He cried *aloud* to God.

Not just silent prayers.

Not just mulling over thoughts to himself.

Not just wishful thinking.

David cried *aloud*.

He said to God, "When my spirit grows faint within me, it is You who know my way" (v. 3).

He said, "You are my refuge, my portion in the land of the living" (v. 5).

He said, "Set me free from my prison, that I may praise your name" (v. 7).

God did answer David! God had plans for him, just as He has plans for each of us! In fact, God's plans for David even included Jesus Christ being his descendant! Who knows what God has planned for us?

Scripture says,

"No eye has seen
no ear has heard,
no mind has conceived
what God has prepared for those
who love him." (I Corinthians 2:9)
God has plans for you!
God has plans for me!
He notices us.
He is concerned for us.
He knows us.
He cares for our lives.

Dear God, I cry aloud to You today for myself and for all those who feel unnoticed, unknown, or uncared for. Remind us, O Lord, of Your great love for us, and of Your individual plan for each of our lives. Help us to remember David, and how You helped him, and even used him to bring Jesus Christ into the world for us as his descendant! What great plans You have prepared for us, O God! In Jesus' name, Amen.

Psalm 143 "I spread out my hands to you; my soul thirsts for you like a parched land" (v. 6).

Picture this with me.

A parched desert land with cracked ground. God is pouring water onto it. Watch what happens to the earth; to the soil. Watch how it becomes mud, soft, squishy, and moldable. Think of how it feels. This is a picture of our souls.

Our souls, our inner persons, can become parched. They can become dry and cracked like desert ground.

"I spread out my hands to you; my soul thirsts for you like a parched land."

When we spread out our hands to God, He gives us a drink. He pours living water into our souls, and we thirst no more (John 4:13-14).

Sometimes we may need to sit with God for a long drink in order to be refilled. We may need to spread out our hands in earnest before God. We may need to grab on to God's coat tails and not let go until He answers. We may need to wrestle overnight with God like Jacob did, until He gives us His blessing (Genesis 32: 22-32).

God *will* water the parched ground of our souls. He will soften us and make us moldable. Soft and squishy. Muddy. Pliable clay.

That's what God likes to work with.

That's what God likes to use.

Filled up, stuffed, self-satisfied Christians are not those God is using. God is delighted with those who "hunger and thirst for righteousness, for they will be filled" (Matthew 5:6).

How about it? Are we satisfied with where we are? Do we mind being thirsty or hungry? Are we willing to spread out our hands before God saying, "Fill me, Lord?" Do we want to be more like Jesus than we are today?

If so, let us be hungry and thirsty for God! Let us study His word. Let us pray to Him. Let us sit quietly at His feet every day and hear what He has to say to us.

Only then will our dry souls be watered.

Only then will our hungry hearts be satisfied.

Only then will our empty lives be filled.

Dear Lord, water our souls! Feed our spirits! We are weak and in need of spiritual food and drink. We are hungry. We are thirsty. Lord, let <u>new</u> things grow in the watered soil of our souls, after You have poured Your living water on their parched ground. In Jesus' name, Amen.

Psalm 144 "Then our sons in their youth will be like well-nurtured plants, and our daughters will be like pillars carved to adorn a palace" (v. 12).

Sons like well-watered plants.

Daughters like pillars carved to adorn a palace.

I like this imagery especially for our American culture. How many of our sons are "well-nurtured?" How many of our daughters are taught that they are "pillars" in our communities and in society? These terms seem to be used in reverse according to gender roles in our culture.

Nurturing goes with female roles.

Pillars sounds like a masculine term.

God doesn't see it that way.

God desires that our young men be well-nurtured. Only then will they flourish like a plant. A well-nurtured plant is tended lovingly. It is cared for. It is watered often. It is placed in a proper environment, sunlight or shade, depending on its needs.

A well-nurtured plant is not shoved out into the wind and left to be independent. It is not told to be tough. It is nourished and tended lovingly in order to help it grow and flourish.

I believe that as parents, as educators, and as adults in general, it is part of our jobs to nurture our young men.

And our daughters? How are they to see themselves? God says in His holy word that they will be "like pillars carved to adorn a palace."

Pillars are structural. Pillars are strong. Pillars hold up whatever is around them. Pillars are important to a structure. Our daughters need to know that they are important. They are strong. They are *structural* in God's plan. They can hold up those who are around them. Pillars are also carved. They are adorning. They are beautiful. They are gracing. Our daughters need to know that their beauty in not just sexual or superfluous, like lace edging. Our daughters need to know that their beauty is graceful. It is intrinsic. It is both inner and outer. It brings pleasure to God. Beauty makes life more livable. It provides charm and grace.

As parents and educators and adults, it is part of our jobs to teach our daughters that they are pillars. They are structural. They are important. They are strong. They are also beautiful. Beauty is not a sexual decoy or tool or toy. Beauty is adorning to God's house and kingdom.

When will this happen? When will our young people, both men and women, see themselves the way God sees them? Psalm 144 says it will be when we are "rescued and delivered from the hands of foreigners whose mouths are full of lies, whose right hands are deceitful" (v. 11).

I believe that the word "foreigners" here has nothing to do with skin color, accent, or place of origin. I believe it has to do with *ungodly* versus *godly*. When God's people in the Old Testament were attacked by foreigners, they were made captives. Their worship of Jehovah, the One True God, was infiltrated and contaminated with idol worship. False gods were brought in. They were told lies. They were treated deceitfully.

Today in America, I believe that media advertising is, in a way, a foreigner. It makes us captives. Advertising gives us false gods. It confronts us with idol worship. "Worship the tough, athletic, masculine sports hero." "Worship the sexy, young, thin, feminine make-up model." We are told lies. We are treated deceitfully.

May we be rescued and delivered from this way of thinking. May we instead see ourselves, and our young people, as well-nurtured plants, and as pillars carved to adorn a palace. May we break free from the captivity of our culture. May we say with the psalmist:

> *Then our sons in their youth*
> *will be like well-watered plants,*
> *and our daughters will be like pillars*
> *carved to adorn a palace.*
> *Our barns will be filled*
> *with every kind of provision.*
> *Our sheep will increase by thousands,*
> *by tens of thousands in our fields;*
> *Our oxen will draw heavy loads.*
> *There will be no breaching of walls,*
> *no going into captivity,*
> *no cry of distress in our streets.*
>
> *Blessed are the people of whom this is true;*
> *Blessed are the people whose God is the Lord.*
> *(Psalm 144:12-15)*
>
> *In Jesus' name, Amen.*

Psalm 145 "One generation will commend your works to another; they will tell of your mighty acts. They will speak of the glorious splendor of your majesty, and I will meditate on your wonderful works" (v. 4-5).

One of the things I like best about my husband is that he believes in redemption.

Redemption is one of God's "wonderful works." Psalm 145 says that we are to "meditate" on God's "wonderful works."

I remember learning in Catechism class as a child that three wonderful works are attributed to God, the Holy Trinity. To the Father is attributed the work of creation. To the Holy Spirit is attributed the work of sanctification. To the Son is attributed the work of redemption.

All Christians know and believe that Jesus died on the cross to *redeem* us from sin and death. Redemption means "to buy back;" "to salvage;" "to win back;" "to retrieve." But how about in our *daily lives*? Do we really believe that Jesus *redeems*?

My husband does. He reminds me of it all the time. I'll say something like, "This day is ruined. I got behind schedule; now nothing will get done."

And my husband will say, "No, it isn't. This day isn't ruined. Let's pray right now and ask God to redeem the time. Let's ask Him to salvage this day; to buy it back."

We've prayed prayers like that together hundreds of times, and do you know what? God *always* redeems those days! He somehow makes up for our lost time. He salvages the day! He helps everything to get done that needed to get done!

The same it true in relationships. My husband and I have had some fights. We argue. We disagree. We say things that are hurtful which we wish we hadn't said. At those times, I often wallow in guilt. Even after we've said we're sorry to each other, and we've told each other, "I forgive you," I still feel a need to wallow in guilt. I can't seem to get over it.

At those times, too, my husband often reminds me that God is a God of *redemption*. God redeems. He restores. He buys back. He retrieves. He salvages.

Even bad times.

Even fights.

Even angry words.

"Dear God," we can pray at those times, "Please redeem this relationship. Restore it to where it was before we fought. Before we disagreed. Redeem us from guilt, Lord. We forgave each other. Let us go back now to being in love."

We don't need to wallow in guilt! God bought us back from that when Jesus died on the cross! Condemnation is not from God! *Conviction* is from God, but it leads to repentance, not to guilt. If we turn around from our sin and ask for forgiveness, there is no more guilt! Our situation is redeemed! It is salvaged and restored!

I am so good at thinking, "But I screwed up. I deserve to suffer. It wouldn't be right to feel good again so soon; at least until tomorrow, or next week."

God says, "No! I redeem *daily* situations! You can be over that sin *now!* Be happy! Be at peace!"

Psalm 145 says, "One generation will commend your works to another."

God's works of redemption in our lives are worthy of being commended to future generations. To "commend" means "to entrust for care or preservation." Remember when Jesus said on the cross to His Father, "Into Your hands I commend my spirit?" Jesus entrusted His spirit into God's hands for care and preservation.

Let us do the same with God's wonderful works in our lives. Let us tell others! Let us commend God's works of redemption in our lives to the next generation! What has God done in our lives? What situations has He redeemed? In what areas has God created in our lives? In what areas has the Holy Spirit sanctified, bringing cleansing, or holiness? These are all wonderful works of God, to be commended by us to future generations.

Oh Lord, I meditate today on your wonderful works in my own life. Thank you for redeeming times and situations and relationships in my daily life. Only You could salvage those things. Thank you for Your most wonderful work of all: redeeming us to Yourself through Jesus. In His name, Amen.

***

Psalm 146 "Praise the Lord. Praise the Lord, O my soul. I will praise the Lord all my life; I will sing praise to my God as long as I live" (v. 1-2).

What an affirmation!

"I will praise the Lord all my life; I will sing praise to my God as long as I live."

There was a man named Levi in my Bible study group years ago who did just that. He praised God as long as he lived.

Levi was in his eighties. He was dying of cancer. He was so sick that each day could've been his last. Yet he was praising Jesus.

We had our Bible study at Levi's house, because he couldn't leave his home anymore. He was a lifelong bachelor who lived with his brother and sister. They lived in a big, square farmhouse at the edge of town. For months, Levi had been so sick that at times he couldn't leave his bed. He often could not eat. When he sat up, it was only for an hour or so at a time. Yet when our Bible study group came over, he asked to be brought out into the living room. He sat in a big recliner chair with his feet propped up and his eyes often closed. Levi wanted to hear the music. He wanted to hear us sing hymns. He asked for his favorites to be sung over and over each week. He wanted to hear us read from the Bible, to hear the words of God. He wanted to hear us pray.

Often is the middle of Bible study, Levi interrupted with spontaneous praying or praising of his own. The Holy Spirit filled his soul, and Levi would say, "Praise you, Jesus! Precious Jesus! Bless each loved one here tonight."

I heard him say these words of affirmation over and over. I will never forget them.

Levi was in great pain and discomfort, yet his spirit was praising God as long as he lived.

His praise of God was a testimony to me, and to my husband. If we live to be old, or are one day dying in pain or discomfort, we want to be witnesses to Jesus like Levi was. We want to praise Jesus as long as we live.

Sometimes Levi interrupted our Bible study more than once. He couldn't hear very well, so he would break into prayer or praise while the rest of us were talking or were in the middle of something else. It didn't matter. We knew that Levi's praise to God was more important, so we all just stopped and listened. We closed our eyes and prayed, too. Levi would say, "Precious Saviour. Precious Jesus. We love you, dear Lord. Father, Son and Holy Spirit, we bless you. Bless each loved one here tonight."

We listened.

We waited.

We praised.

Levi was praising Jesus as long as he lived.

Dear Jesus, I have such respect and awe for someone who praises You as long as they live. In pain, in trial, in suffering, in old age. What a testimony to Your great love,

God! What an affirmation of Your faithfulness. May I be given the grace to praise You all my life; as long as I have my being. In Jesus' name, Amen.

❧ ～◇ℓℓℰ ～

Psalm 147 "The Lord sustains the humble... He covers the sky with clouds; he supplies the earth with rain and makes grass grow on the hills. He provides food for the cattle and for the young ravens when they call. His pleasure is not in the strength of the horse, nor his delight in the legs of a man; the Lord delights in those who fear him, who put their hope in his unfailing love" (v. 6a, 8-11).

A measure of progress may here be defined as, anything that makes us more "God-reliant."

Psalm 147 makes it clear that God's delight is "not in the legs of man." Man's self-reliance does not delight God. Man's strength and technology do not delight God.

God delights in those who fear him.

God delights in those who put their hope in His unfailing love.

God delights in the humble.

All our lives we are taught to be more self-reliant. "Be independent," we're told. "Be strong." "Be tough." "You can do it."

God is not impressed.

I like what the NIV Bible text notes have to say about Psalm 147:7-11: "The God who governs the rain and thus provides food for beast and bird is not pleased by man's reliance on his own capabilities or those of the animals he has domesticated (or the technologies he has developed); he is pleased when people serve him and trust his loving care."

More technology is not always progress.

When my oldest daughter was about twelve years old she said to me, "Mom, I wish everybody was Amish."

We had been reading books by Amish people. We had also read books about the Amish life-style.

The Amish believe in a simple life-style. They have no electricity in their homes. They do not use automobiles of any kind. They do their farm work with horses. They follow the same God of the Bible that other Christians do, but their life-style is

slower-paced and simpler. They have not embraced each and every
new technology that man develops as progress. They see that some progress actually
makes us more self-reliant and less God-reliant.

When my daughter, Jessica, said, "I wish everybody was Amish," I said,
"Why?" One of the reasons she gave me is that there would be less pollution. I
agreed. One of man's biggest problems with developments in technology is that we
do not properly handle the side effects.

With automobiles comes more pollution.

With medical innovations come ethical questions.

With farm chemicals come environmental and stewardship concerns.

With more luxurious life-styles comes the need for more income.

With two-parents-working households comes more stress.

Do we see the connections here?

God does.

He says, "My pleasure is not in the strength of the horse, nor is my delight in
the legs of man."

Next time we are faced with decisions concerning new technologies or life-styles
or progress, let us ask ourselves:

"Is this really progress?

How do I define progress?

Does it make my life simpler?

Does it give me peace?

Does it have positive side effects for the environment or for the people around me?

Does it make me more reliant on God?"

If the answer to these questions is "No," then perhaps that new technology or
life-style change is not progress after all.

'Tis the gift to be simple;
'Tis the gift to be free;
'Tis the gift to come down
Where we ought to be;
And when we find ourselves
In the place just right,
'Twill be in the valley

Of love and delight.

When true simplicity is gained,
To bow and to bend we shan't be ashamed;
To turn, turn, will be our delight,
'Till by turning, turning, we come 'round right.

(from "Simple Gifts," a Shaker melody and lyric)

Psalm 148 "Praise him, all his angels, praise him, all his heavenly hosts" (v. 2).

How familiar are we with the "heavenly hosts?" The word "hosts" suggests "a large number;" "a multitude." (Webster's New Collegiate Dictionary)

Luke 2:13, the account of an angel's appearance to the shepherds near Bethlehem, says that there appeared suddenly, with that angel, "a great company of the heavenly host, praising God."

Luke 2:15 says, "When the angels had left them, and gone into heaven, the shepherds said to one another, 'Let's go to Bethlehem and see this thing that has happened, which the Lord has told us about.'"

God's heavenly hosts spoke to men on that occasion about God's glory and about His peace to men on whom His favor rests.

Psalm 91:9-12 tells us that if we make the Most High our dwelling, no harm will befall us, "For he will command his angels concerning us to guard us in all our ways; they will lift us up in their hands, so that we will not strike our feet against a stone."

Here, angels actually touch people with their hands. They lift us up and keep us safe from violence, harm and danger.

Many people speak of angels having helped them in car accidents, in other dangerous situations, and in surprising circumstances.

The Bible says that some people who have entertained strangers have really entertained angels without knowing it! (Hebrews 13:2).

In these cases, people and angels are interacting without the people even being aware of it!

Psalm 148 tells us that God created angels, and all heavenly hosts, as well as all beings on earth. The psalm says, "He commanded and they were created" (v. 5). *All* of God's creation is to praise Him!

The angels and heavenly hosts are praising God right now! They never stop!

"Let all God's angels worship him," says Hebrews 1:6.

The Bible makes it clear that Jesus Christ is superior to the heavenly beings. "The Son is the radiance of God's glory and the exact representation of his being, sustaining all things by his powerful word. After he had provided purification for sins, he sat down at the right hand of the Majesty in heaven. So he became as superior to the angels as the name he has inherited is superior to theirs." So says Hebrews 1:3-4.

No matter what we learn of angels, or how we are touched by their ministering spirits in our earthly lives (Hebrews 1:14), we are not to worship them. Only Jesus is to be worshipped!

We are, however, to be aware of and to acknowledge their existence and presence. In Matthew 18:10, Jesus calls a little child and has the child stand among the disciples. He then says, "See that you do not look down on one of these little ones. For I tell you that their angels in heaven always see the face of my Father in heaven."

We all have angels who constantly see God's face! That is comforting! That is reassuring! God "commands them concerning us" (Psalm 91). That is exciting news!

One day, we human beings will even judge angels. I Corinthians 6:2-3 says, "Do you not know that the saints will judge the world? . . . Do you not know that we will judge angels?"

That verse humbles me. It says that I will one day be among those who will judge angelic beings. Heavenly hosts whom I have not yet met. Beings whose forms I have not yet seen, whose ways I do not yet understand or comprehend. That is hard to imagine. Yet God has written it and His word does not lie. God has ordained it, so when that time comes, He will grant complete understanding.

Until then, I will simply pray to become more familiar concerning God's heavenly hosts. I will thank God for His ministering angels. They, and I, will do as we are charged in Psalm 148: We will praise the Lord!

Angels from the realms of glory,
wing your flight o'er all the earth;
ye who sang creation's story
now proclaim Messiah's birth:

Come and worship, come and worship,
worship Christ, the newborn King.

(from "Angels From The Realms Of Glory," by James Montgomery, 1816)

Psalm 149 "For the Lord takes delight in his people; he crowns the humble with salvation. Let the saints rejoice in this honor and sing for joy on their beds" (v. 4-5).

I have always enjoyed pleasing people. I like to send greeting cards and imagine a smile coming across the face of the person who opens it. Giving gifts has always delighted me more than receiving them. (Although, don't get me wrong, I like to receive them, too!) But there is something about pleasing others that makes me happy.

I like to sing and play the piano and direct children's choirs in front of an audience. Knowing that something we have done has delighted the audience or ministered to them gives *me* pleasure, too.

If knowing that we have pleased others is a good feeling, how much more joy it can give us to know that we delight God! Psalm 149 says that "the Lord takes delight in his people" (v. 4).

Can't you just imagine God sitting up in heaven and being delighted with us? It's like when a mother or father watches their children at play. They are delighted just to watch! Or when a teacher sees the accomplishment of a student. What a delight! Or when a boyfriend or girlfriend brings flowers or a special gift to one another. What a pleasing surprise!

God delights in us!

He delights in our play times, even as adults!

He delights in our words of love.

He delights in our singing and dancing and music-making.

He delights in our accomplishments.

He delights in our humble attitudes.

On top of all this, Psalm 149 says that God "crowns the humble with salvation."

God's delight in us and His crown of salvation for us through Jesus Christ is reason to rejoice and to "sing for joy on our beds!"

We have pleased God, dear saints! Because of Jesus living in us, God sees us as His sons and daughters! He is our loving parent, looking down on us with delight!

If we cannot picture God that way, let us read Zephaniah 3:17. "The Lord your God is with you, he is mighty to save. He will take great delight in you, he will quiet you with his love, he will rejoice over you with singing."

God loves us so much that it makes Him sing!

Usually we think of it the other way around. *We* love God so much that it makes *us* sing! But let us remember that *God loved us first!* (I John 4:19). "We love because He *first* loved us."

Hebrews 2:11-12 says, "Both the one who makes men holy and those who are made holy are of the same family. So Jesus is not ashamed to call them brothers. He says, 'I will declare your name to my brothers; in the presence of the congregation I will sing your praises.'"

Jesus sings over us, too!

He is not ashamed to call us brothers and sisters!

We are in the same family!

Let us rejoice today and sing for joy on our beds because God takes delight in us!

Dear God, it makes me smile to think that I make You smile. Thank you for singing over me. Thank you for delighting in me. What an honor to be able to please You! I love You, God! In Jesus' name, Amen.

Psalm 150 "Praise the Lord. Praise God in his sanctuary; praise him in his mighty heavens. Praise him for his acts of power; praise him for his surpassing greatness. Praise him with the sounding of the trumpet, praise him with the harp and lyre, praise him with tambourine and dancing, praise him with the strings and flute, praise him with the clash of cymbal, praise him with resounding cymbals. Let everything that has breath praise the Lord. Praise the Lord" (all verses).

What a journey this book has been! In the course of writing it, dear relatives have died, and several other friends have also gone to be with Jesus. Our lives have changed, as have yours, dear Christian readers, as God continues to change all of us "from one degree of glory to the next" (II Corinthians 3:18).

Finishing a book is in some ways a picture to me of God's acts of completion in our lives. Each accomplishment, each goal attained, is another reminder of what God is doing in the "big picture" of our lives. Philippians 1:6 says, " . . . he who began a good work in you will carry it to completion until the day of Jesus Christ."

Just as we finish books and projects and phases in our lives, so God finishes His works. He has begun a good work in each of us, dear saints; that is, the work of saving us. God is in the process of completing that work in each of us. Each step of our lives is yet another step closer to seeing Jesus! On that day, the work begun in us will be completed!

It is God's work, not ours.

It is His grace that saves us.

It is His mercy.

It is His Son.

It is my hope that this book has strengthened us on our journey. It is my hope that God's words in the psalms have fed us and nurtured us. It is my hope that these devotions have brought us closer to Jesus. It is my hope that these words have been "words of life."

Sing them over again to me,
Wonderful words of life;
Let me more of their beauty see,
Wonderful words of life;
Words of life and beauty,
Teach me faith and duty.

Beautiful words, wonderful words,
Wonderful words of life;
Beautiful words, wonderful words,
Wonderful words of life.

(From the hymn, "Wonderful Words Of Life," by Philip P. Bliss, 1874)

Judy (Langemo) Roth
(Cover Artist)

Judy (Langemo) Roth lived in Wheaton, Minnesota from 1968 to 1973 while her father, Rev. Martin Langemo, was pastor of St. John's Lutheran church. Judy and Linda were both in first grade at Wheaton's elementary school when they met one day at the hallway water fountain. Judy asked, "Do you want to be best friends?" Linda replied, "Sure!" The two have been best friends ever since!

While she no longer lives in Minnesota, Judy is sure to visit at least three times a year to enjoy time with family and friends. Her parents and siblings all live in the Twin Cities area, and visiting each of their homes is one of her greatest joys! Judy would like to credit her parents, and their penchant for limiting television time, as major catalysts in helping her to grow as an artist. Drawing and craft materials were always present, and she and her sister and four brothers were able to develop talents in the visual arts as well as in music and performing arts.

Today Judy lives in Philadelphia, Pennsylvania with her beloved husband Dan, a United Methodist pastor, and their two cats, Deacon and Indy. A former teacher, she now leads the worship band and ministers to neighborhood children and youth at their inner-city church. A favorite pastime is to retire to her third floor studio where she continues to learn and evolve as an artist and painter. She also enjoys traveling with Dan, reading, and riding her bicycle around Philadelphia.

Linda Winter-Hodgson is available for speaking engagements and personal appearances. For more information contact:

Linda Winter-Hodgson
C/O Advantage Books
PO Box 160847
Altamonte Springs, FL 32779

info@advbooks.com

To purchase additional copies of this book or other books published by Advantage Books call our toll free order number at:
1-888-383-3110 (Book Orders Only)

or visit our bookstore website at:
www.advbookstore.com

*A*dvantage
BOOKS

Longwood, Florida, USA
"we bring dreams to life"™
www.advbooks.com

Breinigsville, PA USA
28 September 2010
246257BV00001B/3/P